Hard Man
Hard Knocks

For Jordan

Hard Man Hard Knocks

Terry Yorath

With Grahame Lloyd

Celluloid

Published by Celluloid,
12 Chargot Road,
Llandaff,
Cardiff CF5 1EW

ISBN 0-9545961-1-0

A CIP record for this title is available
from the British Library

Printed and bound in Great Britain by
CPD Wales, Ebbw Vale

Contents

Foreword
by Ryan Giggs

When I made my international debut against Germany in October 1991 at the age of 17 years and 321 days, I became the youngest footballer to play for Wales. I was very proud to hold the record for seven years – taking over from one of my heroes, the late John Charles – and it was an honour which I have to thank Terry Yorath for because he was the Welsh manager at the time.

Terry had picked me as a substitute for a European Championship qualifier in Nuremberg and although we lost 4-1, I'll never forget the six minutes I was on the pitch. We were getting beaten and I was sitting on the bench dying to get on so I could try to change things. When my big moment arrived and I replaced Eric Young, I didn't feel overawed but with so little time left, I only managed about three touches of the ball. I did feel before then that I could have been given my debut a little sooner. I thought I was ready but Terry was the manager and perhaps he was right to bring me on as a substitute for my first five caps – after all, I was only 17.

I made my full debut 18 months later against Belgium in a World Cup qualifier at the old Cardiff Arms Park and scored our first goal in a 2-0 win. I volunteered to take a free-kick just outside the box on the right and bent it with my left foot over the wall. It's one of my favourite goals of all time and when I scored you could have heard the noise at Wembley 150 miles away! What made it better was that so many of my family were there. It made me try harder and I produced one of my best performances for Wales.

I won the last of my 11 caps under Terry when we lost 2-1 to

Romania at Cardiff Arms Park and missed out on the chance of going to the 1994 World Cup in America. Realistically, it was the best chance we'd had for years and we'd blown it but Terry was brilliant. 'Listen,' he said, 'it was the best you could do. We came so close.' I remember feeling so desperate because we could have been on our way to the United States. We had the makings of a strong side and we understood Terry and the way he worked so we couldn't believe it when his contract wasn't renewed.

I always got on well with him and all the lads respected him because he was a former Welsh captain and a fine manager. He and his assistant, Peter Shreeves, always had a good laugh with the lads and treated us like adults. But, immediately after the World Cup campaign, after Terry had done so much, he was kicked out. Something should have been done to allow him to stay as manager – everyone wanted him to carry on because it looked like we could build a serious challenge for the European Championship. Instead, he wasn't kept on and it upset the whole balance of Welsh football.

Over the last 10 years, Terry has gone back to club management and also had a spell coaching the Lebanese national side. I was really pleased when, as Peter Jackson's assistant, he helped Huddersfield win promotion in our home city of Cardiff in the Third Division play-off final in May 2004. I will always look back and be grateful to Terry for giving me a chance to play for Wales. It was something I had dreamt about as a boy and I hope I didn't let him down.

The Heart of the Matter

At first, I thought Daniel was joking. We'd been out playing in the back garden for an hour or so when I kicked the ball into the long grass near some apple trees about 25 yards away. Daniel went to fetch it and as he stepped back on to the lawn, he just fell flat on his face. I stood there for what must have been about a minute. I was convinced he was mucking around so I kept shouting 'Come on! get up!' Eventually, when Daniel didn't move, I went across to him and I could tell straightaway that something was wrong. I picked him up and saw the blood running from his nose. He let out a groan as I held him in my arms and the next moment he had gone. There was a spent look in his eyes: they were open but he was staring lazily into space and I knew then that he was dead.

The memory of that dreadful day will stay with me for the rest of my life. It's as if the events of 25th May 1992 – the Bank Holiday Monday – happened only yesterday: the hot weather, the game of football, Daniel keeling over, my next-door neighbour trying to give him mouth-to-mouth resuscitation, the rush to the hospital with me vainly massaging his heart in the ambulance and then the doctor telling us there was nothing they could do.

As we struggled to understand how a boy as fit as Daniel could collapse and die so suddenly, we soon found out that the cause of death was hypertrophic cardiomyopathy – a rare hereditary disease which causes a thickening of the heart muscle. Not long after his funeral, the whole family – my wife, Christine, our daughters, Gabby and Louise, our son, Jordan and I – underwent a series of tests to check if any of us were affected. It was a bit scary – especially for Jordan who was only six at the time – but luckily nothing was found. He has since been back twice for further tests and he's still in the clear. Although I'm delighted that we've been able to help the Cardiomyopathy Association in their work into sudden death syndrome, I don't think I will ever be free from the after-effects of Daniel dying.

He was the light of my life. Christine called him my soul brother and he was more than just a son to me – he was my best mate. We did everything together. Daniel loved sport and, in particular, football and he would come to international and club games with me. He had just signed associate schoolboy forms with Leeds United, the club that I'd begun my career with, also as a 15-year-old, in 1965. He was elated because it was what he'd always dreamt of. I knew he had the makings of a very good footballer and everyone I spoke to at Leeds or at his school talked so highly of his ability and his potential.

Daniel's death has had a lasting impact on my life because I've never managed to get rid of my grief – I've never been able to handle it. His death knocked me to bits but while Christine underwent coun-selling and consulted mediums, I didn't do any of that on the same scale. She did suggest that I went with her so I saw a couple of mediums but they weren't any help to me. They only told me things I already knew and I didn't want to share my pain with anyone. I wasn't prepared to go and talk to a stranger about Daniel – I just wanted to try and contain my grief, to deal with it myself. Looking back, I should have gone to the counselling sessions with Christine. Twelve years after Daniel died, his name only has to be mentioned and I'm finished, I'm out of it.

Christine is very strong and I think the counselling helped her deal with Daniel's death. She's been a wonderful mother, she's a very suc-cessful businesswoman who runs her own property, interior design and beauty care products companies but sadly, we've gradually drifted apart over the years. We separated just before Christmas in 2003 and I'm now living by myself in a flat not far from the family home in Leeds.

Drinking has always been a big part of football's culture and to try to cope with Daniel's death, I began drinking more – something that has been instrumental in the break-up of my marriage. When you acquire a taste for something, it becomes bigger and bigger and you find yourself not having one or two drinks but more like three, four or five. Sometimes, I drink to relieve the pain, sometimes to hide my grief or the things that are going on in my personal life. To the outside world, I've just been getting on with my job and doing things that I normally do but if you haven't got a very happy personal life then the drinking becomes stronger.

The problem came to a head on the night England played Portugal in Euro 2004 when I stupidly drove my car home with three times the legal limit of alcohol in my blood and knocked down a young woman, Raziya Aslam. I was so ashamed because I could have cost that girl her life – and, after losing Daniel, that's something I could never have forgiven myself for. I committed the crime and I have been rightly punished. I know that when my 30-month ban ends, I will never drink and drive again.

I have dedicated this book to Jordan because I feel in some ways, he has paid the highest price for Daniel's death. One of his sisters, Gabby, is a famous TV presenter and the other, Louise, is modelling in Las Vegas. His father was once pretty well-known in football, his mother is a high-profile businesswoman and his brother was signed by Leeds just before he died. Jordan has to live up to all that and sometimes he finds it very difficult – especially as he wants to be a footballer too. I feel that I've not really been the father I should have been to him. I've been too upset – even obsessed – by Daniel's death to devote enough time to Jordan. I always watch him play football but there are other things I could have done which I haven't – simple things like just being there for him when he needed me. It's true that I've had a few setbacks – like being sacked by Wales and then having to retreat to a coaching job in Lebanon to try to come to terms with life after Daniel. They have taken me away from home but I know the truth. I think I could have tried to form the same sort of relationship with Jordan as I had with Daniel.

Christine and I were going to put a bench in the garden to mark the spot where Daniel collapsed but we decided to plant a weeping willow tree there instead. It's thriving now but it struggled at the beginning – no matter how much we fed and watered it – and it looked as if it too was going to die. One day, the tree suddenly came to life and it produced one of the most wonderful feelings I've ever known. The football we'd been playing with on the day Daniel died was left at the bottom of the willow tree until the next-door neighbour's dog came in and took it – and we haven't seen it since!

The willow tree is not really a comfort to me but it's nice to know it's there and that it's flourishing. In fact, I'm the one still doing the weeping – I can't help myself. When I look back on the time we had with Daniel, I'm very grateful for his 15 years on this earth and I have some great memories because he was a lovely boy. I'm pleased that some good has come from his death and that the problem of hypertrophic cardiomyopathy has been brought to the public's attention through the Daniel Yorath Appeal Fund. We're still involved with the campaign but nothing can help me cope with losing him. It's no comfort to me that Daniel died from something I could have done absolutely nothing about. Although it's said that time cures all things, even the strongest grief, I'm afraid that this wound just won't heal.

Cardiff-born, Leeds-bound

There was no debate. 'No you're not!' they both cried. 'You're going to play football!' And that was that – the end of the discussion. My father and my brother, David, laid it on the line. There was no room for doubt – and no way I would be allowed to choose rugby ahead of football. The shape of the ball I'd be kicking in future would be round rather than oval.

As I stood in front of them both as a 14-year-old schoolboy, the seeds of my career as a professional footballer were sown. My father David – with a little help from big brother who was two years older than me – had pointed me in the right direction – and I've never regretted letting them make the decision that so shaped the rest of my life.

For more than a century, the argument about the national sport of Wales has divided my nation but nobody has yet come up with a definitive answer – probably because there isn't one. Rugby may dominate in the south but football certainly rules the roost in the rest of the country. Forty years ago, I found myself having to choose between the two games at a very crucial time in my life.

I'd been selected for the Cardiff Schools senior side at both codes after unofficially becoming involved with the football team a year earlier. I'd gone to watch my brother play for them and because they were a man short, they asked me to help out, gave me a pair of boots and stuck me out on the right wing. The next year, they invited me back for a trial – as did the people who ran the Cardiff Schools rugby team. When I found out that I'd been picked for both codes, I went home and proudly announced to Dad and David that I wanted to play rugby.

It was all very well for them to tell me what to do but can you imagine how I felt having to go and let the head sports master know that I wasn't going to play rugby for Cathays Grammar School anymore? I was quaking in my shoes when I finally summoned up enough courage to break the news to him. In fact, I didn't actually say I wouldn't play rugby – I just said I was going to play football for Cardiff Schools. I was immediately banned from the school rugby and cricket teams and I was told to go swimming all year instead! I felt left out of everything and swimming became pretty boring. I've always had a stubborn streak and, with the prompting of my family, I'd made up my mind up to go down the football road. When I was banned, my friends were just flabbergasted – they thought I was being very hard done by. For me, there was no going back and my treatment by the school made me more determined than ever to become a professional footballer.

I was born in Cardiff Royal Infirmary on 27th March 1950 and, as I've since found out, I share a birthday with, among others, Sir Henry Royce, the co-founder of the Rolls-Royce motor company, and Jim Callaghan, the former British Prime Minister who was actually my local MP. I spent my first few weeks living with my parents, David and our elder sister, Pauline, just around the corner from the hospital in my grandfather's home, a typical two-up-two-down terraced house in Pontypridd Street in Splott, near the centre of the city. Splott was one of three working class areas in Jim Callaghan's Cardiff South constituency and the city's docks and local steelworks at East Moors were the main employers at the time.

Yorath is the English version of the Welsh name, Iorwerth, which Christine and I decided to call our first house after we married. Dad's family came from Splott – his father, Ben, was a docker – while Mum's were from Tiger Bay, the area around Butetown where the cosmopolitan workforce lived as Cardiff became the biggest coal exporting port in the world in the nineteenth and early twentieth centuries. Her maiden name was Sigallias – her family had come over Salonika in Greece. Her brother, my Uncle Mike, spent a lot of time researching the family tree and now lives in Cyprus. Mum's father, Jim, was a bookie who never wrote anything down but kept it all in his head. He was so sharp he remembered every bet he'd ever taken. Dad followed in his father's footsteps by becoming a docker while my mother, Mary, was everything. She used to clean in a bank, then look after a friend's two children all day before working as a barmaid at night. That's what she felt she had to do if she was going to help provide for the family. When I was still a baby, we moved to Llanishen, a suburb in north Cardiff, and we lived there as a family until 1963. I went to Rhydypenau junior school where David and I both played for the football team. He was a good all-rounder because as well as representing Cardiff Schools at football, he also played in their baseball and cricket teams. Baseball was – and still is – very popular in Cardiff. We were two sports-mad brothers, always kicking, throwing or hitting a ball around whenever we could. I was a right-sided midfielder-cum-forward whereas David played all over the place before settling down at full-back where he represented Welsh Schoolboys.

We loved playing for the Rhydypenau school side and during one season we scored 56 goals between us. I've still got a team photo taken in the 1957-58 season in which everything looks normal – until you look down at our feet. There I am in the front row, arms folded, smiling proudly at the camera but I'm the only player in the team not wearing boots. I'd forgotten to take mine into school that day and I had to put something on my feet so I borrowed a pair of wellies instead! The best schoolboy side in Cardiff were Gabalfa. They had the best kit – a silky, yellow shirt with a black cuff on it, black shorts with a yellow stripe down the side and yellow and black socks – and every time I played against them I thought to myself: 'Wow, they really look like a football team!' Their sports master, Doug Lewis, was very good at coaching schoolboys and he was involved in selecting the Cardiff Schools junior team. When I was about nine, a new school was being built on our estate and after we'd played Gabalfa once, Doug said to me:

'If you don't want to go to that new school, come to ours.'

Now it may just have been a throwaway remark to him but it lodged very firmly in my young brain. I knew the new school wouldn't have a football pitch for a couple of years so I went home and thought about it. Even at that age, football had taken a grip on me and I told my parents that I'd like to go to Gabalfa. The school wasn't exactly on the other side of the city but it wasn't very near and I remember turning up there on the first day of term when everybody was in assembly. I hung about for a while and then asked one of the teachers where I could find Mr Lewis' class. They showed me the way and when I knocked on his door, Doug nearly fell over. I'd taken his remark at face value and, at that age, I hadn't realised that I needed permission to go to Gabalfa because we didn't live in the school catchment area. Doug quickly put the wheels in motion for me to officially become a pupil and I stayed there for the next two years.

Doug was a good man who helped me develop my sporting skills so that I played for Cardiff Schools junior team at football, baseball and cricket. In the 1960-61 season – my last year at Gabalfa – I captained the soccer side when we became joint holders with Merthyr of the Tom Yeoman Shield after beating Newport, Mountain Ash and Rhondda on the way to the two-legged final. As well as being involved with my sport, Doug helped me to pass the 11-plus which meant I went to Cathays Grammar School. Looking back, it was the worst thing that could have happened to me!

I really did hate school – I just couldn't stand it. I think it was because I just wanted to be out playing sport all the time. I don't see why kids can't go to schools where sport plays a bigger part in the curriculum – like it does in North America – because not everybody's going to be academic. I still regard myself as quite intelligent – even though some of the things I've done may not suggest that – but I just think if I'd have gone somewhere that was more sport orientated, then maybe I wouldn't have been so unhappy – and I could also have become a better footballer or cricketer. I tried my best at schoolwork and although I was OK at English, history and geography, subjects like physics, biology, chemistry and maths all went either through or over my head. I remember that in one year, our first lesson on a Thursday morning was maths with the headmaster followed by music. As soon as the headmaster left, I would go out of the classroom, jump over the wall and spend the rest of my day either in a museum or walking around the city centre. But despite that, I ended up getting 56% in the music exam that I never took! The mark put me 12th in a class of 30 – I don't know what the other boys had been doing and I haven't got a clue how it happened. Perhaps the teacher couldn't remember me? That exam result still makes me smile when I think about it.

When I was 13, we moved again – leaving Llanishen so that my parents could run The Cambridge pub in Tyndall Street in the Irish part of the docks area of Cardiff. We lived above the pub and I found the life completely different to anything I'd experienced before. Although I was captain of the school's football, cricket and rugby teams, I was basically quite a shy boy. So it was a bit of a shock to find myself in an environment where I sometimes had to serve behind the bar – it made me grow up very quickly. The kids I mixed with there were amazing – very street-wise. The area was next to Tiger Bay where I'd spent a lot of time as a child with my grandparents and as all the lads around were Catholic – some of them altar boys – I started going to church with them. The priest, Father Mac, took me to my first race meeting at Chepstow. I wasn't a Catholic then but I converted later. You had to know how to look after yourself in that part of Cardiff but I didn't very often get involved in any fights – apart from on the football pitch!

Some people say that your schooldays are the happiest days of your life but I'm afraid they weren't for me – mainly because of the attitude towards pupils who liked sport at Cathays Grammar. Before I went for the trial for the Cardiff Schools football team, the head sports master was taking assembly one day when he made it clear what he thought of my ambitions. I'll never forget what he said:

'We've actually got a boy in this school who thinks he's going to make a living out of playing football.'

I look back now and I just have to laugh but, at the time, it wasn't very funny – I was very serious about wanting to play football for a living. When I won my first full Welsh cap in 1969, the school didn't put up a photo of me in my kit on the wall – like they did when Billy Raybould, a former head boy, had played rugby for Wales against England two years earlier. It was the one thing I always wanted but they wouldn't do it. In fact, since those long ago days, the school have written to me many times asking me to present prizes but I've never gone back. Every time I went to see my mother before she died in April 2004, I'd pass the school and have a little chuckle to myself.

Like David, I was pretty good at most ball games but choosing Cardiff Schools football rather than rugby meant I was barred from playing cricket for Cathays. My last game was in a cup competition and I scored about 40 not out to help the team reach the semi-finals.

The cricket teacher was also a football man and he asked me to keep playing.

'You know I'm banned,' I said.

'Yes...but I want you to play,' he insisted.

Being stubborn, I refused. My view was that if I couldn't do what I wanted to do at school, why should I do what they wanted me to do? I took no pleasure from seeing the team being beaten in the semi-final and even without me I'd have preferred them to have won. That obstinate streak has stayed with me throughout my life.

As for my aborted rugby career, I was a tenacious scrum-half and I really think I could have made it at a pretty high level – given the chance. I used to take penalty kicks using the 'round the corner' technique – as perfected by the great Barry John – but the sports master who later banned me didn't approve. One day before school, he pulled me to one side and warned me that if I carried on taking kicks like that, I wouldn't be taking any more. It turned out to be a pointless threat in the end because when I was forced to choose between rugby and football, it didn't really matter which method I used. Although I loved playing both games, I did what Dad and David told me to do, chose soccer – and never looked back.

In my first year with the Cardiff Schools senior side, John Toshack, the former Wales, Cardiff and Liverpool striker, was also in the team. 'Tosh' was a year older than me and went to Canton High School in the west of Cardiff. He had an amazing record with the Cardiff Schools team – hitting 47 goals in 22 games – and became the youngest player to appear in a League match for Cardiff City when he scored on his debut against Leyton Orient at the age of 16. I was later made captain of the schoolboys team and I was training with Cardiff City at Ninian Park twice a week. It might have seemed obvious that they would come in for me but Leeds were the only team in the country who were actually interested.

The move came about through Jack Pickard, the part-time scout for Leeds in South Wales who discovered, among others, John Charles, Gary Sprake, Leighton Phillips, Carl Harris and Byron Stevenson. One day in December 1964, I came home from school and walked into the pub to find Jack sitting at the bar. But it was my mother who spoke:

'Would you like to spend a week of your Christmas holidays up at Leeds?'

'Leeds? What do you mean?' I said incredulously.

'Well...that gentleman,' she said, pointing at Jack, 'is a scout for Leeds United Football Club and he wants to take you there.'

I really couldn't believe what I was hearing but it was true: Leeds wanted me to go for a trial. Jack was the man who set me on the road to becoming a professional footballer and I'll always be grateful to him. One of my most prized possessions is a letter he sent to my parents on the eve of my first game as skipper of the full Wales side at Ninian Park in October 1974. He described my 17th cap against Hungary as 'the greatest match' of my career to date and said that it fulfilled his prediction that I would captain my country. As it happened, I didn't have my trial with Leeds over the 1964 Christmas period. The trip was postponed because of snow until the following Easter when I travelled up to Elland Road with Leighton Phillips. Like me, Leighton, from Briton Ferry near Neath, was playing for the Welsh Schoolboys team. We'd been in Belfast for a match against Northern Ireland the week before and when we were on the ferry, one of the teacher-selectors came up to us and said he understood we were going to Leeds for a trial. He then looked at me and said:

'The only reason you're picked for Wales is because you can take a corner!'

It was typical of some of the rather disparaging remarks that have been made about my footballing ability over the years but I tried not to let it get to me as Leighton and I went up by train at the start of our big adventure to Leeds. It was a long, six-hour journey and when we finally arrived, we were met by the late Maurice Lindley, then chief scout at Elland Road. He took us to a hotel where Leighton, myself and the eight other hopefuls stayed for the week. It was very enjoyable and they treated us like apprentices so we trained in the morning and then carried out chores around the ground in the afternoon.

My job was to clean out the referee's room and on the last day of the trial, I noticed a pile of letters lying on the desk. The first one I picked up contained an offer of an apprenticeship to one of the boys with me so I naturally thought that mine must be in there somewhere and I went looking for it. But when I found the letter addressed to my parents, I was devastated. Apparently, I'd done well but not well enough. It was a 'thanks but no thanks' type of letter. But, fortunately for me, there was a twist at the end of my trial at Leeds.

One of the other lads with us was a Newport boy, Alan Smith, who also played for Welsh Schoolboys. He was being offered an apprenticeship by Leeds but his twin brother, like me, was one of the unlucky ones. When their parents were told that the club would take only one of their sons, Mr and Mrs Smith took umbrage. They said Leeds would have to sign both their boys or Alan wouldn't join them. It was all or nothing. But Leeds dug their heels in so my parents received a completely different letter to the one I'd come across lying on the desk at Elland Road. I found out what had happened shortly after the letter arrived at our pub because South Wales schools football was such a close-knit community. Cardiff played Newport about four times a year so I learnt all about the Smith family's part in my career when the two teams next met. I'm very grateful to Mr and Mrs Smith!

After being taken on by Leeds through the back door, I now had the problem of sorting out school. I was desperate to pack it all in but I was still only 15 and in those days, you needed £100 to buy yourself out if you didn't want to stay until the official school-leaving age of 16. My parents couldn't afford that sort of money so Leeds sent it down to us. When I took it into school, the possibility of going to Millfield, the sporting scholarship public school in Somerset, was mentioned but my mind was made up. I went to hand the money to the headmaster and he told me to give it to my parents – which, after all the aggro they'd given me, was a nice gesture on the school's part.

Having been turned down by Leeds, Leighton Phillips joined Cardiff as an apprentice a year later. There was never any rivalry or animosity between us. We were friends then and we remain very good friends now. Leighton went on to establish himself as a first-class defender with Cardiff, Aston Villa, Swansea, Charlton and Exeter before becoming player-manager at Llanelli. He won 58 caps for Wales – only one less than me.

The twice-weekly training sessions with Cardiff City were run by Ronnie Stitfall, the former Cardiff and Wales full-back, who was looking after the kids at the time. Ronnie used to drink at The Three Arches pub in the Heath area of Cardiff where my mother worked and

Dad often drank – even though they ran The Cambridge on the other side of the city. After we'd received the letter from Elland Road, my father ran into Ronnie there and he wanted to know if I was going to Leeds. Dad told him the good news and then asked why Cardiff weren't interested in signing me. I've always been intrigued by Ronnie's reply:

'Oh...we always thought somebody else would take him.'

I'm not sure, but I think my brother was behind Ronnie's assumption because David wanted me to go anywhere but Cardiff who he'd signed for as a 15-year-old apprentice. Although Arsenal and Nottingham Forest were interested in him, my mother, being a mother, didn't want him to leave home. David should really have gone to one of those other clubs and although he didn't make a League appearance for Cardiff, he did play in a Football League Cup game before joining Crystal Palace on a free transfer in 1966. He later moved to non-League Margate where he made nearly 300 appearances – usually at right-back but sometimes on the right wing and in midfield. He also played for Tonbridge, Romford, Dover and Ramsgate. The local papers referred to him as being 'utterly resolute', 'a brilliant overlapper', ' a subtle blend of resolution and elegance' and 'the epitome of modern full-back play.' He was once described as 'steaming up the right flank like a cavalryman to support his infantry.'

Those comments seem to back up my mother's judgement because she always said David was a better footballer than me. We used to have fantastic rivalry and I think he was just unfortunate – probably a classic case of being in the wrong place at the wrong time. Whenever Ronnie Stitfall asked about me, David would always say I was going somewhere else. I don't think he felt threatened by me but they had this culture at Cardiff in those days of finishing training and going to Canton Liberal Club, about half a mile from Ninian Park, and staying there all afternoon drinking and playing snooker. David got caught up in that and perhaps he thought I would have become involved in it too if I'd have joined him at Cardiff. I think he felt he was doing me a favour. He liked his social life, he loved being around women – and the feeling was mutual. He was a very smart, good-looking footballer but I think if he'd had his time over again, he'd have been more dedicated. After seeing what happened to him, I understood the kind of dedication required when I went to Leeds but then they were a completely different club where discipline was rock solid. Anyway, it was always going to be Leeds for me once I knew they were interested. No disrespect to Cardiff, who had finished in the bottom half of the old Second Division, but Leeds had just missed out on winning the First Division championship to Manchester United only on goal average. It would have been no contest had Cardiff ever made a serious attempt to sign me.

Elland Road may have been more than 200 miles from home but I was desperate to make it as a footballer and although a lot of tears were shed in the Yorath household when I finally left the pub to travel north, I was really looking forward to starting my new career in a new city. I wasn't to know it then but joining Leeds turned out to be the best thing I've ever done in my life.

Norman Hunter's Mum's New Lodger

When I arrived in Leeds, the club put me up in digs with a Mr and Mrs Turner at their house in Beeston, an area of the city about a mile from Elland Road. There were four of us – two to a room – and I shared with a lad called Paul Peterson from Luton. It was a home from home but Mrs Turner was a typical British landlady. She ran her lodgings for Leeds players in a very strict way – she was a fearsome woman and a real stickler for discipline. Everything had to be in its place and she wouldn't stand for any mucking around. When her husband, Ernest, used to come to our room and tell us a joke or two, she was soon shouting at him to get out – that wasn't part of the service they were providing to Leeds United's young footballers. One of the other boys, Maurice Parkin from Sheffield, was always the one getting into trouble. She went berserk once after he'd wiped his shoes on one of her precious curtains.

Then there was the time we came back from a night out at the local youth club, where, incidentally, I met my wife, Christine. I later found out that her mother, Sheila, had a connection with the football club in that she used to run the café next to the fish and chip shop straight opposite the main gates at Elland Road. The youth club was an old Catholic church building which we used to visit a couple of times a week. As usual, we went to raid the fridge as soon as we arrived home but, on this particular night, at around about 10 o'clock, we discovered that Mrs Turner had cottoned on to what we were up to – she'd taped up the fridge door so we couldn't open it.

I'll never forget my first day as an apprentice with Leeds at the start of pre-season training in the summer of 1965. By then, the renaissance under manager Don Revie was well underway and after returning to the old First Division, the club had just failed to pull off a remarkable League and cup 'double' by finishing second to Manchester United and Liverpool respectively. I'd watched the FA Cup Final defeat by Liverpool on the television at home in Cardiff as a Leeds supporter because I knew I would be joining them in the summer. By the way Don carried himself, nobody was left in any doubt that he was the boss – not only of the football team but of the whole club. He was 'Mr Leeds United'. After arriving as a player from Sunderland in 1958, he played 80 games before taking over as manager when director Harry Reynolds persuaded the board that Don should replace Jack Taylor in March 1961. Don immediately set out his stall by looking for some advice from Matt Busby at Manchester United and then changing the first team's strip from blue and gold to all white in homage of the then greatest club side in Europe. 'We shall be like Real Madrid,' Don had told the press. 'Feared by everyone, challenging for everything.' It may have seemed a little ambitious but it was Don's way of letting every-one know that Leeds meant business. The possibility of a second successive relegation receded when the team won one and drew four of their last nine games to finish 14th in the old Second Division.

With Harry Reynolds having taken over as chairman, there was a very tight finish to Don's first full season in charge – only a 3-0 win on the last day at Newcastle kept them up – but then a crop of promis-ing youngsters started to make their mark. Rookies such as Gary Sprake, Paul Reaney, Norman Hunter and Billy Bremner were intro-duced alongside the more experienced players like Jack Charlton and Bobby Collins. When right-winger Johnny Giles and centre-forward Alan Peacock joined from Manchester United and Middlesbrough respectively, everything fell into place. The Second Division champi-onship was won in 1964 as club records were set for most points and away victories and fewest defeats. Leeds were on the move.

Following the lead taken by Reynolds, a steel magnate who believed in making everybody working at Elland Road feel important, Don fos-tered a family spirit within the club. He made sure he got to know everyone and it was that attention to detail that helped to make him so successful as a manager. He was a father figure to us all – from the players to their wives and girlfriends to the cleaners – and his inclusive, paternalistic approach meant that many parents, including mine, were happy for their sons to join Leeds. They knew the club would look after their children and Don knew every one of his new charges by name. After my parents had received the letter saying that Leeds were going to take me on as an apprentice, I played for Welsh Schoolboys against Scotland at Cappielow Park, Greenock Morton's ground. Don was in the stand and during the national anthems, I looked up and saw him and he waved at me! For someone like him to do that was fantastic, especially when you consider his other commitments at that time. It was something I never forgot.

Despite the disappointment of missing out on the 'double', the players were in a pretty upbeat mood when they returned for the start of the 1965-66 season to Fullerton Park, alongside Elland Road. It was the club's training ground for the first team and reserves and the youth team played their games there. I can remember Billy Bremner going up to Bobby Collins, the club captain, shaking him by the hand and wishing him good luck and then Don held a meeting at which he told the players what he was expecting of them. I was absolutely petrified because I didn't know if I was good enough to be at Leeds or how I'd be treated. I just sat there listening like a schoolboy – which, of course, is what I was.

After Don had finished, the young lads were told to report to the groundsman, Ces Boyd, who then lectured us on what he was expecting. I was allocated the job of putting out the first team's kit in their dressing room. Ces's assistant was John Reynolds, who'd come up to Leeds as a highly rated centre-half in 1952 from Briton Ferry in South Wales, also on the recommendation of Jack Pickard. John's career ended after he damaged cruciate knee ligaments in a youth cup match. John is a lovely man who's still at Elland Road. My original nickname at Leeds was 'Yogi' – I suppose because it began with the same letter as my surname – but I later became known as 'Taff' and it was great to have someone from Wales to talk to in my early days at Leeds.

When Ces and John had finished with us, we went out training with the first team which meant travelling by coach to Roundhay Park – a huge area with its own natural bowl. We would run around a big lake, up the steep hill to the bowl from where you could see the coach that had brought us to the park in the distance – it was the finishing line.

On that first day, I thought I was up there with the big boys: I thought I was the bee's knees. When we got to the top of the hill, I looked across, saw the coach and started to head for home. But I had nothing left so I crawled in last. From then on, I knew the level of fitness I had to reach if I wanted to make it with Leeds. After this we had to collect up all the kit, put it in the laundry and then lay out another strip for the afternoon session. My job also involved running and then cleaning the baths for the players as well as sorting out anything else that needed doing – like polishing boots and painting or wiping down seats back at Elland Road. Sometimes, we even had to put our hands down the toilets to clean them! I daren't refuse so I just did it.

As part of his pre-season training programme, Don would split everybody – including the apprentices – into four mixed teams in the afternoon after we'd done all the hard work in the morning. When I'd been there for a year or so, I happened to find myself in Jack Charlton's team – it was a nightmare. Jack had joined Leeds in 1952 and spent 21 years at Elland Road. He played a huge part in the Revie Revolution. He made a record 629 League appearances for the club before retiring and becoming manager of Middlesbrough, Newcastle, Sheffield Wednesday and then the Republic of Ireland. Although he'd just helped win the World Cup as England's centre-half, Jack was never the greatest runner and by listening to the other players, I had the feeling that our team was the worst of the four. We would play eight-a-side on a full-sized pitch in a round-robin format so we'd all have three games. On this particular day, we were getting well beaten and Jack was just standing about up front, not doing much, so I shouted across to him:

'Are you going to do some running around?'

I thought nothing of my remark – made in the heat of the moment during a pretty competitive game – and carried on playing but afterwards, as I was carrying some balls across the car park back to the main building, I felt a hand on my shoulder.

'When you've won a World Cup medal,' said an obviously irritated Jack, 'then you can speak to me like that.'

I wouldn't say he held the comment against me but Jack didn't speak to me for two years – even though I was cleaning his kit during all of that time! I remember another incident after Don announced that he wasn't happy with the way the training kit was being thrown on to the ground. He wanted the players to hang up their own kit after a session but they thought it was too much trouble for them. So Johnny Giles, who was signed as a right-winger before eventually replacing Bobby Collins in midfield, his partner in the centre of the park, Billy Bremner, and a couple of the others said they'd pay me to do it for them. I can't remember how much I was offered and I don't think it was very much but as I was earning only £5 a week, it was a nice little bonus. I hung up their kit for about a week but they didn't bother paying me. So I decided to do it for another week and see what happened. Again, I received nothing so I started to leave the kit lying on the ground where they'd dropped it. Don went ballistic and for the next three weeks, the players regularly threw me, fully clothed, into the team bath.

Until I was 18, I only occasionally worked with these fantastic footballers because the first team looked after itself and I was in the youth side and then the reserves where I played at right-back and central defender before being pushed into midfield when I grew stronger. If you were asked to train with the first team then it was seen as a great honour. We used to have some tremendous games against sides like Sunderland and Newcastle and I remember playing against the future England forward, Frank Worthington, when he was starting out at Huddersfield. At the end of the first year of my apprenticeship, I was involved in an incident that I suppose sums up what a ruthless club Leeds became during the Revie era from 1961-74. Winning was everything – whatever the standard of the competition.

In October 1965, Bobby Collins broke his leg against Torino in an Inter-Cities Fairs Cup tie and he was in a plaster cast from his groin right down to his toes. My job was to make sure that he was able to climb into the bath and then help him out of it and dress him. This went on for months until his plaster was taken off. Bobby then started to get himself fit before being put in charge of the youth team and eventually returning for the final League game of the 1965-66 season at Old Trafford. He was the original pocket dynamo, a pint-sized midfield player who Revie had bought from Everton for £25,000 in 1962 to help turn the club around. Bobby was the man who pulled all the threads together as Leeds started to take on Manchester United and

Bill Shankly's Liverpool. Although only 5ft 4in, he intimidated opponents through his tenacious tackling but, like Johnny Giles, he also had a delicate, sometimes devastating, touch.

In the youth team's last match of the 1965-66 season, we had to beat Hull at Fullerton Park to win our league. Their left-winger was giving our right-back, Bobby Sibbald, the runaround and Bobby Collins wanted him sorting out. So when the ball went out of play, he called me over to the touchline.

'You move to right-back,' he said, 'and the first chance you get, 'do' him.'

My instructions were clear: I had to take the Hull winger out – so I did. My concern was just to get him off the park. The ball got thrown to this lad and I just went whack! Straight into him. He was carried off on a stretcher with a broken leg – although I didn't know it at the time – and we ended up winning the game. I don't feel very good about it now but it was the kind of thing that went on in those days. I will admit that I severely damaged the career of a fellow professional but Bobby was held in such high esteem at Leeds that I felt I was doing it for him and the club. In Bobby's eyes, the end justified the means – we won the league. I didn't think about it at the time but, over the years, I've given it a lot of thought and it's not a pleasant memory. I don't know who the lad was – we didn't have team sheets in those days – but I never came across him in the game again so I could well have ended his career. It's not something I'm proud of but you have to remember the times. If you didn't see at least two or three instances of players going over the top of the ball in a game, then you weren't watching the right type of football. I still see Bobby Collins quite a lot these days and he always reminds me of the incident:

'Remember that tackle?' he says. 'That won us the league'.

I admit it's not a nice story but it just shows how the competitive spirit under Don Revie had affected everyone at Leeds. You had to be prepared to put your foot in where it hurt for the good of the team. In many ways, Bobby was my mentor. He showed me that I needed strength and determination as well as skill to succeed in a man's game. I looked up to Bobby and it was a privilege for me to look after him when he was injured. I love Bobby dearly and I'm very grateful to him for the start he gave me in the game.

After I'd been lodging in Beeston for about a year, the Turners decided to put up the rent by 10 shillings in old money – that's 50p nowadays. The rise meant half my weekly wage would go on rent and as I was determined not to pay the increase, I quickly started to look around for alternative digs. Derek Montgomery, a boy from Chester-le-Street in County Durham, told me there was a place at his lodgings – provided by the legendary Norman Hunter's mother in a club house in Kirkdale Gardens, not far from Elland Road. Jimmy Greenhoff, the skilful forward who later blossomed at Stoke and Manchester United, had just moved out and Derek suggested that I could replace him. Mrs Hunter was running the boarding house because Norman had been such a thin lad when he came down from the Gateshead area in 1959. It's hard to believe when you think what he developed into later on in his career but when he arrived at Elland Road the club thought he needed building up so they installed his mother in the club house to look after him. At first, Don Revie insisted Norm should be fed a diet of sherry and eggs but gradually home cooking started to do the trick. Although his fighting weight was never more than 12 and a half stone, Norman became one of the most formidable defenders in the game as he was pretty soon given his notorious 'Bites Yer Legs' nickname. I jumped at the chance of moving in – even though it meant me being the only Welshman among three Geordies – Norman, Derek and another lad called John Price. Norman's mum was a wonderful woman who looked after us really well and I shared a room with Derek – or 'Titch' as we called him. It was fantastic because Norman had already been a first-team regular at Leeds for four years and I quickly learned what you could and couldn't do as a professional footballer. It was the start of a longstanding friendship that led to us rooming together on away trips when I made it into the first-team squad.

Towards the end of my second year at Elland Road, I became a full-time professional. It was the proudest moment of my short career when I was called into Don Revie's office to sign the contract in March 1967. I went in with the youth-team coach, Cyril Partridge, and the manager told me I'd done well and then gave me a lecture about the right way to live. He stressed the importance of having good digs and, as he did with all players, he later encouraged me to get engaged as soon as possible. He felt he would get more out of us if we had settled home lives. I was so pleased to have achieved my immediate ambition by turning pro even though I knew a lot of hard work lay ahead before I could say I'd finally arrived.

I spent all of the 1967-68 season playing in the reserves before making my first team debut in the last First Division game against Burnley at the age of 18 in May 1968. All the reserves knew we had a chance of playing because it was a nothing game. Leeds had already won the League Cup by beating Arsenal 1-0 but they couldn't win the First Division title and finished fourth in the end – five points behind the champions, Manchester City. In fact, we reckoned that taking part in five-a-sides at Leeds was more nerve-racking than playing in the first team. The standard was unbelievable and I was nervous just being on the same pitch as people like Billy Bremner, Johnny Giles, Norman Hunter and Jack Charlton. I'd been playing at the back for the reserves and when Don announced the team in the Turf Moor dressing room, I found myself marking Andy Lochhead, one of the most consistent goalscorers in the old First Division. The former England and Everton defender, Brian Labone, once described Andy as his toughest-ever opponent – and I soon found out why he felt that way! It turned out to be a pretty frightening experience on a mud heap of a pitch. The match will always be special to me, not only because I made my debut but for a remark I overheard just after I'd dumped Andy over the touchline and into the arms of our trainer, Les Cocker, in the away dugout.

'Who the hell did that, Les?' asked Andy, as I congratulated myself after pulling off such a thumping tackle.

'His name is Yorath,' replied Les. 'He's Norman Hunter's mum's new lodger!'

I may have won that particular battle but Andy ended up winning the war by scoring his 100th League goal for Burnley in their 3-0 win that afternoon before later moving on to Leicester, Aston Villa and Oldham. So, not the best of starts to my first-team career but on the way home, Don congratulated me and then rewarded me at the end of the season. We had to go and sit in an outer office to the manager's to find out if we'd been offered contracts and after making my debut at Burnley, I came out of that room with a broad grin on my face. My first wage as a professional had been £17 a week and I was now being given a pay rise of £8. There were no negotiations – I'd be on £25 a week from now on. To be honest, I was so delighted that I wasn't bothered about the money. The new contract was a sure sign that I was making progress from the Northern Intermediate League to the reserves to the fringes of the first team.

In the reserves, I came into contact with Syd Owen. His title of first-team coach was a bit misleading because the first team were in the hands of Don and his trainer, Les Cocker. Syd was a really hard taskmaster as I found out when I started training with the reserves in the afternoons. Before we worked on an exercise, he'd show us how it should be done. For example, we would chip the ball up to the centre-forward, then lay it out wide to the winger who would then knock it forward and cross it for someone else to score. Syd would then stand behind the first kid who, because Syd had played for Luton and England, would be trembling in his boots. If any part of the move wasn't perfect, Syd would make his displeasure known by tutting to himself. That kind of pressure was put on you from a very young age. Some of the youngsters resented Syd because it was thought he ruined more careers in the game than he helped to make, but I always felt that if you got past Syd, you were into the first team!

Having made my debut in May 1968, I was in the squad for the second leg of the Inter-Cities Fairs Cup Final against Ferencvaros in the Nep Stadium the following September. Leeds had really taken to European football, reaching the semi-finals of the competition in 1966 and then losing to Dynamo Zagreb in the final the following year when the two legs were actually played at the start of the 1967-68 season. The same format was being used in my debut season as Leeds saw off Spora Luxembourg, Partizan Belgrade, Hibernian, Rangers and Dundee on their way to the final against the Hungarians. Elland Road was half-empty when we beat Ferencvaros in the first leg through a first-half goal by Mick Jones, who'd joined Leeds for £100,000 from Sheffield United a year earlier. For the second leg a month later, there were 76,000 spectators in the Nep Stadium in Budapest – and only 50 of them were from Leeds. In those days, Hungary was a communist country and the Cold War was in full swing. On the night before the game, Don Revie called all the squad together around a table and spoke to us in a very low voice.

'Be careful what you say,' he said, rather furtively. 'There are people everywhere. You don't know who you're talking to.'

To an impressionable 18-year-old lad like me, comments like that only added to the excitement of my first European away trip with the first team. It was also the first time I'd ever been to the Nep Stadium and that was an experience in itself. There was a training ground alongside 'The People's Stadium' with very tall statues of soldiers with guns and workers with hammers and sickles. The oak-panelled dressing rooms were magnificent – the armchairs and flowers on the table made them seem just like somebody's lounge – and it was fabulous being there. I got to know the stadium quite well over the next few years when I went back there with Leeds and Wales.

The game itself has rightly become part of Leeds United folklore. We mounted an incredible rearguard action, having to defend for most of the match and being pinned back in our own penalty area. We almost scored when Peter Lorimer's deflected shot was beaten away by the goalkeeper and then Mick Jones headed against the crossbar but my abiding memory is of Gary Sprake's heroics to keep us in the lead on aggregate. He pulled off an absolutely outstanding save from a free-kick – considering the poor view he had with 10 defenders in front of him – and I was particularly pleased that Gary had helped Leeds to win their first European trophy. He had come up from Swansea in 1962 and eventually played 507 matches for Leeds – a record for a goalkeeper – and because we were both Welsh, he'd taken me under his wing when I arrived at Elland Road.

I spent the whole of the 1968-9 season in the reserves as we won the First Division championship for the first time after drawing 0-0 at Liverpool in our last but one game. We needed a point to make sure while a home win would have meant Bill Shankly's team still being in with a chance of winning the title for the first time since 1966. I was sitting in the stand at Anfield as two teams at the very top of their game did battle in a 0-0 draw in front of a crowd of nearly 54,000 spectators. It was a great occasion because the Kop were sportingly chanting 'Champions!' to the Leeds players when they went over to acknowledge their applause. We used to have mammoth battles with Liverpool in those days. The games were just awesome – a bit like Manchester United versus Arsenal today.

I didn't play for the first team in the League again until the 1969-70 season when I made 11 appearances, four of them as substitute. It was strange because I was captaining the Welsh Under-23 team and yet still playing for United's reserves. It was frustrating but it's worth recalling what a fantastic group of players I was part of at Leeds. Gary Sprake's miraculous save against Ferencvaros was one of many he pulled off during his 10 years at Elland Road. He was a natural goal-keeper and an excellent shot-stopper but I'm worried that he'll always be remembered for some of the high-profile mistakes he made through his occasional lapses of concentration. I will defend Gary against anybody who criticises him because football is littered with brilliant goalkeepers who all make the odd mistake. It's unfair and it was just unfortunate that the cameras always seemed to be there when he made his howlers. Gary had this image of being blonde, good-looking and brash but, in fact, he was a very nervous character and when he made mistakes, they were big ones. His most famous gaffe was when he inadvertently threw the ball into his own net during a game at Anfield in 1967. There was snow on the pitch and the throw-out was intended for Peter Lorimer out on the right. When Peter saw the Liverpool full-back bearing down on him, he made it clear that he didn't want the ball. Unfortunately, as Gary went to pull the ball back to his chest with his right arm, it flew between his left arm and his body and into the net. Gary's team-mates didn't realise what had happened until they heard the crowd roar. To add insult to injury, the Des O'Connor song 'Careless Hands' was played over the tannoy during the half-time interval and the crowd sang along. Gary was eventually replaced by his understudy, David Harvey, in 1973 and it broke his heart to leave Leeds for Birmingham where he picked up a bad back injury and retired two years later.

At right-back, Paul Reaney was a tremendously quick athlete whose battles with George Best were just that in the 1960s and early 1970s. George and Leeds just didn't go together and Bestie could never get a kick of the ball when Paul was around and when he wasn't, then Paul Madeley would take care of George. Paul Madeley was a Rolls Royce of a player who, more than anybody else, kept the Leeds team together because he could slot in anywhere – he was so unselfish. He ran so effortlessly and he was so quick that he glided over the ground. I'm sure if he'd had just one position, Paul would have played many more times for England. As with many all-rounders in any sport, his versatility was his greatest strength and his greatest weakness. Paul Reaney's broken leg kept him out of the 1970 Mexico World Cup while Paul Madeley turned down the chance to join the England squad because he was exhausted and thought he'd only be making up the numbers.

On the left side, we had Terry Cooper who'd been converted by Don Revie from a winger to full-back. He wasn't that quick but he had a great left foot that scored the goal to win us the 1968 League Cup – our first major trophy. I only ever saw Terry torn apart by one player and that was the legendary Celtic winger, Jimmy Johnstone. He played out of his skin in both semi-final legs of the European Cup in 1970 as Celtic beat us 3-1 on aggregate.

Our two central defenders were as rough and ready as they came. Big Jack Charlton was a late starter with a steely streak who carved out a fantastic career at Leeds. Apparently, he'd been an awkward cuss who didn't appreciate being given advice but, after settling his differences with Don, Jack settled down to become the lynchpin of our defence. He was OK with me when I got into the first team but he could be very abrupt. During the 1972-73 season, when I started 16 games because of injuries to Billy Bremner and Johnny Giles, I picked up a hamstring strain. I didn't know how bad it was so I carried on playing even when it started to affect my back. But that was typical of the Leeds players – they were so committed to the cause that they'd do anything for the club and for Don.

I remember receiving some treatment for my hamstring problem at Elland Road on a Saturday morning after the manager had agreed that I needed a rest. Suddenly, the phone rang: I was needed to play at Manchester City that afternoon. Because I didn't drive, I had to take my boots and catch a train to Manchester to meet up with the squad in the Midland Hotel. I walked in just after Don had begun his team talk and he was going through the team... 'Sprake, Reaney, Taff, Billy, Jack, Norman...' right through to number 11, Eddie Gray. When Don finally finished, Jack piped up:

'Er Boss...who's left-back?'

'Taff,' replied Don.

'Fucking Taff! Left-back?' cried Jack.

For a moment, I felt awful. I'd just made the journey across from Leeds by myself and this was the reception I was being given! But that was Jack – no messing around, straight to the point. He wasn't taking the piss – he was being serious in that he didn't rate me as a left-back. Had it been Johnny Giles then the comment would have knocked my confidence but because it was Jack just being his normal blunt self, it didn't bother me. He was the last person in that team who I ever thought would become a manager. He didn't seem to be interested at all in coaching but, unbeknown to us, he had been taking his badges. I admire Jack because he's had the courage to walk away from a couple of big jobs with Middlesbrough and the Republic of Ireland when he's had enough.

His partner at the back was a different kettle of fish. When I tell people that Norman Hunter was a very honest player, they look at me and think I'm daft but he was. OK, if Norm kicked you, you stayed kicked but he wasn't trying to hurt you. The only person I saw him really hurt was Burnley's Paul Fletcher at Burnley who he tackled off the pitch. Everybody at Leeds loved Norm – you'd always have him in your side and he was a great character. He was so unlucky with England because Bobby Moore was in front of him but he never once complained about not being in the side. If it hadn't been for Bobby, he'd have won more than 28 caps for his country. As a kid, I used to quiz Norm when he came back from international duty about the England players like Bobby and Jimmy Greaves and I learned so much from him.

Billy Bremner was a fiery little Scotsman who, after being snapped up from under Celtic's noses, became the talisman of Don Revie's teams. At one stage, the manager threatened to resign when the board were thinking of selling him – I think Don idolised the scamp in Billy because he was a cheeky chappy. When Johnny Giles arrived in 1963, Billy moved from either right-wing or inside-right into the centre of midfield. He was happiest in that position and it was from there that he scored so many important goals on the big occasions for Leeds – the winners in the FA Cup semi-finals of 1970 and 1973 are two that stick out for me. Under Don, Leeds were a fabulous footballing side who knew how to mix it as well. His teams were a classic combination of brain and brawn: at times, we could turn it on but when we needed to, if say we went 1-0 up, we could close down games by simply smothering our opponents and killing everything stone dead. Billy summed up that approach in that he could do both jobs so well. For example, he had the knack of looking one way and then passing the ball the other but he was nearly always involved in the niggly side of the game. Billy was inspirational as a captain and without having favourites, he was a good friend to us all. The players knew that he was idolised by Don and it was fitting that after everything he did for the club as a player over nearly 17 years, a statue of Billy should be put up outside Elland Road after he'd died from a heart attack in 1997.

Johnny Giles had felt he wasn't appreciated at Manchester United so he joined Leeds for £35,000 – and what a buy he turned out to be. He really came into his own when he replaced the injured Bobby Collins to play alongside Billy in the centre of midfield two years later. Johnny was a very shrewd footballer, a great tactician who always wanted to be the best and he was a wonderful passer of the ball over 20, 30 or 40 yards. He wasn't frightened of anything or anybody and he could turn nasty when he wanted to. But the game was different in those days. Today, you can't tackle from behind but then you could – in fact, you could tackle from anywhere and Johnny, like Billy, knew how to look after himself.

Soon after I'd joined Leeds, Johnny told me never to say sorry because it was a sign of weakness. In the 1972-73 season, we played against a Turkish side, Ankaragucu, in the European Cup Winners' Cup. They were a nasty bunch and one player, round about Johnny's size, was particularly unpleasant during the 1-1 draw at their place. In those days, teams like that would be given the warning that we'd see them back in Leeds. In the return leg, which we won 1-0, there was a mêlée in the first five minutes when half a dozen players all went in for the same ball. At the end of it all, our little Turkish 'friend' was lying on the ground and had to be carried off on a stretcher. After the game, Johnny, Mick Bates and I were in the bath when the injured player passed through our dressing room on his way to the bathroom. He lifted up his trouser leg, pointed to a bandage and said to Johnny:

'Hole, Giles – hole.'

He wasn't being nasty. I think he was trying to say that Johnny had done what he said he was going to do.

'Fuck off out of here!' replied Johnny.

Mick Bates, who was a real prim and proper lad, immediately piped up:

'John, there's no need for that!'

'You fuck off as well!' said Johnny. And that's the way he was – a very competitive man who was so influential. But off the pitch, he had a great sense of humour and was terrific company.

Out on the right, we had another Scot, Peter Lorimer, who still holds the record for being the youngest Leeds player to make his first-team debut – 15 years and 289 days. He's also the club's top League scorer having racked up 168 goals during his two spells at Elland Road. Peter was a great crosser of the ball who didn't have tons of pace but somehow got past full-backs. He was known for having the hardest shot in English football and although his left foot was more for standing on, his right was lethal – especially from free-kicks. During training, Peter's shooting was so dangerous that we had to warn him to be careful not to hit us!

Our left-winger, Eddie Gray, was the third member of the Scots colony in the first team. He was the complete opposite to Peter because he was a real twinkle toes. Eddie was so unlucky in the early part of his career with injuries to his thigh and then his shoulder. I was lucky enough to be on the same pitch as him when he scored that famous goal against Burnley at Elland Road in April 1970. We'd put out a weakened side because we were playing Chelsea in the FA Cup Final a week later so I found myself in the team. We won 2-1 with Eddie scoring both goals. His first was pretty special because he lobbed the goalkeeper from 40 yards and if that wasn't enough, he then scored one of the great goals of all time. He went into the penalty area, out of the area, over to the corner flag and back in, dribbling past six or seven players in the process, before casually stroking the ball into the net. I saw a video of it recently and our other winger, the South African, Albert Johanneson, was actually lying injured in the box and Eddie dribbled around him twice! A week later, on that noto-riously bad Cup Final pitch at Wembley, he made a fool out of Dave Webb who then had his revenge by scoring the winner for Chelsea in the replay at Old Trafford.

Our two main strikers could hardly have been more different. Mick Jones, signed for £100,000 from Sheffield United, was the most down-to-earth player I've met – he was just one of the lads. He never wanted or asked for anything and worked very hard to improve his game with Don Revie arranging special training sessions to help him. He was so unselfish – he didn't care if he didn't score as long as the team won. He averaged a goal in every three games at Leeds and as a hard-working, old-fashioned centre-forward, he was the perfect foil to Allan Clarke.

'Sniffer' Clarke was always a predator and if there were chances to be had, his goalscoring instincts would spot them and then, more often than not, take them. Don broke the British transfer record by paying Leicester £165,000 for him after he'd impressed in their 1969 FA Cup Final defeat by Manchester City. 'Clarkey' could be very cynical about anybody he thought couldn't play – you had to be the best. He'd annoy defenders by rubbing them up the wrong way and in a one-on-one with the keeper, I don't think I've ever seen anybody better. He was lethal anywhere near goal but he always admitted that he wouldn't have been as effective without Mick alongside him. He and Billy Bremner became big mates and when Billy died, it broke Clarkey's heart.

Waiting in the wings was a group of substitutes known as 'The Pie-testers'. In those days, teams were allowed only one substitute so the other players in the squad used to sit in the stand and when we went into the dressing room after the game, the players who'd been chosen would ask us what the pies were like! The group was made up of keeper David Harvey, midfielder Mick Bates, the late Terry Hibbitt, who was an Eddie Gray-type winger, centre-forward Rod Belfitt and me, a jack-of-all-trades. Although I played in every position apart from goalkeeper during my time at Leeds – I suppose I was the poor man's Paul Madeley – midfield was always the place to be. The main difference between me and Paul was that I never had any pace – which he had in abundance. All the books about the Revie era have described me as 'hard-tackling, versatile, whole-hearted, willing and industrious' and every single one of those words sums me up perfectly.

We didn't mind being stand-ins because it was a privilege to be involved. The good thing about the whole squad was that everyone got on so well. We were good mates who looked out for each other. The first team took some breaking into and when one of the reserves did manage to force our way in, there was even more pressure on us to perform.

The hardest period for me was when I was aged between 18 and 23. I was on the edge of the first team but I couldn't seem to crack it. Although other clubs were interested in me, I knew I had to be patient because the players in front of me were world class. It wasn't as if I could go to Don Revie and ask him why I wasn't in the first team. I knew why: I wasn't as good as them. I used to put in regular transfer requests – probably one a fortnight – but Don always insisted that I was going nowhere and he'd look after me at the end of the season which, to be fair, he always did. He told me to bide my time and assured me that my chance would come – and he was right on that score too as Leeds became one of the most consistent and most criticised teams in English football. As we threatened to win at least one trophy every season, people either loved us or loathed us – there wasn't any middle ground. Sadly, the record books show that, invariably, it used to all end in tears.

Bridesmaids Revisited

So why did a team of winners keep coming second so often? With Don Revie as our inspirational manager and so many internationals in our squad, how come Leeds didn't win more trophies between 1964 and 1974?

Looking back at the record books, I'm reminded of just how close we came to completely dominating English football under Don. I suppose it's fair to say that in the 1964-65 season, our first back in Division One, we perhaps weren't quite ready for the big time. We lost 1-0 to Manchester United in a crucial game at Elland Road in late April which led to them beating us to the title on goal average and we seemed overawed by the occasion at Wembley – eventually losing 2-1 in extra-time to Liverpool in our first FA Cup Final.

That double near miss set the pattern for the next decade when we would be in the running for at least one of the domestic and European trophies every season. We won the First Division championship in 1969 and 1974 but finished runners-up in five other seasons including three on the trot from 1970-72. We followed a League Cup win in 1968 with victory in the Inter-Cities Fairs Cup which we won again in 1971 before lifting the FA Cup in 1972. Apart from those six successes, we lost another six finals! In all, we were in at the death for a staggering 17 trophies! We won our fair share of silverware but we also lost our fair share. There has to be a reason for that. I think it was a combination of bad luck, bad mistakes and, on more than one occasion, some very bad refereeing.

I suppose we did put ourselves under pressure by trying to be successful on so many fronts – we wanted to win every competition we entered. We set very high standards and we were very competitive. Certainly, our congested fixture list took its toll in terms of injuries to star players at key times. You also have to remember that nearly everybody in the country hated us because we were in contention for so many trophies. We were known as 'dirty Leeds' because people didn't like the way that we imposed ourselves on opponents. We were accused of grinding them down by using a mixture of strong defence and intimidation – some critics described it as outright thuggery. It was said we were too professional because we put pressure on referees, questioned decisions and disrupted play by feigning injury. This hatred was used to fire up opponents as they set their hearts on beating us. As a result, they often played out of their skins against us in important matches.

We also put a lot of pressure on ourselves through the aura of invincibility that our success created. We were so determined to win that the expectation became too much at times. Some of that was down to Don himself through his tendency to over-prepare and emphasise the strength of our opponents too much. The dossiers were not originally his idea – his assistant, Maurice Lindley, introduced them – but Don loved them. They were pages and pages long and he read them out to us before every game in the hotel during the team meeting which lasted anything between half an hour and 45 minutes. Don spotted more things on a football field than almost any other person I've known. We would be given the information during the week and play a practice game against the reserves who copied the style of the opposition. Everything was reinforced on the day of the game. More often than not, the dossiers would tell us everything good about the opposition. Their weaknesses came out in the team talk but Don mainly concentrated on their strong points by going through all their free-kicks and their players individually. Having built up the opposition, he would do the same for us. He told us what we had to do – one by one – and he'd explain how he wanted us to play but perhaps he was guilty of building up our opponents too much so that the seed of doubt – the fear of losing if you like – was always there. I wonder if Don was worried that he didn't know absolutely everything there was to know about our opponents? Perhaps something crucial had been missed so he included everything he had in the dossiers? But

I think he was too thorough – he gave us too much information. Don was too preoccupied with detail and perhaps that caused him to take his eye off the bigger and more simple picture.

Don wanted cogs that fitted into his overall team machine and if information was given to you about your particular job, then you had to take it in – that's what the dossiers were for. We felt that if he'd gone out of his way to gather in all the information from his scouts, then we should take it on board and act on it. If you'd been told that your opponent was left-footed, then Don wouldn't expect that player to be allowed to get a shot in with his left foot. You'd have to show him on to his right foot. That you could be forgiven for but not if you let him fire in a left-foot shot. If Peter Lorimer was up against a full-back whose strength was on his left side then Peter would automatically try to take him on his inside. When we played Chelsea, Jack Charlton was always told not to let Peter Osgood come off him. If he did, we knew we'd be in trouble. If you didn't follow Don's instructions to the letter, then you'd get a bollocking as I found out after we'd played Plymouth at Elland Road in the fourth round of the FA Cup on our way to Wembley in 1972. We were winning 2-0 through goals from Clarkey and Mick Bates but I let one of their players pull the ball inside me before crossing it for Derek Rickard to score. After the game, Don told me in no uncertain terms that, after listening to his briefing, I should have stopped the cross.

Looking back, I think we had the balance between being aggressive and being a good football team about right. Sometimes, though, we were restrained by Don. He let his caution get the better of him. If he'd let us express ourselves individually a little more, then it could have been different. Everyone had to play within the team structure and although I'm sure he didn't restrict the flair players intentionally, if he'd realised just how talented his footballers were then I think we would have won more trophies. It wasn't until Don managed England that he realised that what he'd left behind was far better than what he'd taken over.

As well as being thorough and well-organised, Don was very punctual. He'd always be at Elland Road at half past eight every day so if you wanted to see him, you went in about nine. You knew he'd be there because he never turned up late and he didn't expect anyone else to.

Most people involved in football are superstitious but Don had it off to a fine art. In fact, he was obsessed to the point it made him eccentric, paranoid and uptight. In 1967, he brought a gypsy over from Scarborough to get rid of a curse hanging over Elland Road that he thought was bringing the team bad luck. It's said he once told Billy Bremner to go down on one knee every night and thank God for being blessed with such talent. He didn't like ornamental elephants and his phobia about birds eventually led to the peacock being dropped from the Leeds club badge. His whole build-up to games had to be just right – from the ritual of taking the same route to the dugout to wearing the same blue suit and sheepskin coat. As I was a substitute or in the squad so many times, I saw Don's superstitions in action at first hand.

During a match, he would sit in the dugout and take three puffs on a small cigar. Then he'd unwrap a Nuttall's Minto and suck it for about a minute before throwing it out and replacing it with gum that he'd chew for about 10 minutes. That went on continuously throughout the game: cigar, mint, gum – strictly in that order. Don was a slave to routine and strange traditions – he would do anything to cut down the chance of Leeds being hit by bad luck. Before one home game, he realised he'd left a dossier at home. He only lived about five minutes from the hotel where we used to meet up but he insisted on taking me with him in his car. When we arrived, he told me to go and knock on the door and ask his wife, Elsie, for the dossier.

'Why do I have to go in, Boss?' I asked. 'Why can't you?'

'Never go back in the house once you've left it,' he replied.

Another time, we were playing at Derby and just before kick-off, one of our players wanted to change their boots.

'Taff – go in and get his other pair,' Don said to me, 'but count to 10 before you go in.'

This was another example of his idiosyncratic superstitions. For some inexplicable reason, he felt it would bring the team bad luck if I went straight in. So I did as I was told and stood outside the away dressing room at the Baseball Ground with the groundsman looking at me as if I was stupid. The whole club was superstitious – it was just something we all got caught up in. Don used to rub Terry Cooper's back with liniment before every game – because he'd done it once and we'd won. Jack Charlton insisted on being the last one to leave the dressing room and he and Norman Hunter had to head the ball back to each other 20 times before going out. If we won a game, we all had to wear exactly the same suit and tie for the next one – it was just one of those things. It may sound crazy but if you keep on winning, then you don't think it's silly. Whatever prepares you for winning a game is right. If you feel happy preparing a particular way, then that's what you do.

I came a cropper once when I tried to prepare the Johnny Giles way. Just after I'd joined Leeds, I saw him putting some really hot liniment on his groin. But I forgot one key thing: Johnny had done it with his jockstrap on. I didn't and I nearly burnt off my privates! A quarter of an hour before we went out, I was still in the bathroom on fire! I had to have an early shower before the game to sort it out.

Although we were superstitious as a team, we never felt we were jinxed when we kept falling at the final hurdle – even when, after winning the League title in 1969, we came second for the next three years. More than 30 years down the line, the list of near misses under Don seems incredible. At times, we just didn't seem to get the rub of the green. Take the 1969-70 season which was shortened because England wanted to go to Mexico early to defend their World Cup. We were chasing an unprecedented treble of First Division championship, FA Cup and European Cup. As the fixtures piled up, so our chances of pulling it off dramatically disappeared – especially as there was little or no help from the Football League in rearranging our fixtures. As a result, we played 17 matches in March and April, nine of them in the space of 22 days. Don had to give up any hope of catching Everton so he fielded weakened sides full of reserves in League games as we concentrated on the two cup competitions.

In the first leg of the semi-final of the European Cup on 1st April, Celtic won 1-0 at Elland Road and then 24 hours later, Paul Reaney broke his leg in a meaningless League defeat at West Ham. Eddie Gray's two fabulous goals then gave us a win against Burnley and a week later we played Chelsea at Wembley. I was in the squad but not the team and watched Eddie tear them apart on what was probably the worst pitch in Wembley's history after the Horse of the Year Show had been staged there earlier in the week. After Jack Charlton had given us the lead in the 20th minute, Sprakey let Peter Houseman's long-range shot go under his body but a Mick Jones goal with seven minutes to go looked like winning us the FA Cup for the first time. It wasn't to be because Ian Hutchinson's header with just four minutes left produced the first FA Cup Final replay for 58 years.

Four days later, we travelled up to Hampden Park for the second leg of our European Cup tie against Celtic in front of 136,000 fans – which is still a crowd record for the competition. I was chosen as substitute for one of the most amazing matches of my career. Billy Bremner put us in front but John Hughes headed the equaliser just after half-time and then when Sprakey had been carried off after colliding with Hughes, David Harvey replaced him. His first involvement in the game was to pick Bobby Murdoch's shot out of the net. When I was getting warmed up, I realised just how jam-packed the ground was. In those days, Hampden was like a cauldron and when I looked into the crowd, there were so many faces that all I could see one big face. I just don't know how they managed to cram so many people in that night. It was a big game for Leeds not only because Celtic were the opposition but because Don Revie's wife was Scottish and so was our skipper, Billy Bremner. I couldn't really describe the electricity being generated in the stadium that night. At one stage, I was all stripped and ready but Don decided not bring me on and Celtic ended up winning 3-1 on aggregate.

Between that defeat and the FA Cup Final replay, we lost a couple of League games against Manchester City and Ipswich and then had eight days to prepare for the second game against Chelsea at Old Trafford. I wasn't involved at all this time but another hard man was to play a key role for Chelsea. As soon as we saw the teamsheets – with Ron 'Chopper' Harris at right-back and Dave Webb as central defender – we knew what was going to happen. After his performance at Wembley, Eddie would be a marked man and, sure enough, within five minutes, Chopper had sorted him out. We had no chance of protecting Eddie. We'd get the ball to his feet and whack! That was it – in came Chopper and out of the game went Eddie. There was no way he could give Chelsea the runaround as he had done at Wembley. It was a real battle with some rating it the dirtiest final since 1945. Mick Jones had given us the lead in the first-half but Peter Osgood scored with a brilliant diving header 12 minutes from the end and Webb popped up with the winner in extra-time. We were devastated when his header went in at the far post because we felt we had played well enough both at Wembley and Old Trafford to have won. It was just one of those occasions when a freak goal beats you. I remember Don being very disappointed but not too downhearted in the dressing room afterwards. As he smoked a cigar and chatted to the Chelsea chairman, Brian Mears, and one of their directors, the actor, Richard Attenborough, he said it was better to be involved as we had been rather than not being involved at all. And then he told us to go away on holiday and start all over again after the summer.

There was another heartbreaking end to the next season when we were the victims of one of the biggest FA Cup upsets in the competition's history. Having needed a replay to beat Rotherham in January, we knocked out Swindon and were drawn against Fourth Division Colchester in the fifth round in February 1972. We stayed in a hotel at Felixstowe and Don used the manager's lounge for his team talk where he announced that Mick Bates would be substitute with me as 13th man. He then looked at Sprakey, who wasn't in the best of form, and said:

'Gary, this is your last chance!'

Now I don't know if this ultimatum was meant to gee up Sprakey but if it was, it didn't work. I think Colchester knew Gary was going through a bad patch so they bombarded him with crosses and it paid off. I was sitting in the dugout along with Don, Les Cocker and Mick and I remember the pitch seemed even smaller than it actually was because chairs and benches had been placed around the edges. Colchester's veteran striker, Ray Crawford, who'd always seemed to score against us when he was at Ipswich, did the damage by giving them a 2-0 lead. He headed the first from a free-kick out on our right and then took advantage of a defensive mix-up between Gary and Paul Reaney when a ball was crossed from the right. Sprakey must have called for it because Paul seemed to duck. The ball hit him on the back and fell nicely for Ray who, although lying on the floor, tucked it away.

During his half-time team talks, Don would raise his voice but he didn't so much rant and rave. He was more constructive than anything else. Sometimes he'd encourage us by saying things like 'You've got him on toast, you can go by him any time you want to', other times he'd criticise us in the hope of getting a response. He was a good motivator but he couldn't get the team going against Colchester and when they scored a third goal with less than an hour gone after Gary and Paul had got themselves into another tangle, I felt we were never going to come back. Goals from Norman Hunter and Johnny Giles gave us hope of salvaging a replay but Colchester held out.

The atmosphere in the dressing room afterwards was shocking. We were gutted and Don had a face like thunder. We were embarrassed and we couldn't get out of there quickly enough. We knew what sort of reception we'd get from the press because of our reputation – and we weren't wrong – but at least Don was generous in defeat when he spoke to journalists before we left Layer Road. We had been without Billy Bremner through injury and Liverpool had just become the first team to win at Elland Road that season but Don offered no excuses. He said Colchester hadn't played above themselves because they were a difficult side to beat at home. They had done very well and that was the story of the match.

After a bad display at home, Don would hand out his bollockings and then walk across to the mirror in the changing room, comb his hair and look at Les Cocker and say:

'Tell them they're in tomorrow at 10 o'clock.'

He would then walk out. This time, we had to endure a long – and very quiet – coach journey back to Leeds.

The heartache wasn't over for that season either. 1971 will always be remembered as the year of Arsenal's 'double' triumph but we felt we were robbed of the title after losing 2-1 to West Bromwich Albion at Elland Road. With four games left, we led the First Division table by two points and Albion hadn't won away for 16 months. I'd spent most of the season in the reserves – starting only twice for the first team – and I was again watching from the stand. We were losing 1-0 when Norman Hunter's misplaced pass to Johnny Giles ricocheted off the Albion forward, Tony Brown, and ran over the half-way line. As Tony hared off towards our goal, the linesman flagged because Colin Suggett was clearly offside by at least 10 yards. Everybody stopped, including Tony and all our defenders but, amazingly, the referee, Ray Tinkler, waved play on. Tony, having paused again, couldn't believe his luck so he kept going before squaring the ball for Jeff Astle, who was also standing offside, to sidefoot into the net from about six yards. We were 2-0 down – and virtually out. Tinkler refused to disallow the goal maintaining that Suggett wasn't interfering with play. His decision led to a spontaneous pitch invasion – mainly by middle-aged men rather than teenage hooligans – as Tinkler was surrounded by our protesting players. As usual, Billy Bremner was involved but I remember Terry Cooper being particularly het up. There were 32 arrests and a linesman was hit on the head by a stone and although we pulled one back through Allan Clarke, Jeff's goal turned out to be the winner.

When the incident was shown on that evening's Match of the Day, the commentator, Barry Davies, came out with immortal line 'And Leeds will go mad! And they have every right to go mad because everybody stopped when the linesman flagged.' His assessment was spot on. Millions of viewers then saw Don Revie lose his composure. Normally, he could control himself but this was one injustice too many. After raging against the referee on the touchline, he then marched on to the pitch with the linesman, urging him to speak to Tinkler. As he trudged back to the dugout, Don looked to the heavens in disgust and shook his head in disbelief. He was livid because, as he said afterwards, Tinkler had ruined nine months of hard work. It wasn't a pretty sight seeing Don actually going on to the pitch and the incident confirmed our feeling that the world was against us. It cost us the title because although we won our last three games – including a 1-0 win over Arsenal at Elland Road – the Gunners finished a point clear after beating Spurs 1-0 at White Hart Lane in their final match. It was typical of the things that seemed to happen to Leeds then. Barry Davies also said that Tinkler's decision – or 'non-decision' as he called it – would be talked about for years and, again, he wasn't wrong.

At least that season ended on a high when we won the Inter-Cities Fairs Cup by beating Juventus on the away goals rule in early June. Again, I wasn't involved in either of the two legs but I was delighted that one of the Piemen, Mick Bates, scored the all-important goal. The first leg in Italy had to be abandoned after 50 minutes because of heavy rain. When the match was played again 48 hours later, we twice came from behind with Mick smashing home our second equaliser. An Allan Clarke goal in the home leg meant it ended 1-1 so we won the trophy for the second time. Because it was then replaced by the UEFA Cup, we were given the chance to hang on to the Inter-Cities Fairs Cup for good by playing Barcelona, the first winners of the competition, but we lost 2-1.

I still wasn't getting a regular game in the first team – in fact, I made only 12 appearances, including four as substitute, in all competitions during the 1971-72 season. This turned out to be almost as controversial as the previous one. We didn't make the best of starts after being made to play our first four 'home' games at Huddersfield, Hull and Sheffield Wednesday because of the West Brom pitch invasion the previous season. We collected six points out of the eight on offer and I scored my only goal of the season in 5-1 hammering of Newcastle. But the two dropped points in early draws against Wolves and Spurs turned out to be crucial in the long run.

There were some real high points during the season including the 7-0 humiliation of Southampton in March 1972, which included that cheeky flicked back-heel from Johnny Giles as we played 'keep-ball', and the 2-1 win over Spurs at Elland Road in the sixth round of the FA Cup a fortnight later. Don always had a thing about the national press and he loved it when we beat teams from London – especially on their own patch – because he felt we were unfairly treated by Fleet Street's football writers. He really hated the hacks so he was very pleased when a report in the *Daily Telegraph* talked about us showing 'an awe-inspiring and quicksilver grace that had a majesty and scope unequalled in Britain since Real Madrid beat Eintracht in 1960' to beat Spurs. Don's homage to the great Spanish team didn't look so ambitious now and the icing on the cake was our 1-0 win in the centenary FA Cup Final over another side from the capital, Arsenal, just down the road from Highbury at Wembley. Once again, I was in the party but not the team and I watched from the stand as Mick Jones crossed for Allan Clarke to score the winner. The down side of the goal was that Mick dislocated his elbow as he fell on the turf after crossing the ball. I remember that rather than just defend our lead, we then pushed forward for the goal that would have killed off Arsenal and we fully deserved to win the FA Cup for the first time. The sight of Mick struggling up to the Royal Box to collect his winner's medal with his arm heavily strapped is one of my most lasting FA Cup memories.

Naturally, he wasn't available when the four-horse race for the championship between Leeds, Derby, Liverpool and Manchester City reached its climax at Wolverhampton just two days later. We needed to draw to take the title and so complete the 'double' for the first time. If we didn't, then Derby would win their first First Division championship. In 1970, it had been England's World Cup preparations, this time it was their European Nations Cup campaign that partly scuppered our chances. Even though so much was resting on it, the Football League refused to reschedule the game because they said it would have interfered with Alf Ramsey's plans and the second leg of Wolves' UEFA Cup Final against Spurs. It could never happen now – can you imagine the Premiership saying to Manchester United or Arsenal that they had to play a vital League game two days after the FA Cup Final!?

The day after our win at Wembley, a Sunday newspaper published allegations that Wolves had been offered bribes by Leeds to lose the match and there was also a rumour that Derby were going to pay the Wolves players a lot of money to win the game. I was there that night so I know what happened and I remember the Wolves fans telling anybody who wanted to listen that their team hadn't played like that all season. They were certainly fired up by all the talk of us doing the 'double' – including Bobby Charlton's comment on BBC Television that there was no way Wolves could hold us. Frank Munro and Derek Dougan scored for them with about 20 minutes left but we hit back almost straightaway when Billy Bremner fired home from close range. It was like the Alamo until the end of the match and as we pushed forward for the equaliser, our first-team coach, Syd Owen, jumped into the Wolves' dugout and called them cheats after we'd had two penalty appeals turned down. I came on as a substitute and I remember the ball dropping near me when I was about six yards out. If I could have got my head to it, it would have hit the back of the net and we'd have won the League. But it just flicked the top of my hair – which I had then – and dropped behind the goal. It was another typical anti-climactic Leeds occasion. Everything seemed to be stacking up against us again and we lost out on the title by a single point for the second successive year. Derby were actually sunning themselves in Majorca when they heard they'd won the championship. I know that the Wolves players have always denied being tapped up by anybody but when we played them at Molineux during the next season, we obviously remembered that defeat. During games, all players say things to opponents just to wind them up and I mentioned the bribe rumour to one of their players. His reaction was one of pure guilt but I'm not prepared to say who he was. You can't be bribed to win – only to lose – but you can be offered an incentive to win. Nothing was ever substantiated or proved and the Football Association later announced that, after advice from the Director of Public Prosecutions, they considered 'no useful purpose' would be served by holding an inquiry so I suppose we'll never get to the bottom of it.

As Don began to re-build his squad during the 1972-73 season, I started to feature more in the first team – making 23 starts with about half as many appearances as substitute. David Harvey took over from Gary Sprake in goal while Joe Jordan arrived from Morton and centre-half Roy Ellam and full-back Trevor Cherry were both signed from Huddersfield. Gordon McQueen joined from St Mirren in September 1972 and made his debut the following March.

Joe was a big, bustling centre-forward who was signed from Morton on the recommendation of their manager, Bobby Collins. I got on very well with Joe and in fact, he became a close family friend and godfather to Gabby, our eldest daughter. He was bought as cover for Mick Jones who was becoming more and more injury-prone. Joe didn't score as often as Mick but he was more aggressive and held the ball up well. I also became friendly with Trevor who could play almost anywhere in defence and sometimes in midfield. We teamed up together when he became manager at Bradford in the early 1980s. Roy Ellam didn't make the grade at Leeds and, after a handful of appearances in the first team, he returned to Huddersfield two years later. Gordon McQueen eventually took over from Jack Charlton to become the mainstay of the Leeds defence for five years before, like Joe, moving on to Manchester United.

Once again, we were involved in virtually everything as the 1972-73 season reached its climax. By the end of April, Liverpool had edged clear at the top of the First Division – I replaced Johnny Giles for our 2-0 defeat at Anfield when they actually won the title – but we were back at Wembley. As well as beating Wolves 2-0 at Molineux in the

League, we knocked them out of the FA Cup when Billy Bremner scored the only goal in the semi-final at Maine Road. Nearly a year on from our controversial defeat in Wolverhampton, revenge was sweet that afternoon in Manchester.

During our run to the final against Sunderland, I'd come on as a sub in the second replay against Norwich and started against Plymouth in the fourth round and against Wolves. It was a choice between me and Mick Bates for the substitute's spot at Wembley. He'd got the nod in 1972 and I was hoping it was going to be my turn now. We prepared in the usual way by staying in the same hotel just outside London and during the team meeting on the Thursday, Don told me the good news – I would be sub. Obviously, it was a big blow to Mick – as it had been to me the previous year – but I felt marvellous. On the day itself, I was a little nervous when I woke up but felt calmer after our pre-match meeting and meal. The coach ride to Wembley, as always, was quiet.

Everybody expected us to win, but everybody – outside Leeds – wanted Sunderland to win. They'd beaten Notts County, Reading, Manchester City, Luton and Arsenal to reach the final. We were over-whelming favourites but their performances made them the people's favourites. It was classic David and Goliath but there was no feeling of complacency in our camp – it wasn't a case of us thinking we were only up against Sunderland from the Second Division. We knew they had some good players and it was really a question of us getting out there and doing the job as professionally as possible. Ten of our team were appearing in their second successive final and, with me as sub-stitute, all but one of our named players were full internationals. Sunderland hadn't been to Wembley since 1937 while under Don we'd been in nine finals in as many years. It may have looked all done and dusted but Sunderland, led out by Bob Stokoe in his tracksuit, had dif-ferent ideas. I remember that Don, wearing his lucky suit, was more uptight than usual.

After losing our last three League games at Liverpool, Southampton and Birmingham, we weren't in the best of form and, to be honest, a few players didn't perform on the day – which can happen. I think Sunderland were out of the starting gate quicker than us and that gave them the upper hand psychologically. When I look back to the start of the game, I remember the ball coming back to Johnny Giles and it being blocked. It then came back to Norman Hunter and it was blocked again. All of a sudden, Sunderland were in our half straight from our kick-off. They'd seized the initiative and we'd hit a negative straightaway. I sometimes wonder if that's why we lost – because that opening minute of play set the pattern for the rest of the game?

After a pretty tense first half-hour in which they hustled us out of our stride, Sunderland suddenly scored from a corner when Ian Porterfield cushioned the ball on his left thigh and then smashed it home with his 'wrong' right foot. Don just slumped forward on the bench. I don't remember him saying anything – his body language said it all. The goal obviously came as a bit of a shock but we still had time to get back into it. We thought we should have had a penalty in the second half when Billy Bremner looked to have been tripped in the area by their defender, Dave Watson, but it wasn't given. We kept plugging away – only to find their keeper, Jim Montgomery, playing out of his skin. First, he dived to his left to keep out Trevor Cherry's header and then amazingly scrambled to his knees to push Peter Lorimer's pile-driver from all of five yards on to the underside of the bar. When the ball bounced back into play, it was cleared and, unbelievably, we were still behind. Down on the bench, we couldn't take in what was happening. Although the final has gone down in history for that double save, I still maintain that if Trevor had stood up after his diving header, he would have tapped the ball into the back of the net. Instead he was lying on the ground watching while everything was going on.

I came on for the last quarter of an hour for Eddie Gray in what I thought was a baffling substitution. It's true that he'd had a quiet game and hadn't played for the team for a while because of injury but I couldn't understand why Don was sending me on. Eddie was far more likely than me to win us a game or take it to extra-time. Don just told me to get on and play in midfield. There was nothing astute tactically about the change – it was a straight swap. I did OK and I remember firing a weak shot straight at Montgomery but it just wasn't to be and, for the second time in three seasons, we were involved in an FA Cup upset – one of the biggest ever in a final.

Back at the team hotel, Don was so annoyed that he pulled three of us to one side – myself, Mick Bates and Eddie's younger brother, Frankie, who'd made his first-team debut in the previous February. He said there were going to be changes and we would become the nucleus of the new team. But it didn't happen and the squad was largely the same the next season.

We seemed to have got the Sunderland result out of our system when we put six past Arsenal at Elland Road four days later to finish third in the First Division behind them and the champions, Liverpool. A week later, we desperately wanted to round off our first season in the European Cup Winners' Cup by winning the trophy. We'd knocked out Ankaragucu, Carl Zeiss Jena, Rapid Bucharest and Hajduk Split to reach the final against AC Milan in Salonika but injuries and suspensions now started to kick in big style. Billy Bremner, Johnny Giles, Allan Clarke and Eddie Gray were all missing, I kept my place after starting the two semi-final legs against Hajduk Split and Frankie and Mick came into the team. As we travelled to Greece, the mood of uncertainty in the camp wasn't helped by a rumour that Don was seriously thinking about joining Everton.

The game against AC Milan still rankles with me to this day because we were cheated by a corrupt referee. Christos Michas was nothing short of a disgrace and his performance cost us the match. When we came out of the airport at Salonika, a journalist told us about a strong rumour doing the rounds: the referee had been bought. As it turned out, he had so we weren't only playing a great side in AC Milan but the referee as well. It started to go wrong for us almost from the kick-off when Paul Madeley was penalised for what seemed like a fair tackle in the fourth minute. It was a diabolical decision and we were made to pay for it straightaway because Luciano Chiarugi's indirect free-kick was deflected and ended up going into our net via a post. It went on from there. Romeo Benetti and I were at it hammer and tongs all night, the Italians were all doing their usual play-acting and Michas was helping them. As we pushed forward more and more, he turned down three stonewall penalties when our players were brought down in the box. Joe Jordan, in particular, took a real kicking that night. Even the Greek supporters in the crowd were shouting 'Cheats!' all through the game. Just before the end, it all proved too much for Norman Hunter. After being hacked down by Rivera, he finally snapped, lashed out and was sent off.

By that time, I had been substituted by Gordon McQueen.

It was a miserable night, the rain was pouring down and I'll never forget the Milan players being slaughtered by the Greek crowd when they went off on a lap of honour. My other memory of that game is the distraught face of a Leeds fan after the final whistle as he looked at it all through a fence. He was crying his eyes out because he and all our supporters knew what was going on – it just wasn't real but there was nothing we could do about it. It was little consolation that the Greeks made us feel like the winners on the night or that, this time, the corruption allegation was later investigated. Michas was immediately suspended and then banned by UEFA when it was found out that he had been bribed but we were never given the chance to set the record straight on the pitch. And, of course, the defeat meant we ended up with nothing.

It all came right for me and the club during the 1973-74 season when we finally got our hands on the First Division championship for the first time in five years. Don's rejection of Everton's overtures in the summer seemed to galvanise everybody and he decided it was time for Leeds to become as white as our kit – if not whiter. Our disciplinary record had been so bad during the previous season – Norman Hunter and Trevor Cherry had picked up eight bookings each – that the Football Association hit us with a £3,000 fine. It was suspended as long as we cleaned up our act and as our first full-time public relations officer started work, Don made it clear what his number one priority was for the new season. The effect of so many near misses since 1964 had concentrated his mind and his first team talk of the season was very upbeat. He told us we'd been the best team in England for the past decade and that because we'd finished the previous season with nothing, we would, in typical football fashion, just be concentrating on the League. In fact, like Alf Ramsey predicted with England and the World Cup in 1966, Don said we would win the title. What's more, he raised the possibility of us going through the whole season without being beaten. Did we think we could do it? We all looked at each other in silence and then said we thought we could. Every team starts off aiming to win every game at the start of a season but to actually set it as a target was different. We decided to go for it and the results started to flow. We won our first seven League games, scoring 19 goals and conceding just four. Among the newspaper cuttings I've kept over the years is a report by John Arlott in *The Guardian* of the last win in that run – a 2-1 defeat of Southampton at The Dell with Allan Clarke scoring both goals.

'Wearing the white strip of a blameless life,' Arlott wrote, 'Leeds moved in a ceaseless flow, back in packed defence, competing for the midfield, sweeping forward and with backs overlapping. Yet it was all so controlled, almost amiable...so free from the aura of violence they used to generate.'

The turning point for me came in the very next game when we drew 0-0 at home to Manchester United in late September 1973. It was a roughhouse of a match and Eddie Gray picked up an injury that kept him out for virtually the rest of that season. I ended up making most of my 33 appearances on the left wing as his replacement while Mick Bates and Joe Jordan were drafted in when injury kept out Johnny Giles and Mick Jones. Although it was hard luck on Eddie, I found my feet in that wonderful 1974 championship side – the best team I ever played in.

After the draw with Manchester United, Don played the first of his mind games with us. He said the board had given him money to spend and if we didn't improve, then he'd bring in new players to strengthen the squad. The wake-up call worked and the unbeaten run continued – although we had to start grinding out a few draws.

We were knocked out of the League Cup in our first game by Ipswich but we were making progress in the UEFA Cup having beaten Stroemsgodset 7-2 on aggregate. In the second round, we faced Hibernian and after drawing 0-0 at Elland Road, we were in danger of losing our bonus for staying in the competition when we travelled to Edinburgh for the second leg. A few of us liked to gamble and we noticed that the bookies were offering generous odds of 9-4 on Hibs to win the return leg. As we were putting out a very weakened side, there was some typical half-hearted and light-hearted dressing room talk about backing Hibs before we went out but nobody did. Billy played sweeper and I remember him being in a very cheeky mood that night. After chipping the ball over their centre-forward back to David Harvey, he later took up his usual position on the line for a Hibs corner. When the ball was headed towards goal, Billy stopped it on the line and then back-heeled it across the goal to Frankie Gray – much to Frankie's horror! It ended 0-0 so it was all down to a shoot-out. We asked Don what we should do.

'We win on penalties don't we?' he said. Pat Stanton, who Billy knew well from their experiences with Scotland, stepped up to take the first Hibs spot-kick.

'Pat,' said Billy. 'You do realise that the whole of Scotland is looking at you now?'

Billy's trick worked a treat because Pat missed his penalty and we went through 5-4. The next UEFA Cup game was against Vitoria Setubal who we beat with a rare Trevor Cherry goal at Elland Road and we then stretched our unbeaten League run to 18 games through a 2-2 home draw with Queens Park Rangers. Don called us together again and went through each player's performance individually. He started with David Harvey and told him he wasn't doing it. He carried on in the same vein with the rest of the team apart from when he came to Billy and Norman Hunter. Those two, as usual, were the exception. We all walked out of that meeting wondering what more we had to do! In fact, it hardened us up and I immediately hit a little purple patch of my own by scoring two goals in three games as we beat Ipswich and Chelsea away and Norwich at Elland Road in the first half of December. I was really chuffed with my performance in the 3-0 win at Portman Road because after putting us ahead with a dipping drive from the edge of the box, I then set up the second goal for Mick Jones with a cross from the left.

After the Ipswich game on the Saturday, we stayed in London overnight and took our golf clubs with us over to Portugal. We'd never done that before but it was typical of the relaxed way in which Don was approaching this game. We knew the League championship was his priority – like us, he was fed up with being beaten in Cup finals and missing out on trophies – and so he wasn't too worried about how we did in Europe. On the Monday, we trained for a bit and then played some golf at Estoril. The press boys were wondering what was going on – especially as we did the same on the Tuesday. The players who went out on to the pitch that Wednesday night wanted to win the game but the preparations for it – especially being allowed to play golf – had never been so laid-back. During the game, we knew we weren't going to go through because Vitoria Setubal weren't a bad side and they deservedly won 3-1 on the night, 3-2 on aggregate. There was one anxious moment for Don when Gary Liddell, whose son, Andy, now plays for Sheffield United, came on as substitute, burst through the middle and then scored with a shot off the post. He's the only player I've known who's been bollocked by his manager for putting the ball in the back of the net! Don was worried that we might get another one and go through on away goals. We didn't so we were out and free to carry on with our campaign to win the title.

Our season briefly hit the buffers during a week in late February when our FA Cup jinx struck again and we lost our first League game. After drawing with Second Division Bristol City at Ashton Gate in the fifth round, they dumped us out by winning the replay 1-0 at Elland Road and then we went down 3-2 at Stoke. We had stayed unbeaten for 29 games until then – despite Johnny Giles being out for four months with a groin injury. We were without Mick Jones, Gordon McQueen, Paul Reaney and Eddie Gray against Stoke and Don's gamble to play Johnny seem to have paid off. We were coasting at 2-0 at the time when his injury flared up again and he was taken off. It made sense for Johnny to be kept for the run-in but after he was substituted, it all fell apart. Stoke were level by half-time and then scored the winner with a quarter of the match left. It just showed how important Johnny was to the team.

It was wonderful watching Arsenal go through the 2003-04 season without losing a League game but 30 years earlier for us it was primarily just about winning the title – and we showed that we had the steel and the determination to do it. Although we eventually lost our unbeaten record, we were playing so well that we didn't think about losing and it was a shock when we went down at Stoke in the way we did.

I don't think it's fair to compare the 1974 Leeds side and the 2004 Arsenal team because modern-day football is so different – especially with the number of foreign players in the game. Premiership teams have got the pick of so many different nationalities and the modern footballer is more of an athlete. We felt we were athletes back in the 1970s but the current players have terrific technique, most of them are very big and quick and the game itself is so much faster.

After the Stoke setback, we steadied the ship with a couple of draws and a win before three successive defeats set the alarm bells ringing again. At one stage, we'd been nine points clear of Liverpool but our lead was gradually being whittled away. After being beaten 1-0 at Anfield in the first of those defeats, I remember Don coming over to me when I was sitting by myself on the coach journey back to Leeds. It was unusual for me to be on my own because I was normally a regular member of the card school but I was feeling sorry for myself. I didn't have any pace to go by anybody, I didn't have a trick and all I could do was shuffle the ball further up the field and give to either Johnny or Billy or slot it into Clarkey's feet.

'What's the matter with you, Taff ?' asked Don.

'I don't feel I'm any use, Boss,' I replied. 'I'm going up and down that left wing and I call myself 'The Wall'. They pass the ball to me and I pass it back to them.'

'You're doing a fantastic job for the club,' said Don and I felt OK after that. But despite his comforting words, our form was anything but reassuring. We crashed to a 4-1 home defeat by Burnley and then lost 3-1 at West Ham. As he later admitted, Don was worried we might have blown it again and he certainly aged a few years during the final couple of months of the season. But this time, we avoided a last-minute slip-up. As Liverpool started to wobble themselves, we stopped the rot by beating Derby 2-0 at Elland Road, picked up two points with 0-0 draws against Coventry and Sheffield United and then rounded off the season with three straight wins over Sheffield United, Ipswich and Queens Park Rangers. I was in and out of the team at that stage with Eddie Gray returning for the 3-2 win over Ipswich at Elland Road that effectively won us the title. Even then, we managed to make it difficult for ourselves in front of an expectant crowd of more than 44,000. After Peter Lorimer and Gordon McQueen had put us 2-0 up, Ipswich were level 10 minutes after the break. With 20 minutes left, Allan Clarke scored the winner – even though Ipswich claimed he'd handled the ball – and with Liverpool drawing at Everton, we were virtually home and dry. To stand a chance of pipping us to the title, Liverpool had to win their last three games but four days after we'd picked up those two points against Ipswich, they lost to Arsenal at Anfield and it really was all over.

I came on as a sub for Paul Reaney in our 1-0 over QPR in front of 35,353 spectators – which is still Loftus Road's biggest crowd – as Allan Clarke's goal meant we won the title by five points. Understandably, we were all very relieved – especially Don. I remember him saying that he felt as if someone had just lifted six tons of coal off his back. He was very proud of us for bouncing back from the three defeats before Easter and said he felt he was walking on air. 'This is the greatest moment of my life' he told the press – and I could only agree with him.

I was especially pleased for Don because I had him to thank for my career in football. His decision to just concentrate on winning the First Division had been vindicated and his obsessive planning had paid off too. Our second championship made up for some of the heartache created by those second places between 1970 and 1972 and it helped Leeds get rid of some of the 'dirty Leeds' reputation which had dogged us for a decade. Don hated that tag. It's funny how players change when they become managers. In Don's case, he was an arrogant midfield player who liked to pass the ball and never really got stuck in. Then when he turned the page and took over as manager of Leeds, he became a different kind of character who, according to our critics, would go to any lengths to win.

The 'dirty Leeds' tag didn't affect us as players in any way whatsoever. We went about our job in the most professional manner that we could. I admit we were cold and some people called us ruthless. One or two teams tried to match us but they couldn't. We certainly intimidated our opponents and we knew they were frightened of us. When I was on the edge of the first team in 1969, we played West Ham at home in midweek. They were staying in the Queens Hotel, right in the centre of Leeds, and we'd been booked in there for an afternoon nap. I found myself in the lift with two of their international players. Obviously, they didn't know who I was because one of them turned to the other and said:

'I don't know why we bother coming here. We might as well just telephone them and give them two points and stay at home.'

I thought that was an amazing comment to make and, needless to say, we beat them 4-1. But teams weren't just frightened by the way we went about winning games – they were afraid of our ability. They knew they couldn't come to Elland Road and win very often. As well as being defensively strong, we played a lot of expansive attacking football and we knew how to close down games. We would never give the ball away – if we were 1-0 up, we'd keep it and it was up to the opposition to try to get it back off us.

In saying that, I can't deny that we were a side that went very close to the edge quite a few times. We stood up for each other to a man and we knew how to get our opponents at it – to wind them up with strong verbal comments and digs. We looked after each other in the sense that if one of us were fouled, his team-mates would realise that the opponent would be close to a booking. We would then go in and rough him up to try to get him booked through retaliation or committing another foul. Then he'd be only another yellow card away from a red. Nobody ever told me to do it: it was just an unwritten and unspoken code of conduct that we would look after each other out on the field. Looking back, I don't see anything wrong with that. If you go over the mark – which I did on a few occasions – then you should be prepared to take your punishment.

Don didn't encourage us to be dirty. He taught us to be professional and not pull out of a tackle. Nobody from numbers 1 to 11 would do that. 'Be honest, be professional and use your ability' – that was his message. He never told me to go over the top of the ball or to 'dig out' an opponent although I'd often be given a man-marking job on people like Alan Ball or Colin Bell, the two England internationals. In fact, one of the best games of my career was against Manchester City when I didn't give Colin a kick of the ball.

Don never criticised me for the way I played for Leeds and I was never sent off in a first-halfteam game. The only time I got a bollocking was when I was captaining the Welsh Under-23s against England early on in my career. I had a few scuffles and a few words with Peter Osgood who must have gone into the dressing room and complained to Les Cocker, the England and Leeds trainer. Les must have said something to Don who pulled me in and told me I couldn't behave like that in an international. I had to conduct myself better. I was about to start telling Don about the passion and pride I felt in captaining my country but I stopped. I realised that if I opened my mouth once he'd spoken to me, then I could be looking at not being picked for the first team for two months or so.

Thirty years on from that 1974 championship win when we proved what a great, all-round side we were, the shame is that the 'dirty Leeds' tag is still brought up all the time. Even today's Leeds team are hit with it if they commit a couple of bad tackles. Winning the First Division title turned out to be a watershed for the team and our manager. We won a few friends because we'd turned over a new leaf and played some fabulous football and Don felt free to leave, having kept his word and steered Leeds to the biggest prize in English football.

In retrospect, I suppose it was the perfect time for Don to go. There was nothing more he could have done with an experienced but ageing team. It needed rebuilding and perhaps he didn't have the stomach to end the careers of so many legends – although another tilt at winning the European Cup must have appealed to him.

We all knew the Football Association were looking for a permanent replacement for Alf Ramsey as England manager after Joe Mercer's caretaker spell in charge and Don made it clear that he would like the job. But we were surprised when he took over because the most often used word around Elland Road was loyalty. Obviously, if you're offered the England job then you take it. But ever since I'd known him, Don had always preached loyalty. He'd received it from the club and from his players and then suddenly he was gone.

Don's decision to accept the England job couldn't have come at a worse time for me personally. I was on £125 a week and I'd had such a good season that before he left, Don said he was going to double my wages. Now it was something I would have to take up with the new manager. Little did I, or any of the players, know that Don's successor would be his arch rival – Old Big 'ead himself.

Clough and Tumble

At least Brian Clough held his hands up. In his autobiography, *Walking on Water*, he admitted that he blew it. Leeds weren't for him and he wasn't for them. After going at the job 'like a bull at a fence', he was sacked after just 44 days in charge at Elland Road. Far from walking on water, Cloughie sank without trace.

Brian Clough taking over from Don Revie at Leeds? I suppose it would be a little like Sir Alex Ferguson succeeding Arsène Wenger at Arsenal. As players, we just couldn't understand it. We were well and truly gobsmacked. Don's departure for the England job might have been a shock but it was nothing compared with the board's decision to replace him with Cloughie who, after resigning from Derby, had moved to Brighton. We first heard the news on television – nobody had bothered discussing the situation with us, the people who would have to work with the new manager. It was a bizarre decision because of the very bad blood that existed between Leeds and Derby and the personal bitterness between Don and Cloughie which all came out on television after Cloughie was sacked by the Elland Road board.

He had described Don's team as one of the most cynical and dirty yet most talented sides he'd ever seen. He said he admired Don but had serious reservations about the way we sometimes went about our business. Cloughie claimed we had paid a price for being 'dirty Leeds' because our over-physical approach had undermined public respect for our achievements.

So you can imagine how the players felt when we heard the news – especially as when Don left, he had strongly recommended to the board that Johnny Giles should take over. The two had worked together for 10 years and Don obviously thought it would be a much smoother transition to a new era if one of the old guard rather than an outsider were in charge. But the board thought they knew better. The Football Association had paid a lot of compensation for Don and the Leeds directors decided they were going to spend it on one of the biggest names – and certainly the biggest mouths – in English football. I was more surprised about Brian Clough coming than Don leaving because, after Don had gone, I'd played a round of golf with Johnny, Norman Hunter and Mick Bates. We'd only got about 50 yards up the first fairway when Johnny said to me:

'Taff...what would you think if I became manager?'

'That would be absolutely fantastic,' I said.

But that's as far as it went at that stage. For whatever reason – and there were rumours that not everyone in the squad was behind Johnny – the board went for Cloughie and the players went ballistic. Speaking personally, I was utterly amazed when I heard that he was the new manager – I thought it was a wind-up. It was a hell of a shock.

When Cloughie arrived for his first day's work at Elland Road in July 1974, it was, as he says in his book, like walking straight into an ambush. He says he was confronted by a 'seething, resentful and spiteful' dressing room and I wouldn't disagree with that assessment, but he didn't help himself by having a go at his first team meeting. He told us to throw all the medals we'd won under Don into the dustbin because we'd got them by cheating. He then made a couple of limp wisecracks including his remark to Eddie Gray that if a racehorse had suffered as many injuries as Eddie had, he'd have been put down months ago. It was downhill all the way from there and, in the end, Cloughie was shown the door – partly because he was too hasty and disrespectful and partly through player-power.

I was one of the first members of the squad to come into contact with Cloughie because I needed to sort out my new contract. I knocked on the door of assistant manager Maurice Lindley's office.

'Maurice, is the manager here?' I asked

''Boss' to you, son,' came the reply from around the corner where Cloughie was sitting.

'Is it possible to see you?' I said.

'Yeah, sure.'

So I went into his office and told him my contract had run out but that Don Revie had promised to double my wages.

'What?' said Cloughie.

'Don Revie promised that he'd double my wages to £250 a week.'

'Why would he double your wages?'

'Well…I played more than 30 first-team games last season and we won the First Division title for only the second time in the club's history.'

'Who else knows about this?'

'The chairman.'

A week or so later, Cloughie called me into his office where a cleaner was going about her work.

'About your contract…' he began before I interrupted by pointing to the cleaner.

'She won't tell anybody.'

'I'd still rather discuss it in private.'

'I've talked to the chairman,' said Cloughie, once we were alone, 'and he says he knows nothing about it. But I think he does so I'm going to double your wages.'

He was more or less saying that the chairman, Manny Cussins, was telling porky pies but I wasn't going to argue with him. I just wanted my money so I signed a new contract. We also had a contract to cover bonuses and if you didn't sign your new one at the start of the season, then the club were entitled to pay you the previous year's amounts. Soon after sorting out my main contract with Cloughie, I caught gastro-enteritis and I was in bed for more than a week. Just before the 1974-75 season started, I received a phone call from Maurice Lindley.

'You've got to come to the ground to sign your bonus sheet today,' he said, 'otherwise we'll be going by the old one.'

If Don Revie had still been in charge, he'd have sent someone up to my house with the form because I was ill. But I had to drag myself from my sick bed and go down to Elland Road. I looked a right mess – I was wearing a T-shirt and I hadn't shaved for a while. When I arrived at Cloughie's office, his son, Nigel, who was then eight, was running around the place.

'You're looking well!', said Cloughie. 'Do you want a beer? Nigel, go and get him a beer.'

Off went Nigel and then came back with a bottle of Newcastle Brown. I politely declined and Cloughie took it instead. I signed the bonus sheet and went back to bed. That was the way he operated.

Like all new managers, Cloughie wanted his own people alongside him so although his former assistant, Peter Taylor, had decided to stay at Brighton, the ex-Derby coach, Jimmy Gordon, arrived at Elland Road along with midfielder John McGovern and centre-forward John O'Hare while Duncan McKenzie was signed from Nottingham Forest for £250,000.

Cloughie and I were on a collision course from the word go. I suppose our relationship was always going to be prickly once he decided that I would be missing another trip to Wembley. Although I'd been a regular in the team that won the championship, he left me out of the party for the 1974 Charity Shield against Liverpool. Instead, Cloughie made me play for the reserves at Witton Albion so I missed seeing Billy Bremner and Kevin Keegan being sent off in one of the most unseemly curtain-raisers to a new season. That explosive start earned Billy a £500 fine and an 11-match suspension and put the pressure on John McGovern as his replacement.

We'd never come across a character like Cloughie before. When we travelled to Stoke for our first League match, we stayed in a hotel alongside the M6. He walked the players down towards the motorway, sat us down on the embankment of the slip road and then gave his team talk. It was really strange with all the lorries going by and it didn't seem to work too well because we lost 3-0. I'd been in the squad but not the team and I was still out of favour when we played Queens Park Rangers in our first home game of the season but I went down to the dressing room to have a chat with a few of the lads.

'Young man,' Cloughie said to me, 'take your hands out of your pockets!'

That was typical of the way he talked to the players and it went from bad to worse. About 45 minutes before kick-off, there was a knock on the door. It was Eddie Gray who asked me, in a whisper, to ask Peter Lorimer if he had managed to sort out a couple of tickets for him. Because Leeds had always operated an open-door policy in the dressing room, I motioned Eddie inside.

'Come in and ask him yourself,' I said.

'Young man,' boomed out Cloughie. 'I'll invite who I want into this dressing room – not you!'

I turned around, looked him in the face and said:

'Well, I'd better fucking go hadn't I?' and I walked out. As I sat watching the game from the stand, I started to read the match programme and I noticed Cloughie was still having a pop at Don Revie's team. 'The club has to be sold to the public,' he wrote, 'because what they achieved on the field was not enough to win over the public's hearts. People have begrudged them their success.' He just wouldn't let go.

The next day, I picked up *The Sun* newspaper and read a story by Cloughie's mate, John Sadler, who would later ghost-write *Walking on Water*. It said that Everton wanted to buy me. I immediately went round to the manager's office where I decided to apologise for my outburst the night before.

'I'm always the same before games whether I'm playing or not,' I said. 'I get geed up and the adrenaline starts flowing.'

Cloughie didn't seem to bothered about that and said that, despite the story in the paper, he didn't want to sell me. I missed our first win of the season when Allan Clarke scored the only goal against Birmingham at Elland Road but then found myself being picked as the ball-winner in midfield in our next match – away at Queen's Park Rangers. And what a way to mark my return to the first team! The ball came to me about 30 yards out and I just chipped Phil Parkes in goal. I was delighted to have put us 1-0 up but they then equalised. In the Revie era, we would have taken the draw away from home so when I next picked up the ball on the half-way line, I just knocked it back to our keeper, David Harvey. In the dressing room afterwards, Clough tore me off a strip:

'That was the old Leeds not the new Leeds!,' he shouted. I looked at him in amazement. I had chipped in a lovely goal to put us in front and all I got for my efforts was a bollocking for trying to make sure we hung on to a point!

After that draw and a 2-1 defeat at Manchester City, the anti-Cloughie campaign started to gain momentum – in the boardroom and in the changing room. The players had been holding meetings – occasionally at first and then twice a week – because we were getting fed up with Cloughie's attitude towards the job and us. He would turn up at the ground at half past nine in the morning in his squash kit when we'd been used to Don being there an hour earlier. The training wasn't as thorough as we'd been used to and it seemed to be all off the cuff. It wasn't very organised or planned and his team talks weren't as thorough as Don's. I think Cloughie was jealous of the Leeds set-up, the players and the many cups we'd won, but in his mind, we had achieved everything in the wrong way. I remember him saying to Duncan McKenzie that he'd be sitting in the stand watching a real striker play when Allan Clarke was on the pitch. Clarkey was singled out by Cloughie in his autobiography as just about the only player who wasn't hostile towards him at Leeds but, as far as I'm concerned, everybody felt the same. We were all unhappy about the way he treated players who had been at Elland Road for a long time. Take nothing away from Cloughie, he was a great manager – as he went on to prove by winning successive European Cups with Forest. But his methods weren't right for an established squad like ours. I felt he always worked better with younger players who he could cajole and manipulate to his way of thinking – people he could be rude to and dominate. Cloughie was a verbal disciplinarian but players like Billy Bremner and Johnny Giles were too old and experienced for that. They were too far down the road in their careers to be expected to put up with that sort of treatment but Cloughie ploughed on regardless. As he says in *Walking on Water*, his boat was sunk when he told David Harvey that he wanted to sign Peter Shilton as a replacement keeper.

It all came to a head when the board decided to discuss the worsening situation with the players and the manager after a 1-1 draw with Luton at Elland Road in early September. We had won only one of our first six League games, we were 19th in the table and we were only in the League Cup because a late Peter Lorimer goal had won us a replay against Third Division Huddersfield. Sam Bolton, one of the leading members of the anti-Cloughie group, was the driving force behind a momentous meeting. Cloughie was an unusual manager – and an unusual bloke too. He wouldn't sit on a chair as most normal people do. Instead, he turned it round to face him and sat with his arms across the back of it and his legs on either side. As he settled into his seat, the meeting began.

'I say, I say, I say,' began Manny Cussins. 'Something's telling me things aren't right.'

'Never mind that crap, chairman,' interjected Sam Bolton, a typical gruff Yorkshireman. 'We want to know what's going on here.'

Although Billy was the captain, Johnny was always our spokesman. Brian Clough might have wanted Johnny out of Elland Road because he'd been recommended by Don as his replacement but Johnny wasn't the ringleader – and he wasn't after Cloughie's job. As a group of players, we had settled on our stance before the meeting and Johnny said we were happy to talk – on one condition:

'We'd like Mr Clough to leave the room and when he comes back, we'll tell him everything we've said.'

Now, Cloughie was an intelligent man and I think you have to wonder why he agreed to our request. Was his mind on the money at that time because if he walked out of the room, then he was hardly likely to walk back in, was he? And if he had returned, how would he know that the players were going to repeat, word for word, everything they'd said in his absence? After he left, Johnny began to describe how unstable the situation had become. He explained that we just weren't happy with Cloughie. As well as being disrespectful, he'd created a rod for his own back through the history between him and Leeds when he'd been very rude about our style of play in public. Johnny was a good speaker and he was trying to be constructive with his criticism as he put forward our point of view. Sam Bolton's last comment was 'That'll do for me, Chairman' and that was Cloughie done for – although he wasn't sacked straightaway. During training later that day, Cloughie was, as usual, practising his own shooting. When Billy dummied as he was about to knock the ball into him, Cloughie's comment was very revealing:

'Yeah, I've been the biggest dummy around here.'

He obviously knew something was happening. Just before he left, we had a meeting in the Queens Hotel in the centre of Leeds and Cloughie looked around the room:

'I've been a bit of a mug here but there have only been three players who have been honest with me. Him,' pointing at John McGovern, 'him', pointing at John O'Hare, 'and him' pointing at me. Jimmy Gordon said something similar after Cloughie had left:

'I think you've been absolutely disrespectful – you haven't treated the man right.'

I thought it was great that he'd stuck up for his boss but, as I've explained, Jimmy's complaint about us was also one of our main gripes against the manager.

Whatever he felt about the attitude of the players, Cloughie could have no complaints about the way the board treated him. He later admitted that his final pay-off was about £100,000 – four times as much as he was expecting under the terms of his four-year contract. The money made him financially secure for the first time in his life and he knew he'd be able to do his next job with complete peace of mind. So he came out of it pretty well and went on to become a true legend in the game. But what about Leeds United?

After the emergency board meeting which led to Cloughie being sacked in September 1974 after just six weeks in charge, Manny Cussins explained the reasoning behind the decision:

'The Leeds United club and the happiness of Leeds United players must come first.'

Although the board denied that we were behind the sacking, I think, in retrospect, that, on this issue, the players' power was too strong and the board were too weak. If the board had turned round and said to us: 'Look...we've got him – you've got to work with him' then we would have had to because we were under contract and we were professional footballers. Brian Clough left Elland Road claiming 'it was a sad day for Leeds United' and maybe he had a point. But if you were being really ruthless, I think you can date the decline of the club to the moment when the board hired Cloughie. How different could it have been if they had followed Don Revie's advice and appointed Johnny Giles?

As it happened, the board realised they'd made a mistake and did offer Johnny the job. The day after Brian Clough was sacked, Johnny was phoned by Manny Cussins at seven o'clock in the morning and he arranged to meet the board two hours later. Apparently, Billy Bremner had also informed them that he was after the job – something that Johnny only became aware of by lunchtime that day. But before Johnny's next meeting with the board, Billy had withdrawn his interest and so Johnny was offered the job. The problem was that he knew the decision had been made only on a 3-2 majority vote. He was being offered a job he hadn't even applied for and he was getting pretty fed up with the whole thing. He felt that with two directors already against him, he was being handed too much of a poisoned chalice so he turned it down. There was a rumour that Billy had told the board that he wasn't prepared to play under Johnny but although they didn't mix socially, there was never any rivalry or animosity between them. Johnny was an avid golfer, Billy played when he felt like it. Johnny was a strong character within the club and he had his disciples – people who would hang on to every word he said. Billy, on the other hand, kept his own company and mixed with people like Jack Charlton and Allan Clarke. But as quickly as the rumour surfaced, it was forgotten.

Not for the first time, Maurice Lindley stepped into the breach as caretaker-manager until Jimmy Armfield was appointed three weeks later. As a player, Jimmy had a great pedigree, having been captain of England before Bobby Moore and won 43 caps and, as a manager, he'd just taken Bolton to the Third Division championship. He really was the perfect choice because, more than anything else, Leeds needed a nurse, somebody to heal the wounds. Jimmy was a lovely man – a complete contrast to the brash Brian Clough – and he made a great decision in bringing Don Howe in as his number two. Don had helped Arsenal win the 'double' in 1971 and he complemented Jimmy well because they were different types of people. Don was a terrific trainer who got us fit by working hard while Jimmy was very affable. He knew the game, he liked a joke on the training ground and he never really had a harsh word to say about anybody. Maybe he was too nice and, surprisingly, even a little star-struck. The players respected him because of his track record but I don't think Jimmy could really believe he was manager of Leeds with all these wonderful players working for him. He was a completely different character to Don Revie. Outwardly, he was more laid-back but on the inside, I believe he was scared to death about managing Leeds. When he was under pressure, Jimmy used to say little things to us like 'I don't know why I left that Bolton job.'

If you were ever dropped, you'd arrange to see Jimmy in his office and he'd ask you to take a seat. But before you could sit down, he'd start talking about other things. If it wasn't one thing, it was the other.

Jimmy seemed to prefer to discuss the weather or his missus or anything – rather than get down to the nitty-gritty.

'It's a nightmare,' he'd say. 'The mother-in-law's in hospital', or 'the wife's feeling under pressure' or 'that drive over the M62 is doing my head in.'

You'd have been in there for 15 minutes without having a chance to say your piece! So, in the end, I used to stand up and say 'OK Jim, see you later' and walk out. Five yards outside his office, I'd stop and ask myself why I hadn't asked him about being dropped!

Make no mistake, Jimmy was a good manager but I had one or two run-ins with him while we were together at Leeds. – mainly as a result of his bizarre team selections. He steadied the ship after our poor start under Brian Clough and we did well in the FA Cup and in Europe as he re-built both the team and our confidence. John McGovern and John O'Hare were sold back to Cloughie at Nottingham Forest but Duncan McKenzie and his bag of tricks stayed at Elland Road. I was now a regular in the side but I remember once being 'rested' by Jimmy with the assurance that I'd be brought back for the next game. He didn't keep that promise because the team won the match without me. The decision annoyed me but not half as much as one he made in the middle of March 1976.

We'd reached the quarter-finals of the European Cup by beating FC Zurich and Ujpest Dozsa – I scored our third goal in a 3-0 win over the Hungarians – and we now faced the Belgian champions, Anderlecht. After a 3-0 win at Elland Road, we travelled to Belgium for the return leg a fortnight later having drawn 0-0 with Everton on the previous Saturday. Before the game, I joined Eddie Gray and Peter Lorimer who were discussing the likely side in our hotel.

'I think he'll leave the team as it was on Saturday', said Eddie.

'No', said Peter, 'I think he'll bring Taff in and leave out you or me – because we're away from home.'

Johnny Giles then joined the conversation and he agreed with Peter. I'd be in – at the expense of either Eddie or Peter. Not long after, we gathered for the pre-match team talk and Jimmy announced the side.

'We've been here three days,' he said, 'it's absolutely poured down with rain and the pitch is thick with mud so I've decided to bring in

Taff...and leave out Johnny.'

The boys were flabbergasted, but we won the game 1-0 and went through to the semi-finals 4-0 on aggregate. We flew into London and, because we were playing Luton in a League match three days later, we didn't go back to Leeds but stayed in a local hotel. We were all wondering what changes Jimmy might make as he started his team talk before the following Saturday's game.

'We've been here for a couple of days, lads,' he said, 'and, as you can see, it's been pouring down so Johnny's back in and Taff's out.'

So I was dropped for exactly the same reason that I'd been included in Belgium! I went berserk but it was typical Jimmy. Sometimes he could be so indecisive. He couldn't make up his mind which was his best team and then when he did decide on it, his reasoning was occasionally baffling. But no matter what, I got on very well with Jimmy and I'm grateful for the part he played in my career. Under him, I cemented my place in the team and, thanks to him, I achieved one of my ambitions – to play in a European Cup Final. Unfortunately, my memory of that game isn't a happy one – for a number of reasons.

We'd reached the final against the holders, Bayern Munich, after beating Barcelona and the great Johan Cruyff who had inspired Ajax to win the competition three times on the trot in the early 1970s. When David Harvey was injured in a car crash, another Scottish keeper, David Stewart, was pressed into action. A 50,000 crowd packed into Elland Road for the first leg to see Billy Bremner put us ahead but Barca scored a potentially crucial away goal before Allan Clarke gave us a 2-1 lead to take to the Nou Camp where twice as many people saw the second leg. An early Peter Lorimer goal settled us down but Barcelona equalised 20 minutes from time. Gordon McQueen was sent off almost straightaway for throwing a punch before David Stewart really came into his own as we hung on to reach our first European Cup Final.

While I accept that I was one of football's hard men – in that I knew how to look after myself when the going got tough – it saddens me that I may always be remembered for that dreadful tackle I made in the match against Bayern Munich at the Parc des Princes in Paris on 28th May 1975. It's the most high-profile of a certain number of tackles in my career which I'm deeply ashamed of. Like the one that broke the

Hull youngster's leg in 1966, I'm not proud of it and all I can say to Bjorn Andersson, the player who I clattered into in the fourth minute of the match, is that I'm desperately sorry.

At the start of the game, my job was clear: I was just going to get in there and try to win every ball for Johnny and Billy to make use of – that was the only thought in my head. I remember the ball was in the air with at least three players hovering around it. It was loose and it was a case of me going in as hard as I possibly could to win it. I just went in and, in the process, 'did' Bjorn. But the tackle itself wasn't premeditated and I certainly didn't mean to hurt him. My sole concern was to win the ball and I didn't care who, or what, was in the way. I deliberately went for the ball and the man and, as I did, I was thinking 'I hope I get the ball but if I get the man, then hard luck.' I don't know precisely where I hit Bjorn but I think it was somewhere around his knee. He went straight down and was carried off on a stretcher. It's no excuse but it was the biggest game I'd ever played in, we wanted to win it so badly and, if you like, nothing was going to stop me, or us. Nobody said anything about the tackle at the time or afterwards. The incident was a closed door but I know it wouldn't be if it happened today. I suppose I was lucky in that although there were cameras there, we didn't have Sky Television. If we had, the incident would have been picked up and scrutinised in minute detail from six or eight different angles and I would have been slaughtered. In my playing days, those sorts of tackles took place all over the world – they weren't only carried out by me or other players at Leeds.

There was no response at all from any of my team-mates but I became ashamed of what I'd done pretty soon afterwards. Having retired from playing and now moved into management, I don't like to remember that tackle when I'm trying to teach young men how to play football the right way – hard but fair. I know people can look at me and remind me that I was a dirty bastard as a player and I can't deny it. That tackle proved the point. But I've since become a reformed character. I wonder how I'd feel now if the same thing happened to one of the boys who I coach at Huddersfield? I don't want them to do anything like that. I have never asked anyone in my teams to go out and make that type of tackle. In my defence, I believe that tackle has made me become a better coach and, hopefully, a better person.

It's not very pleasant to know that I helped to end a fellow professional's career. After being out for virtually a year with his cruciate knee ligament injury, Bjorn tried to make a comeback but he only lasted another season before retiring at the age of 28. He'd become disillusioned with football, partly because his injury meant he couldn't play at the level he wanted to. Bjorn went back to Sweden and trained as a teacher and while he was helping children with behavioural problems, he took up coaching. In 1995, he returned to Bayern Munich to run their new youth academy before becoming their fitness coach. He now runs their Under-17s team while scouting for Scandinavian players. I'm pleased to say that Bjorn has forgiven me for the tackle. He says he was in the wrong place at the wrong time and that he's never actually seen the tackle on television. I take comfort from the fact that Bjorn says he's never hated me, he doesn't bear any grudges and he's never thought of me as a bad human being. I'm sorry to hear that his knee is still causing him problems nearly 30 years later. I can only apologise again and wish him nothing but the best of luck.

Looking back, the tackle would have meant it would have been immoral for me – but not the team – to have come out of that match with a winner's medal. It remains the one big regret of my career. To play in a European Cup Final and be remembered for that one incident sours the memory of the achievement. Every time I went back to Sweden to play football for Wales, the first question from the waiting journalists was always about that tackle. I've never been allowed to forget it.

The game itself ended in huge anti-climax. As a group of players, we knew that this would be the last chance for people like Billy, Johnny, Norman Hunter and Paul Reaney to win the top prize in Europe. We wanted to do it for them and for Don Revie too because it was basically his team. After Bjorn Andersson had been taken off, we really went at the Germans and had a couple of good penalty shouts – including one when Franz Beckenbauer brought down Allan Clarke by wrapping his legs around him. The referee didn't give it but the next day's newspapers showed very clearly what had happened.

Once again, we were hit by our infamous jinx when a 'goal' by Peter Lorimer was disallowed with about a quarter of the match left. We were about to start celebrating as his volley from the edge of the box screamed past Sepp Maier in the Munich goal but the linesman had flagged for offside so it didn't stand. Why? Well, believe it or not, because Billy Bremner's elbow, as he stood in the six-yard box, was offside! Billy wasn't obscuring Maier's view but the referee decided that he was interfering with play. Beckenbauer later admitted that Bayern thought the match was over when Peter's shot hit the net. So did we. To have it ruled out was typical of the kind of thing that happened to Leeds under Don Revie and now it was happening again. The incident unsettled us, we were distracted and Bayern took advantage by scoring two late goals on the counter-attack through Franz Roth and Gerd Muller. We were caught by two sucker punches and Beckenbauer admitted that Bayern Munich were very lucky winners. Unfortunately, our fans agreed with him. The sense of injustice proved too much for some of them and the closing stages of the match were disrupted by seats being thrown on to the pitch. I was substituted with 15 minutes to go and replaced by Eddie Gray. As I walked past the Leeds fans, seats were flying all around me and a full-scale riot involving the police took place after the match which completely ruined Bayern's lap of honour.

That match was Leeds down to a tee. It had all the sort of controversy that we'd become familiar with over the previous 10 years: the injury to Bjorn Andersson, the disallowed penalties and 'goal', their two late strikes and the crowd trouble which soured the whole occasion. We were banned by UEFA from European football for four years although, thanks to Jimmy Armfield intervening on our behalf, the sentence was later cut in half. We paid the full price for the stupidity of some of our fans and it took years for Leeds to shake off their hooligan reputation. The match also marked the end of an era and the end of the Leeds career of a key player in the Revie Revolution because Johnny Giles then moved to West Bromwich Albion as player-manager.

Under Don, we never went on any end-of-season breaks because he didn't believe in them. He thought the game had taken up enough of our time by that stage and we should be with our families once the last ball had been kicked. But after the European Cup Final, Jimmy decided we were going to Marbella where he wanted to mix a little business with a lot of pleasure. He said that while we were in Spain, he would discuss our contracts with us. Every morning, the players would lie on sunbeds at one end of the hotel pool and Jimmy would be at the other. After lunch, we'd go golfing or have a drink at the bar and nobody was ever called down by Jimmy to talk about their contracts. He liked to sit with me and Frankie Gray – we were the laugh-a-minute merchants – and one day, Jimmy did finally say that he wanted to discuss Frankie's future with him. Frankie asked if it was alright if I came along, Jimmy agreed and we went up to his room.

I poured us all some drinks and lay down on the bed while they discussed the contract. Every time Jimmy offered him something, Frankie would look at me in the mirror and I would either nod or shake my head. I wasn't so much a shop steward as a friend who Frankie liked to discuss things with. In the end, they agreed terms but Frankie was the only player to discuss his contract with Jimmy. On the plane back to Leeds at the end of the break, the three of us were sitting together when Jimmy opened up his briefcase and suddenly realised he'd left all the contracts in his hotel room! That just about sums him up – a wonderful guy but a little absent-minded.

Overall, the 1974-75 season was a big disappointment. Although we'd reached the European Cup Final and the quarter-finals of the FA Cup, we'd finished only ninth in the First Division – the first time for a decade that we hadn't been in contention for the title. On a personal note, I made 51 starts in all competitions – the most in any season at Leeds – and with Johnny now in the West Midlands, I was handed the coveted number 10 shirt before the start of the new season. I must admit I was pleased and honoured because two Leeds greats – Bobby Collins and Johnny – had worn it before me but as time passed, it became a huge millstone around my neck. It was very difficult to live up to their stature as footballers and I began to be given stick by a section of the crowd at Elland Road. I would go to the medical room to warm up on the exercise bike before a game and I came out of there once just as the team was being announced. When my name was read out, the crowd started booing – and that was before I'd stepped on to the pitch! I can laugh about it today but it was awful then. Whenever the press asked me about the crowd's reaction, I would simply explain that I wasn't a Bremner or a Giles. I was me – Terry Yorath. I knew I'd never be as slick as Johnny or as cute as Billy but I would always try my hardest for the team. To be honest, I couldn't really say anything else. I didn't model myself on either of them but I tried to take something from them both and incorporate it into my game. The fact is I never quite reached their standard – I had a certain amount of skill but I just wasn't as good as them.

My last season at Elland Road turned out to be another damp squib. We had lost Johnny, I couldn't fill the void he left and Billy's best years were behind him. We were knocked out of the FA and League Cups early on and although we had a good first half of the season in the League – when top scorer Duncan McKenzie scored the majority of his 17 goals – a slump in form in January and February 1976 cost us dear. We picked up just two points out of 10 and finished fifth in the table.

With the club banned from Europe and the team built by Don Revie starting to break up, I felt it was time for me to go. Elland Road just didn't hold the same attraction anymore and I was becoming increasingly demoralised by all the flak from the crowd. I was only 26 and I thought I'd be better off switching to another club. As the close season began, I went to see Jimmy Armfield and asked for a transfer. He made it clear that he didn't want me to go but when I said I was determined to leave, he told me three teams had made enquiries about signing me – Coventry, Everton and 'some Greek club.' Away from football, my life was about to change too and when nothing materialised on the transfer front, I settled down to prepare for the birth of our third child. Christine and I had married in 1971 and our two children, Gabby and Louise, then aged three and two, were becoming very excited at the prospect of having a baby brother or sister in the summer. Daniel duly arrived on 25th July 1976 in the middle of pre-season training and a month later I became the first in a series of departures by Don Revie's men from Elland Road. I knew it was time to leave the Leeds family because the club I had joined as a 15-year-old had, like me, also changed. It was best for both of us that I moved on.

Life after Leeds

The voice on the end of the line sounded familiar. 'Hello...is that Terry?'

'Speaking.'

'It's John Motson here.'

I wasn't to know it but the BBC Television commentator was about to act as a sort of agent, the middle man in a move which would take me away from Leeds. One famous football personality was going to put me in touch with another. After exchanging a few pleasantries, Motty got to the point:

'Jimmy Hill wants to have a word with you; would you ring him?'

And that was how, on the opening day of the 1976-77 season, I heard that Coventry were officially interested in me. One of the game's most flamboyant and influential figures was on my trail and I must admit I was chuffed to bits. Since turning professional in 1949, Jimmy Hill had been involved in football in some capacity or other...as a player, union rep, manager, broadcaster and the first unpaid managing director of an English club. As chairman of the Professional Footballers' Association, Jimmy had helped to bring about the end of the maximum wage through a long and sometimes bitter fight but when he'd asked Motty to contact me, he had moved on to a different kind of struggle. He was trying to keep Coventry in the old First Division and he wanted me to join his Sky Blue Army.

Motty had tracked me down to Margate where my brother, David, was opening a new pub. I'd been able to take the day off because I was suspended for our first game against Johnny Giles and his West Bromwich Albion side at Elland Road. In my absence, one of the most talented footballers of our generation, Tony Currie, made his debut for Leeds in the 2-2 draw after signing from Sheffield United for £240,000. Although he was obviously a rival for my place in midfield, I think I would have stayed at Elland Road if Tony had come to the club earlier. I'm sure we would have worked well together but sadly we weren't given the chance.

Having taken down Jimmy's number, I thanked Motty for his help and rang Jimmy the next day. He said he'd like to talk to me about a move and I explained that Leeds were playing at Birmingham on the following Tuesday night. Jimmy said he'd be in touch and he was as good as his word. We travelled down to Birmingham on the Monday and in the evening, I picked up this message on the hotel tannoy.

'Would Mr Terry Yorath please go to reception.'

When I arrived there, Jimmy's secretary was on the line.

'Can you be outside the hotel in five minutes', she said, 'and look out for a yellow Jaguar?'

I said I could so I walked out of the hotel lobby five minutes later and waited. Sure enough, the yellow Jag soon arrived with a girl wearing a skirt up to her backside at the wheel. I couldn't take my eyes off her legs. She drove the car around a roundabout and then up a lane before pulling up near a churchyard. Suddenly, out of the back of the car stepped Jimmy – he'd been lying down on the back seat so that he wouldn't be recognised. He immediately started selling Coventry to me by saying how much he wanted me to come to Highfield Road as club captain.

After we'd drawn 0-0 against Birmingham in my only appearance of the season for Leeds, I went back to Elland Road where Jimmy Armfield was still talking to me about staying. To be honest, I'd more or less made up my mind that I wanted to go for two reasons – the crowd abuse I'd received during the previous season and what I thought was a lack of discipline at the club. When you're a professional footballer, getting stick from supporters comes with the job. It's all part of the game – fans pay their money and they have a right to have a go. I had never forgotten something that happened to me as I was breaking into the Leeds first team in the late 1960s. I was always using buses then because I didn't pass my driving test until I was 23. One day after training, I played snooker with the lads in town and then caught a bus to Adel, on the outskirts of Leeds, where I was living with Christine at the time. I was sitting on the top deck at the back when two men in front of me started discussing the previous Saturday's game. Naturally enough, my ears pricked up. They started burning when one of the guys told the other what he thought of our performance.

'They didn't play very well,' he said 'and that Yorath's fucking hopeless!'

As I shrunk further and further down into my seat, I was just hoping they wouldn't turn round and see me! What could I have said? Of course, that kind of thing was bound to happen, bearing in mind how much public transport I was using in those days, but the abuse during the 1975-76 season was very personal and unrelenting. No matter how well I'd played, I couldn't escape it. In the end, I'd simply had enough. Jimmy Armfield knew I was unhappy but he didn't want me to go. I also felt that the way some of the players were conducting themselves wasn't right. We'd been brought up to be punctual, to behave professionally and the discipline was carried through by good pros but they were on their way out. Johnny had gone to West Brom and it wouldn't be long before Billy Bremner left for Hull and Norman Hunter went down to Bristol City. I mentioned my concerns to Jimmy but he didn't agree with me.

By the time Jimmy Hill came a-courting, I was determined to leave and, to be fair, he pulled out all the stops to woo me. He invited Christine and I down to Coventry to meet the rest of the board and their wives. During a big meal they'd laid on for us, the phone rang. Jimmy answered it and then handed the receiver to Coventry's manager, Gordon Milne.

'It's Jimmy Armfield for you, Gordon.'

Gordon and Jimmy Armfield were big mates – they'd played for England together – and when Gordon put down the phone, he turned to me and said:

'Jimmy's just given us permission to speak to you.'

Although I didn't sign there and then, I did agree everything with them that day. As most wives would be in that position, Christine was concerned about where the family – including one-month-old Daniel – were going to live. So Jimmy took us on a short guided tour of the local area. We went out of the ground and drove down Kenilworth Road, a tree-lined avenue full of magnificent houses. Jimmy turned right and went up another road before stopping in front of a lovely white house with a spacious front garden.

'This is where my ex-wife lives,' he said. We went into the kitchen where Heather was with their kids and Jimmy introduced us. He then explained that he'd actually bought Heather the house she wanted just around the corner and we could move in here when she left until we found somewhere to live permanently. In the end, we bought the house and became great friends with Heather. In fact, we adopted her tiny poodle because it kept coming back to the house after she'd gone. As a family, we were very happy in Coventry and made many friends there.

Four days after the Birmingham game, I signed for the Sky Blues for £125,000 on the day they beat Leeds 4-2 at Highfield Road. I watched the match from the stand and saw my old mate, Frankie Gray, and the new boy, Tony Currie, score for my old team. In all, I played 197 first-team games for Leeds and scored 12 goals over nine years. I had mixed feelings after spending so long at Elland Road but I had no regrets about joining Coventry because I really rated Jimmy Hill and what he had done for the club – he was way ahead of his time. He was innovative and inspirational – and I was inspired by his enthusiasm. As a manager, he'd taken Coventry from the old Third Division to the First and his commercial nous led to the whole place being given a make-over. He changed their strip from royal to pale blue and their nickname from the Bantams to the Sky Blues as part of a complete re-branding of the club. Radio Sky Blue was set up and extra money was raised through the club's pub, the Sky Blue Tavern. By 1976, when I arrived at Highfield Road, Coventry had a club restaurant, executive boxes and their own fantastic training ground.

On the pitch though, things weren't quite so impressive. I was one of a crop of new signings as strikers Mick Ferguson and Ian Wallace, defender Bobby McDonald and midfielder John Beck also arrived at Highfield Road. The first day's training was a bit of a culture shock. Some of the established players like Jim Brogan, Tommy Hutchison and John Craven asked the new boys if we wanted to go for some lunch at a country pub just around the corner from the training ground. It sounded like a good idea and, after sinking quite a few pints in the next four hours, we left the pub at about four o'clock in the afternoon. I realised then why Coventry were struggling and Leeds had done well over the last 10 years or so. That sort of drinking session wouldn't have been allowed at Leeds – golf and snooker sure but strictly no alcohol.

I really enjoyed my time at Coventry. Once I pulled on that Sky Blue shirt, I played my heart out for the team as I did for all my clubs. Getting transferred is part and parcel of football, not many people stay at the same club for all of their careers and I felt they had ambition and were going places. Unfortunately, it didn't quite work out but I never felt it was a mistake for me to leave Leeds for Coventry.

Although we didn't have a bad team on paper, we really struggled in the bottom half of the First Division during my first season. Bryan King was in goal and there were plenty of experience in the squad with players like Tommy Hutchison, who'd been with Blackpool, the former Liverpool defender, Larry Lloyd and Barry Powell, the former Wolves midfielder who I played alongside. I got on very well with the manager, Gordon Milne – so much so that when my contract with the Welsh FA ended in 1994, he offered me his club job in Turkey! He was both a good man and a good manager. He included me in a lot of the team preparation. As club captain, every day before training, I would be summoned into Gordon's office where he and the coach, Ron Wylie, would explain what we'd be doing that morning. Gordon and Ron liked good football but they wanted us to get stuck in first and then play – a little like Leeds had done under Don Revie. Nobody could leave the training ground until I'd spoken to Gordon afterwards and he'd said they could go.

In December 1976, we were 10th in the table before a spate of injuries badly disrupted our season. For two months, we were without our two main strikers: Mick Ferguson with ankle ligament damage and Ian Wallace who was injured in a car crash. On the last day of the season, we were in danger of going down – something which the club's long-suffering supporters have had to get used to over the years! It could hardly have been closer. Depending on results, one of Coventry, Bristol City and Sunderland would be relegated with Stoke and Spurs who were already down. All three teams had 34 points and whoever won would be safe. We knew that if the games ended in draws, we'd be relegated because we had the worst goal average and Sunderland the best. While Sunderland were at Everton, we were playing Bristol City at Highfield Road on the same night at the same time. Not only that but who was captain of Bristol City? None other than my old team-mate from Leeds, Norman Hunter! Not surprisingly, Highfield Road was packed to the rafters for such an important match but by kick-off time, not all the 37,000 crowd were in the ground because some Bristol City supporters had been delayed by traffic. On police advice, the referee decided to delay the start by five minutes. Once the game got underway, we went 2-0 up, Bristol pulled one back and then scored again to make it 2-2 in the second half. As the tension mounted, Gordon Milne called me over to the dugout and told me that Everton were beating Sunderland 2-0. I ran over to Norman and explained that if the scores in both matches stayed the same, then we'd both stay up.

'Are you taking the piss?,' asked Norman.

'No, I'm not!', I insisted.

I then shouted over to Gordon that Norman didn't know if he should believe me. But he did a few moments later when the Radio Sky Blue announcer confirmed what many of the crowd knew already through listening to their transistor radios. The final score at Goodison Park was Everton 2 Sunderland 0.

'There you are,' I yelled to Norman. 'You can tell your lads to back off now.'

It seems he told everybody but their substitute, Jimmy Mann, who, as it happened, came from Leeds. Jimmy suddenly picked up the ball, ran through the centre of our defence and hit a shot that touched the top of the crossbar and went over for a goal-kick. I immediately ran across to Norman.

'For fuck's sake, tell him!,' I shouted. So he did – in no uncertain terms. It did the trick and the game petered out. Their goalkeeper would send the ball out to their full-back who Tommy Hutchison would confront and the ball would then be knocked back to the centre-half and so it went on. In other words, Bristol City made no attempt to attack and neither did we during the last five minutes of the match. We both eased up and treated the game like a practice match and why not? We weren't cheating but we knew – quite literally – the score. We were preserving our status in the top division and I'd tell my players to do exactly the same thing again today if we were in that position. That's the name of the game when survival is at stake.

Afterwards, the Bristol players and their supporters were obviously delighted to have stayed up because it was their first season back in the First Division for 66 years. We just sat in the dressing room feeling very relieved. I think it would have been harsh if we'd gone down because it was the first time we'd been in the bottom three all season. That night wasn't about money but just for the record, our bonus for staying up was £11 compared with the £1,100 that Norman and his team were on.

So Sunderland went down but not before the football authorities had held an inquiry into the goings-on at Highfield Road. Although the referee confirmed it was his decision to delay the kick-off, the Football League's secretary, Alan Hardaker, wrote a letter officially reprimanding Coventry for their part in the proceedings. Jimmy Hill led the protest as the matter was put in the hands of the club's lawyers and the board wanted the decision 'rescinded and the stain removed from Coventry's name.' After club officials had attended a formal meeting with the Football League to explain what happened, their version of events was accepted and the matter closed.

At the end of that season, we were on a family holiday in Corfu when I met a Greek water-skiing instructor who was married to an English woman. He was a fanatical Liverpool supporter and he recognised me. During one of his lessons, he asked if AEK Athens had once tried to sign me. I told him that Jimmy Armfield had mentioned that a Greek club were interested when I was at Leeds and he said it was AEK. I then confirmed that my grandfather was Greek and thought no more about it.

The next morning, I went down for a swim about half past eight. As I was having a quick coffee, I noticed a man sitting all by himself. The water-skiing instructor said that he wanted to speak to me. It turned out that he was AEK's secretary – and the club were still interested in signing me. He asked if he could take out Christine and I for a meal that night.

'On Friday, I want to fly you to Athens,' he continued, 'So you can watch our game at the weekend and then you can fly back to Britain.'

I thanked him for his interest and then discussed his offer with Christine. We decided that we didn't want to fly to the mainland because we had the children with us but we would go to dinner with him. We explained our reasoning to him over the meal and then he got around to talking about money. At Coventry, I was earning about £13,000 a year and driving a Cortina. If I joined AEK, I'd be earning the equivalent of £70,000 a year. On top of that, we'd have a villa, a nanny and the kids would go to an English school in Athens.

'What sort of car do you drive?' he asked.

'BMW,' I replied, as quick as a flash.

'Right. There'll be a BMW for you and another one for your wife. And your salary will be tax-free – we will pay the tax.'

It sounded too good to be true but a week later I heard from Jimmy Hill. He knew I'd been in Corfu on holiday and he confirmed that AEK had been in touch.

'We've told them we want £300,000 for you,' said Jimmy.

'But Jim...you only paid £125,000 for me about nine months ago! Why has the price more than doubled to £300,000?'

'Well...that's what we value you at.'

But Jimmy and the board had pitched it too high. No Greek club had ever paid £300,000 for a player before – I think the most was about £150,000 – so the deal fell through. AEK wouldn't come up with the transfer fee so my dreams of playing for a top Greek club and making some serious money in the process had disappeared. My mind went back to the previous summer when Jimmy Armfield had told me that Coventry, Everton and 'some Greek club' were interested in signing me. If he'd told me who it was and I'd made contact then, who knows where I might have ended up?

The 1977-78 season ended in anti-climax but it could all have been so different. With our serious injury problems behind us, we hit some great form. Ray Graydon gave us some width out on the right and Mick Ferguson and Ian Wallace scored more than half our 75 League goals between them. We finished seventh and would have qualified for Europe if Arsenal had beaten Ipswich in the FA Cup Final and gone into the European Cup Winners' Cup. As it was, they didn't and having finished fifth in the table, the Gunners took up one of the available UEFA Cup places and we missed out.

We finished 10th in my last season at Coventry when I spent a lot of the time on the sidelines because of a hamstring injury. In fact, I only played in half our League games. The problem flared up during a 7-1 thrashing by West Bromwich in late October 1978 and my place was taken by a young lad called Andy Blair as we beat Birmingham 2-1 in a West Midlands derby. I didn't play again until early February when we lost 1-0 at Leeds, of all places. I just had to bite the bullet. Andy was a cocky young lad, not a bad player who had about three good seasons with Coventry. I was still playing for Wales and I was trying to be dignified about being left out by my club but it was very frustrating. When I wasn't in the team, Gordon Milne always wanted me alongside him on the bench. When he asked me for my opinion, I'd give it to him and he'd get annoyed if I wasn't there. For example, one Saturday, a friend from Leeds, Colin Farrer, who'd been best man at my wedding, was in Coventry for a birthday celebration. We decided to go to Highfield Road, have a meal in the restaurant and then watch the game. On the Monday morning, I was called into the manager's office and given a right bollocking by Gordon for not being in the dressing room or on the bench for the match. Although the telling-off was supposed to hurt me, I actually took it as a huge compliment.

After the summer break, I came back for pre-season full of beans but once again found myself on the move – just three days before our first League game. The night after Coventry's annual party, there I was, standing in Gordon's office, being told that a transfer to Spurs was on the cards. Would I be prepared to talk to their manager, Keith Burkinshaw?

Now when you're told something like that, there's no point in hanging around – you get out. I was really disappointed because I'd enjoyed my spell at Highfield Road and the timing, once again, wasn't great. I had prepared hard during pre-season to play for Coventry and then suddenly this had come out of the blue. But I realised it had all the makings of a good move because I would be going from a small city club like Coventry to go to a big London team like Spurs. I was really excited by the prospect – especially when Gordon gave me some advice about money. I was earning £250 a week with Coventry and he told me to ask for double that at Spurs.

It was agreed that I would meet Keith in a hotel car park in Leicester but there were no brown envelopes involved! We talked for a while and Keith said that initially he wanted me to play alongside the centre-half – something I was happy with. From what I could gather, he'd looked at his team over pre-season, realised what was missing and decided to bring me in. He asked me what I wanted in terms of wages and agreed to my request for £500 a week. He said he'd expect me down at Tottenham the next day – a Thursday – when I would have to sign by five o'clock if I wanted to play on the following Saturday. Christine was again worried about where we going to live so when we arrived in London, Keith took us out to look at a few houses in the local area. He stopped outside the home of Pat Jennings, the Spurs and Northern Ireland goalkeeper, and I asked him how much it was worth. He said about £125,000 but when I asked Pat himself not long afterwards, he told me it was worth £450,000! Keith was obviously trying to get me to sign before the transfer deadline and it worked because I did. Looking back, the move to Coventry had been good for me at that stage of my career. I'd played about 100 games and scored three goals in my three years there but the best part about it was that it turned out to be the stepping stone for my transfer to Spurs. Just after I'd signed, I remember walking out on to the pitch at White Hart Lane and seeing the cockerel, the club emblem, on top of the main stand.

'You won't understand this,' I said to Christine, 'but that,' and I pointed to the cockerel, 'is fantastic.'

I was referring to the history of Tottenham Hotspur Football Club and their wonderful tradition of playing the game the way it should be played. I was too young to remember Arthur Rowe's 'push-and-run' side of the early 1950s but when I was growing up in Cardiff in the early 1960s, all the talk was of the great 'double' team and the way they entertained football fans all over the country with their dazzling displays. In 1963, Bill Nicholson's side, with the help of one of my boyhood heroes, Jimmy Greaves, went on to become the first British team to win a European trophy when they beat Atletico Madrid in the final of the European Cup Winners' Cup. There was more success over the next decade or so and I considered it such an honour to be joining one of the most glamorous and distinguished clubs in English football.

After I'd signed, we stayed down in London for the night and when we were back in our hotel room, Christine started crying. She had an inkling that Pat's house was worth more than Keith had said. She was naturally worried about us moving to London and having to buy a much more expensive house. Eventually, we decided that the family would stay in Coventry and I would commute. At first, I lived in an hotel and then the club put me up in a house in Enfield in North London. It was great because it overlooked a cricket pitch and it was perfect for both White Hart Lane and their training ground.

My first session at White Hart Lane consisted of a warm-up and a five-a-side game after I'd been introduced to the team. To this day, I still find it amazing that I suddenly found myself amongst this elite group of players. Here I was on first-name terms with three midfield maestros: Ossie Ardiles, Ricky Villa and Glenn Hoddle – a couple of World Cup winners and one of England's most gifted footballers. It was as if I'd died and gone to football heaven! The problem was that we didn't have a decent keeper or a centre-half. Spurs didn't have the same steel as Leeds – in terms of a centre-half like Jack Charlton, a goalkeeper like Gary Sprake or full-backs like Terry Cooper. In goal, we had either Barry Daines and Milija Aleksic – who was very unlucky with injuries – and although John Lacy was a smashing lad and not a bad player, the crowd got to him. I made my debut in central defence alongside John against Middlesbrough at White Hart Lane two days after signing. After a pretty bad overall performance, we lost 3-1 and then Norwich put four past us at Carrow Road. For the next match at Stoke, Keith Burkinshaw wanted to bring in John Pratt to stiffen up the midfield so he called Ossie, Ricky and Glenn out of the team meeting and asked which one of them was prepared to step down. They came back into the room and Keith announced the team with John in it and Ricky as substitute. With that, Ricky looked up and said, quite matter-of-factly:

'Ricky...no substitute.'

'Yes,' insisted Keith, 'you're substitute.'

'Ricky...no substitute,' repeated the big man. 'Ricky love Tottenham. Ricky love Keith but Ricky...no substitute.'

'Ossie,' said Keith, turning to Ardiles, 'talk to him.'

So Osssie started speaking to Ricky in Spanish but then confirmed Villa's position.

'He's not going to be substitute.'

'OK!' declared Keith, 'Don McAllister – you're substitute!'

If I'd have been Don, I would have told Keith where to stick it but he accepted the situation and later came on as a sub. Stoke won 3-1 but the result proved a turning point because we only lost once in our next 12 League games – a 5-2 defeat at Southampton. I only lasted a few games at the back before Steve Perryman took my place and I moved into midfield where I made most of my 33 appearances that season. Stevie was at the heart of everything that went on at Spurs – he was the shop steward who made up and enforced the rules. He was a great player, who should have won more than the one England cap he picked up as a sub against Iceland in 1982, and a great person to be with. We ended up finishing a disappointing 14th in the First Division but the two cup competitions produced some memorable matches against Manchester United. In the second round of the League Cup, we beat them 2-1 at White Hart Lane in the first leg with Glenn Hoddle scoring a wonderful goal. I was playing my first game in midfield and I slipped a free-kick to Ossie who laid the ball off to Glenn and he smashed it into the back of the net. Our young full-back, Chris Hughton, made his debut in that game and although I told him not to worry because we'd look after him, he insisted he'd be alright – and he was. He was a cheeky little sod but he came through very well. We lost 4-3 on aggregate after going down 3-1 in the second leg at Old Trafford but gained revenge by knocking United out of the FA Cup after a third-round replay. Ossie scored in the 1-1 draw at our place and then he got the only goal at Old Trafford where an old Leeds team-mate of mine, Joe Jordan, bundled into Milija Aleksic who went down with cruciate ligament and shoulder injuries. It meant Glenn having to go in goal but we managed to hang on for a great victory.

As everyone knows, Glenn was a fantastic footballer. He was Tottenham through and through and he just wanted to play for the club. He would do things in training which I've not seen anyone else do. He could be looking to his right and then hit the ball with the outside of his left foot 30 yards straight to a team-mate. He was also a great lad to work with. It was terrific playing in midfield with Glenn and the two Argentinians because I knew that all I had to do was to win the ball and give it to them. During a game against Arsenal at White Hart Lane, I went into a tackle and, as usual, my eyes were closed for a split second just before impact. When I opened them, I saw Glenn lying on the ground alongside me.

'What the hell are you doing?' I shouted at him.

'I was tackling!' he replied.

'I fucking tackle,' I said. 'You pass!'

As you often find with flair players, Glenn was invariably criticised either for not tackling or working hard enough throughout his career. The argument about his England credentials was in full swing when I was just beginning my spell as Welsh manager. I remember meeting the Arsenal manager, Arsène Wenger, at the 1988 European Championships in Holland when he was in charge of Monaco. Glenn was with the French club at the time and there was a lot of talk around the hotel about whether he should be in the England team.

'You've managed him,' I said to Arsène, 'and I've played with him – he's a certainty to be picked.'

'Every man has different tastes,' replied Arsène.

Now that was the shrewd view of someone who could obviously analyse the situation. He realised that from a manager's point of view that there might be something stopping Glenn being picked regularly for England. In my view, Glenn, along with Johnny Giles, was the most talented footballer I ever played with. He was extraordinary – he had everything. He could bend the ball in from free-kicks but he was also magnificent in open play with his passing and shooting. Glenn was a rather tall person to play in midfield – unlike Johnny – and was very elegant and smooth on the ball. He was largely responsible, sometimes single-handedly, for bringing back some of the glory days to White Hart Lane when Spurs won the FA Cup twice and the UEFA Cup in the early 1980s. I wasn't surprised at all when Glenn went into management because he knew all about the game from a very young age. I think his strong Christian beliefs changed his life and his character because he'd just been one of the lads who went out for a drink and a meal before he found religion. I reckon Glenn was unfairly ridiculed by the press for using the faith healer, Eileen Drewery, to try to help some England players recover from injury before the 1998 World

Cup. He was seen as arrogant and it was sad when he lost the England job in 1999 after the unfortunate remarks he made about disabled people and reincarnation. Personally, I don't see why anybody in football should be judged by comments made about something outside the game. If he'd called somebody inside football a few nasty names and brought disgrace on his employers, the FA, then OK but surely any manager should be judged on results rather than comments about things that have nothing at all to do with the game?

Ossie and Ricky were as different as chalk and cheese. One little, one large; one game for a laugh, the other more serious; both with great skills. Keith Burkinshaw had pulled off a tremendous coup after Argentina's 1978 World Cup win by persuading them to come to Spurs. They were the first of the current wave of foreign footballers and they paid off Keith's investment with interest. Ossie was one of the best footballers I ever played with. He had a great sense of humour but little grasp of reality. He may have had a law degree but Ossie had no idea about the nitty-gritty of everyday life. He didn't have a clue what you should and shouldn't do. His car broke down once near Arsenal's training ground in North London and he just left it there on the dual carriageway. He didn't realise that he had to phone the police. He once rang up Peter Day, the assistant secretary at White Hart Lane, at half past one in the morning.

'I'm in London, I've come outside and my car is gone,' declared Ossie.

'Where are you exactly?' asked Peter.

'I'm outside the London Sporting Club casino.'

'You parked your car outside there?'

'Yes.'

'The police will have taken it away – it'll have been impounded. You'll have to wait until Monday to get it back. You'll have to get a taxi home.'

And with that, Peter put down the phone and tried to go back to sleep. A couple of minutes later, it rang again.

'Peter,' said Ossie, 'who pays for the taxi?'

Ossie also liked to visit casinos and wherever we went with Spurs, he was always one of the first to find them. I liked the odd gamble with any extra cash I happened to have on me at the time. Although I didn't normally go in for buying and selling anything that looked like it had fallen off the back of a lorry, when I was offered six brand new microwaves at half-price, it seemed a good way of making some easy money. So I showed them to the boys in the dressing room and they snatched my hand off – all six, gone in flash! They paid me the money and we went up to Blackpool for a mid-season break. When we arrived at the hotel, the first thing the guy behind the bar said to me was that it hadn't snowed in Blackpool for 12 years so we weren't expecting any bad weather. After we'd been in one of the casinos for about three-quarters of an hour, Ossie asked me if I still had any of the microwave money. I gave what was left to him and he proceeded to lose it during the next hour. When we came out of the casino, it was blowing a blizzard! So there we were, Ossie and me, absolutely skint, walking back to our hotel, covered from head to foot in snow. We were feeling very sorry for ourselves but it had been a great night out with the man who is still fondly remembered throughout the game for his love of 'Tottingham.'

Ricky was more serious than Ossie and much better at organising his life. During pre-season training, he would have a shower and go home to bed with his wife for an hour and then come back to the ground and carry on with the football. Ricky could be more than a little moody – remember the way he walked off after being substituted in the 1981 FA Cup Final against Manchester City? – but then he showed his tremendous self-confidence by scoring that fabulous winner in the replay.

In the summer of 1980, we played PSV Eindhoven in Holland in a pre-season friendly before going up to Scotland for a couple of games against Rangers and Dundee. Steve Perryman and I always had a thing about Ricky's contribution to the team. We felt that for a person of his ability and strength, he didn't contribute enough in playing terms or mentally. He didn't come with us to Holland because he had what players call 'Dutch calf' – that is, he didn't want to go to Holland. While we were flying up to Scotland, Steve was talking to Keith Burkinshaw.

'You're not going to believe this,' Steve then said to me. 'Ricky's going to be meeting us in Glasgow. He's got his mother and father and wife and kids with him in the car and they're going to follow the team coach and have a tour of Scotland!'

I just couldn't believe it but it was an example of the way Ricky operated. He was able to organise his time so well. That trip to Scotland was a turning point in my career in that I think I played a part in our youth-team coach, Peter Shreeves, being promoted to assistant coach. As I was standing at the bar with Keith in our Glasgow hotel, I had a bit of a go at him on Peter's behalf. I said Shreevesy was different class to the assistant coach but he wasn't being used properly. Keith didn't acknowledge what I said – in fact, he more less talked over it – but about two weeks later, Peter was promoted to first-team coach. I look back and wonder if it was the result of that conversation in Glasgow? Peter's promotion led to a long-standing friendship between us and we later worked together with Wales and Sheffield Wednesday. I didn't know him that well then but I thought that he could do the job and it's nice to think that I might have played a part in him getting his foot on the first rung of the managerial ladder.

Keith Burkinshaw was different class too in that he was the first manager I'd met who was also a human being. Most managers are purely concerned about getting the best out of their players without thinking about them as individuals with specific needs. But Keith was different. He taught me the importance of recognising that there is a world outside football. You shouldn't be too soft with players but they appreciate you asking them about their families and taking an interest in their lives away from the club. I remember sitting down in the dressing room after one game and being told by Keith to have the week off.

'Come in next Friday,' he said.

I looked at him and wondered if he was taking the piss or testing me?

'I know you'll look after yourself,' Keith said, 'so just come in next Friday and be ready for the game on Saturday.'

I thought that was brilliant. I hadn't been able to spend a week with Christine and the kids at our home in Coventry for ages. The break didn't improve my performances on the pitch – they were always the best I could produce on the day – but it improved my relationship with the manager. In January 1980, we played Swindon in the fourth round of the FA Cup. During the 0-0 draw at the County Ground, I had a very heavy cold and I was shaking all over by the time I'd reached

Coventry. I stayed in bed for the rest of the weekend and when I rang Keith on the Monday morning he told me not to move. He said I should forget the midweek replay with Swindon because he needed me for our League match on the following Saturday. We won the replay 2-1 and I was just about to ring White Hart Lane to congratulate everybody when my phone went. It was Keith asking how I was and how I was looking for Saturday. That was the sort of guy he was. Keith really cared about his players – not only because he was the manager but because he was a good person.

After we had beaten Birmingham 3-1 at home in the fifth round, Liverpool knocked us out in the quarter-finals with a single goal at White Hart Lane but we went all the way in the 1980-81 season. I played in the third round when we drew 0-0 at Queens Park Rangers but missed our 3-1 win in the replay. But by the time we met Coventry in the fifth round in the middle of February, I was on my way out of Spurs – mainly because another old club of mine, Leeds, had made a move for me towards the end of 1980. As it turned out, I didn't go back to Elland Road and later chose a new challenge in Canada instead but it really broke my heart to leave Tottenham. It was all sparked off by my old team-mate, Allan Clarke, who, after four defeats in the first five games of the season, had replaced Jimmy Adamson as manager at Leeds. As usual, Maurice Lindley had held the fort for a month or so until Allan arrived from Barnsley. After being bought by Spurs for £300,000 two years earlier, I was now pushing 31 but Leeds were struggling and Clarkey wanted me to play in midfield. He knew what he was getting. I must admit I was very surprised when Keith Burkinshaw told me what was happening.

'I've got to tell you this,' he said. 'Allan Clarke has come in with a bid of £300,000 for you. I've told the board and they've said that, because of your age, they've accepted the offer and you've got to go up there. But, to be honest, I want you and Steve Perryman to stay and come on the coaching side with me.'

I would have loved the coaching job at Spurs but I reckoned I still had a few years of football left in me and anyway the deal with Leeds seemed to be done so I went up to talk to Clarkey. I met him at his house at Collingham, near Wetherby, along with his assistant, Martin Wilkinson, who later went on to manage Northampton. I knew Allan's home very well because I'd babysat for him and his wife, Margaret, when he first came to Leeds. When we started talking about my wages, I told them I wanted £600 a week and a £25,000 signing-on fee. Allan then spoke to the chairman, Manny Cussins, who must have argued with him about the transfer because Clarkey ended up telling me that he would have to persuade the chairman that it was a good deal. I drove back to Coventry and got up early the next morning to drive to the Spurs training ground by about nine o'clock. Keith said Allan had rung to say he was going to sign me and I should pick up the transfer form from White Hart Lane and get myself up to Leeds. I did so and before seeing Clarkey at his office at Elland Road, I bumped into John Reynolds, the Welsh groundsman who'd helped me settle in at Leeds 15 years earlier.

'Great to see you back,' he said. 'We really need someone like you here.'

Comments like that made me feel like I was coming home. But then suddenly everything went pear-shaped. After keeping me waiting for an hour, Clarkey finally turned up and announced that he was now offering me £400 a week and a £15,000 signing-on fee.

'Al, it's impossible for me to do that,' I said. 'There's no way I can sign for that sort of money.'

'Ring Christine,' Clarkey replied. 'Speak to her.'

Because Christine was from Leeds, Allan was banking on her persuading me to sign on the reduced terms. He couldn't have been more wrong. When I rang and told her about the new offer, Christine's reply was brief and to the point.

'Get yourself back here straightaway,' she said.

'Sorry Al,' I said to Clarkey and started to walk out of his office.

'You'll live to regret it,' he said.

'I don't think I will somehow,' I replied as, for the last time during my playing career, I walked out of Elland Road. I was hugely disappointed because I was looking forward to returning to Leeds. My drive up there had been full of great expectations. Tottenham had accepted the transfer fee, they'd already told me that I could leave and I was happy about it all. I had really enjoyed my football in North London – to be honest, you could hardly fail to because it was a fabulous place to play the game – but it felt great to be going back to Leeds. The move

The youngest of three...
with Pauline and David

On holiday with Mum and Dad

A born leader...school captain at the age of nine

The proudest day of my life...Don Revie welcoming me
on to the full-time staff at Elland Road

Johnny Giles...the genius whose boots I could never fill
– no matter how hard I tried

Practising with the professionals...Norman Hunter, Eddie Gray and Jack Charlton

A second Inter-Cities Fairs Cup success against Juventus in 1971...

...and our one and only FA Cup win over Arsenal a year later

Captaining my country meant the world to me

Arfon Griffiths scored against Austria to take us through to the
quarter-finals of the European Championship in 1976

No place to hide...my crucial penalty miss against Yugoslavia at Ninian Park

The Hand of God(father)...Joe Jordan in the dock at Anfield in 1977

Captain and manager...until I moved to Vancouver
and Mike England ended my international career

Promotion celebrations turned to tragedy at Bradford City's Valley Parade

Club and country...managing Swansea and Wales thanks to Alun Evans and
Jack Evans from the Welsh FA and Swans chairman Doug Sharpe

Ian Rush scores his memorable goal against
Germany at Cardiff Arms Park in 1991

would have given me a very good wage but now the last thing I expected was to be asked to take a pay cut. On my way out of Elland Road,
John Reynolds asked me what was happening. When I told him, he
looked distraught.

I've never believed in regretting anything in life. You have to look
forward and get on with it. As I drove south, I decided not to be too
downhearted by the unexpected turn of events. If Leeds wouldn't pay
me what I thought I was worth, then I would go back to Spurs and
keep playing for them. Keith was fine when I arrived at White Hart
Lane. There was no animosity because he hadn't wanted me to go in
the first place and he put me back into the first team. But my life at
Tottenham changed because I realised the board were willing to get rid
of me and I played only 11 games in that season.

There'd been talk of me joining Cardiff as player-coach but
nothing materialised. Then another old Leeds team-mate, Johnny
Giles, got in touch. He'd left West Bromwich Albion and was now
managing Vancouver Whitecaps in the North American Soccer
League. When Johnny offered me a decent salary and signing-on fee
to join him in Canada, I felt it was time to move on again. I was on the
Spurs bench but not used in a 2-0 League win over the 'old enemy'
Arsenal at White Hart Lane in the middle of January and a week later,
I played my very last game for Spurs when we beat Hull, again 2-0 at
home, to reach the fifth round of the FA Cup. My contract was cancelled in February. I made about 50 appearances in all for Spurs
scoring just the one goal and my only disappointment was that, having
played alongside such talented people as Hoddle, Ardiles, Villa,
Perryman and latterly Steve Archibald, we didn't achieve better
results. Mind you, once I'd left, Spurs strangely hit a purple patch by
winning three trophies in four years! I knew I'd be missing out on a
possible FA Cup Final place but I was unsettled at Spurs and the
prospect of living the good life in Canada was very appealing at that
time in my career.

I went to Vancouver mainly because Johnny was the manager and
another Leeds old boy, Peter Lorimer, was due to become his assistant. Johnny came over to England on a recruitment drive with Peter
Bridgewater who was later to become the top man in North American
soccer and they agreed to pay £140,000 for me. Tony Waiters, the

former England and Blackpool goalkeeper, was president of the Whitecaps. At that time, football over there had been through the Pele era when Franz Beckenbauer and George Best also went over and after a quiet period, it was now becoming popular again. Quite a few foreigners were being signed by teams in the big cities. Germans usually played in Chicago while British and Italian players went to Vancouver. When Johnny came in for me, he agreed to release me to play for my country whenever I was needed. I was very keen to make sure my international career didn't suffer because I was leaving English football and I then scored my second goal for Wales in a 3-1 win over the Republic of Ireland in late February.

The North American outdoor season ran from March to November when the indoor league then began. The whole of the Vancouver Whitecaps squad went across to Dublin for pre-season training. While everyone else then went back to Canada, I played for Wales in a 1-0 win against Turkey in Ankara in late March. I flew back to London from Turkey and then out to Los Angeles and on to San Diego where I made my first appearance for Vancouver. It ended in a draw so the game went to a shoot-out. I wasn't involved in this because it was all new to me. As I sat on the bench with my team-mates, I remarked on the impressive size of the crowd.

'That's because the Beach Boys are on after us!' came the reply. I then made another stupid comment:

'What's that smell?'

I hadn't come across pot or marijuana before but the crowd were getting high on the stuff! Welcome to North American soccer – minus the bovril or tea and pies!

To be honest, my first few games for Vancouver didn't go very well. We were playing on astroturf and the pitch was rock hard – just like a carpet over concrete. If you tackled somebody and landed on it, the astroturf would take the skin off your backside. Tackling was three-quarters of my game and I soon found out that I couldn't do it as much over there. Two more ex-Leeds players, goalkeeper David Harvey and striker Ray Hankin, had been signed by Johnny along with the future England and Newcastle forward, Peter Beardsley, former Everton defender Roger Kenyon and Alan Taylor, who'd scored two goals for West Ham in the 1975 FA Cup Final against Fulham. We had

a good team. I took over the number 3 shirt from the Dutch international, Rudi Krol, who was a big crowd favourite. So after inheriting
the number 10 shirt from Johnny at Leeds, I had a similar job on my
hands in Vancouver.

The only bad thing about playing football in Canada was all the
flying involved. I hated it but planes were the only realistic form of
transport in such big countries as Canada and the United States. I got
very nervous even when we just went to Vancouver Island, about a 15-
minute flight. On one trip, as soon as we were in the air, the guy sitting
next to me stated the obvious:

'You don't like flying do you?'

'No,' I replied.

'Well...do you think the pilot wants to die?'

'I don't think so but it's not always the pilot's fault is it?'

As we looked out of the window, he pointed to a piece of land
jutting out from the coastline and said his house was down there.
Apparently, he made that journey every day. Vancouver to San Diego
would take about four hours and I found it extraordinary how
Canadians took all their flying for granted. It was very rare for us to
play an away game and then come home so we'd be on tour for a fortnight at a time. We would go on trips to places like Seattle and Dallas
and then right across country to Tampa Bay in Florida on the East
Coast. It was a fantastic life...staying in wonderful hotels, seeing lots of
places and playing football. If we were due to play Seattle on a
Saturday, we'd fly there from Vancouver the day before, stay in Seattle
for a couple of nights after the game and then catch a plane down to
Dallas on the Monday. We'd play there on Wednesday, stay overnight
and then set off to Florida to play Tampa before flying back up to
Toronto, Montreal, Calgary or Edmonton and then going home to
Vancouver. We'd play no more than four games on one of these enor-
mous trips. I remember once playing at the Dallas Cowboys American
Football stadium in front of just 200 people because the Dallas soccer
team were bottom of the league. The Whitecaps were owned by four
or five very rich people – including a woman who had a home on
Vancouver Island where she would throw a party every year.

I spent four months on my own in Canada until the family joined
me. Rather than rent a two or three-bedroomed apartment like some of

the players, we decided to go for a beautiful house in British Properties, an area up in the mountains overlooking the sea, a lake and the city of Vancouver. It had a big garden and the skiing was five minutes away. It was fabulous! While we were abroad, we rented out a house and an apartment we owned in Coventry. I think Vancouver is God's gift to the world. It's a very clean and friendly place with breathtaking scenery and wildlife. One day we were driving along the motorway to Horseshoe Bay where the ferries leave from for Vancouver Island. You could hire a boat and go fishing or just take the kids out. There was a fish and chip shop and a pub there for any Brits who were missing home. Christine suddenly asked me to stop so I pulled over to the hard shoulder. There, 20 yards away, was a bear eating! When we had bar-becues in the evenings, we'd leave out some scraps for the racoons. We were warned to never touch them because their claws are very sharp and long. They look pretty harmless when they're lying belly up but when you go to stroke them, they can grab you!

Johnny and Peter had moved their families over too so we soon established a little ex-Leeds colony in the Vancouver area. Football always came first because it was my living. When Christine and the children came over to Canada, I'm afraid I wasn't around for their first night in our new home because we had a game in California. Despite the wonderful lifestyle, it wasn't like a holiday for me – it couldn't be if you took your football seriously – but it was fantastic for the family, especially the kids. The Canadians put so much into sport when children are young. The 20 kids in Gabby's ice-skating class were taught by five coaches and it was the same with volleyball. Both Louise and Gabby were good at gymnastics and when we came back, Gabby was picked for Wales in this sport.

After I'd been in Canada for about a month, Spurs reached the FA Cup Final by beating Wolves 3-0 in a replay. On the morning of the match, I was driving along the freeway with the radio on when one of the two sports presenters announced that it was FA Cup Final day in England. He then revealed that I used to play for Spurs and the other one piped up:

'If Terry Yorath put the ball down 10 yards from Wembley and tried to hit the stadium, he'd miss it.'

I just laughed because it sounded funny – for them. Having played in a couple of the early games in the FA Cup run, I was rooting for Tottenham but, on the other hand, Tommy Hutchison was in the Manchester City side. 'Hutchy' had been a good friend of mine since our Coventry days so my loyalties were divided. In the end, I suppose I had the best of both worlds. Hutchy did well – by scoring at both ends! – and then there was the fantastic replay in which Ricky Villa slotted home a great winner after that mazy run through the Manchester City defence. It was incredible – probably one of the most memorable Cup Final goals of all time. But I had no regrets about missing out on the game and I didn't ring up Spurs afterwards to congratulate them. I'm not that kind of person and I don't think Keith Burkinshaw was either. Once I leave a place, I leave it but I was really pleased that the team I'd been part of for 18 months had gone on and won something.

It was great linking up with Johnny and Peter again. Johnny had retired but Peter still played. The Canadians were mad on statistics which showed Peter was the top assists man in my first season with the Whitecaps. I gradually adjusted to the North American form of football and played most of the time in midfield. We won our conference – the western part of the North American Soccer League – and then got beaten in the quarter-finals of the play-offs by San Diego. It was disappointing because we thought we could go all the way. I then coached the indoor five-a-side team in the winter which again involved travelling all over America. Our stadium in Vancouver was next door to the main one and it was full with 4,000 people for every game. When we went down to San Jose, who were the champions, we were watched by a capacity crowd of 12,000. There were certain areas like Dallas where football would never have taken off but then you could go to Chicago – with a big German population – and it would be very popular. Football was big in British Columbia because of the number of British and Italian people living there and it was the same with Florida and their South American population, Boston had their Irish ex-pats and Montreal their French.

I suppose my coaching career had begun at Coventry when, as club captain, I would try to explain to the youngsters what they were doing wrong. But my first spell of serious coaching turned out to be very different because some of the Whitecaps players knew more about the indoor game than me. I needed their help so they had to explain certain rules to me. We played five-a-side on a 60 by 40 metre pitch and it was physically very demanding. It was all about non-stop running. You'd only have been on the astroturf court for a minute or 90 seconds before you were knackered and had to come off. So we would pick two teams with two players of the same ability in each position. It meant you had a partner. I didn't believe you could last only about one and a half minutes but I soon found out it was true. Although there was something inside that made you want to stay on court, your team-mates would shout at you to come off. It was very intense and you didn't see players standing around on a huge pitch watching the game for a few minutes. Everybody was involved all the time. Most of the courts were ice hockey rinks with astroturf placed over the top of them. I remember one game being abandoned at Portland when the ice started to melt and the astroturf began to move.

I enjoyed coaching the indoor team at Vancouver and the family were having a whale of a time. I was on a decent wage but I spent most of it because we were used to a decent lifestyle and, as well as the rent for the house, we spent quite a bit on holidays. When we went to Hawaii, it cost more to go from Vancouver than from England! But after a pretty successful first season, my second year was disappointing. We finished third in our conference and so didn't qualify for the play-offs. I then decided I'd had enough so one day I just said to Johnny I wanted to pack it in at the end of the season. He had a word with Peter Bridgewater and when I arrived back in England for the winter break after my second season with Vancouver, yet another old mate from Leeds, Trevor Cherry, then played a key role in the next phase of my career towards the end of 1982. He was about to take over as player-manager at Bradford City and their chairman rang to ask if I was interested in joining him. I said I was, but I was still owed money by the Vancouver Whitecaps.

A much more difficult stumbling block was Christine and the kids. I had to explain to them why we wouldn't be spending a third year in Canada. Bradford in the north of England instead of Vancouver in scenic British Columbia? For Christine – and certainly for Gabby, Louise and Daniel – it was no contest. They wanted to stay put but I knew it was time for me to go back home – I didn't want to become one of the forgotten men of English football.

Stoking the Dragon's Fire

As Edith Piaf famously sang, 'Je ne regrette rien'. I've echoed those sentiments a few times in this book – I have no regrets. At least, I've tried not to look back and wish I'd done something differently. Most of the time, I haven't but there is one move I made that I now have a few misgivings about – only a few but I wish it had turned out differently.

Going to play for Vancouver Whitecaps was good for my family and our lifestyle but bad for me as a footballer because it spelt the end of my international career with Wales. In retrospect, it would have been better if I'd stayed in English football for a couple of more years. I'm afraid the 18 months I spent plying my trade in the North American Soccer League meant I turned into a classic case of 'out of sight, out of mind'. The one thing I loved doing above all else was playing for my country. In my view, it's the peak of a footballer's career. I got more of a thrill pulling on a Welsh shirt than when I finally made it as a regular in the Leeds first team and my decision to move to Vancouver Whitecaps meant that honour and privilege was denied me.

I had taken the usual international route for a promising footballer living in the Welsh capital in the early 1960s. After playing for Cardiff Schools, I was picked for the Welsh Schoolboys side when I was at Cathays Grammar. Wales didn't have a youth team when I joined Leeds as a 15-year-old apprentice so I had to wait until I was 17 before I made my debut for the Under-23s in a 3-1 defeat against England at Wrexham in 1968. It was a natural progression when I became captain.

Somehow I knew I was going to skipper the Under-23s and then the full side so it didn't come as a great surprise to me when it happened. It wasn't down to ambition – I think I was just born to be captain. It was something in me I enjoyed doing.

I remember reading some favourable press reports of my third international against Scotland in Aberdeen. When I look back now, they seem fantastic, but I must admit that I didn't find it a huge step up going from the Leeds youth team to Under-23 football. My last game for the Under-23s was a 3-0 defeat by England in 1972 when Malcolm McDonald scored a hat-trick. Charlie George, Tony Currie and Kevin Beattie were in the England side while the Welsh team included Leighton James, Leighton Phillips, and Ian Evans who I succeeded as Swansea manager in 1990 and who later became Mick McCarthy's assistant with the Republic of Ireland. By that time, I'd already won eight full caps after making my debut as a 19-year-old against Italy in Rome three years earlier.

We were playing our last 1970 World Cup qualifiers in early November and the Italians had already booked their placed in the finals in Mexico. I was called up as a late replacement after playing for Leeds reserves. As usual, a lot of the squad had pulled out on the Saturday night though injury and there'd been so many withdrawals that another replacement, Wrexham's Gareth Davies, had to be contacted at York and put on a sleeper to London. I was told to meet up with the Welsh party at Heathrow airport the next afternoon but I wasn't given any directions about a specific gate or terminal number. So I was wandering around the airport clutching my two bags – one for my clothes and the other for my kit – before I eventually found the Welsh players and officials. Being with Wales was a bit of a culture shock because Leeds were so professional in their preparation for a match. The Welsh FA were a little Mickey Mouse in comparison as they'd showed during a farcical incident before the previous game – another World Cup qualifier in East Germany a fortnight earlier. When the party gathered at the airport for the trip to Dresden, they realised they hadn't booked enough seats on the plane. The late Gil Reece, a nippy winger with Cardiff and Sheffield United who won 29 caps for Wales, had actually settled into his seat when the FAW realised their mistake. But rather than one of the councillors not boarding the plane, it was decided that the last player alphabetically should get off and take a later flight! That player turned out to be Gil.

After arriving at our hotel in Rome, we were told to be on the coach at 10 o'clock on the Monday morning to go training. When I arrived about a quarter of an hour earlier, I saw a group of our players standing around smoking outside the hotel on the other side of the road to the coach. As the time ticked by, I waited for them. Eventually they put out their cigarettes, came across the road and boarded the coach. Nobody said anything to them about what I thought was a rather causal attitude. It was a hell of a jump from Leeds reserves to international football in the Olympic Stadium in Rome, but switching from a very professional outfit to a part-time, almost amateur set-up actually meant I was far more relaxed about it. I knew early on in the trip that I'd be making my debut in defence rather than midfield when the manager, Dave Bowen, told me I'd be playing alongside the Spurs centre-half, Mike England. Dave had won 19 Welsh caps while at Arsenal and had been part-time manager of Wales since 1964, the year he took Northampton to the old First Division, now the Premiership, after they'd started the 1960s in the Fourth Division.

The training ground was right next to the Olympic Stadium and the first session went well. Mike was winning his 29th cap against Italy and I think his attitude towards me was that if I was good enough to be chosen, I should get on with it – which was fine by me. They were a very friendly bunch of guys and I chummed up with Rod Thomas, the Swindon full-back, because I knew him from the Under-23s.

Before the game, I must admit I was feeling nervous because I was younger than everyone else and I was about to make my debut in front of 76,000 supporters. My Leeds team-mate, Gary Sprake, was in goal and I slotted in alongside Mike England with Rod Thomas (Swindon) and Steve Derrett (Cardiff) at full-back. Barrie Hole (Aston Villa), Graham Moore (Charlton) and Alan Durban (Derby) were in midfield with Dick Krzywicki (West Bromwich) and Ronnie Rees (Nottingham Forest) playing up front with John Toshack (Cardiff), who was winning his eighth cap. Just before kick-off, Gil Reece, who would come on for Ronnie during the game, gave me a few words of encouragement by telling me that I'd find it easier than playing with Leeds. It was good of Gil to take me under his wing. He was a smashing lad with a cheeky smile but like me, he had stubborn streak that occasionally got him into hot water. When Wales played England at Ninian Park in Cardiff six months after the Italy game, Gil heard that he wouldn't even be on the bench for the match so he walked out of the squad's hotel in Porthcawl and went to stay with his mother in Cardiff. His fit of pique meant he didn't play for Wales again for more than a year.

In fact, Gil was right. I did find it easier and it didn't put me off international football in any way – even though Italy beat us 4-1 and the man I was marking, Luigi Riva, scored a hat-trick! Despite all the goals going in – Mike England grabbed a consolation one for us – I felt I'd done alright and the Italian press actually voted me Welsh player of the match. I can't honestly remember if I was at fault with any of Riva's hat-trick but I was quite pleased with myself and my new team-mates congratulated me afterwards. But there was no chance of my performance going to my head. When I returned to Leeds, I was quickly back in my place in the reserves again. It was something I just had to face up to because Leeds had such a big squad. The mickey-taking was pretty ruthless. How could I have been the best Welsh player in a 4-1 hammering when the man I was marking had scored three goals? Nobody at Leeds – coaches or players – would let you get carried away with anything. Mind you, I have to say that Riva is still Italy's record scorer with 35 goals in 42 games so I wasn't marking just anybody!

Despite my encouraging debut, I didn't play for Wales again for another 18 months. I've no idea why Dave Bowen didn't pick me for any of the next six games. After the Italy match, he'd congratulated me and so I was surprised not to be chosen. I kept looking at the squads and wondering what I'd done wrong. To be fair, I did receive a late call-up for one game but I had the flu. Perhaps at that stage, Dave only saw me as a stand-in, as someone who had stepped into the breach when needed but who wasn't quite ready for a regular place with so many experienced internationals still around. Maybe too, my manager at Leeds, Don Revie, had something to do with it. Don always hinted that he didn't like his players going away on international duty – he actually said that he would rather we stayed at Elland Road and the rewards would be better if we did. It was a sort of blackmail but I rarely ever missed internationals once I later broke into the Welsh team. Don was very keen that we maintained our club standards when we played for our countries. He also stressed that although we should never tell our fellow internationals anything about Leeds, we should always listen to what they did at their clubs. Don was always looking to learn from other people without being prepared to give out any of our trade secrets. I thought that was fair enough.

I won my second cap against Scotland in a 0-0 draw at Ninian Park in Cardiff in May 1971 and became a regular in the team from then on. The turning point in my Welsh career came in July 1974 when the Welsh FA appointed Mike Smith as the first full-time manager of Wales. Although his father had been a professional footballer, Mike preferred to stay as an amateur with Corinthian-Casuals and after training at Loughborough College of Education, he decided to concentrate on teaching the game rather than playing it. As the FAW's director of coaching, he'd been in charge of the Welsh amateur and youth teams before taking over the senior side. Mike quickly established himself as an excellent manager. It didn't matter that he was an Englishman, an academic and he hadn't played football for a living because he came in and immediately took control. He was well-organised, he prepared thoroughly and he made the team and the Welsh FA a lot more professional. We were provided with kit bags, new training kit and much better facilities. Mike and his assistant, Cyril Lea, who won two Welsh caps with Ipswich in 1965, struck up a good relationship and worked well together. Besides his huge knowledge of the game, Mike's sheer passion for football was inspirational. He was a great motivator and made you feel as if playing for Wales was the best thing in the world. It was something I tried to do when I took over the Welsh team.

As well as sorting out better working conditions, Mike also knew what he was doing on the training field. He would share his ideas and he often asked me for my contribution. But Mike was more than just the person who picked the team and decided the tactics. He was a shrewd man-manager. He respected the players and the feeling was mutual. No manager can afford to become 'one of the lads' – he'd quickly lose their respect if he did – but Mike became part of the group in that if ever we had a night out, he would quite often come along. He treated me in the way a captain should be treated because he consulted me about everything. In 1977, we played England at Wembley in the Home International Championship. We'd drawn 0-0 with Scotland at Wrexham three days earlier and we were due to play Northern Ireland in Belfast three days later. The night before the England match, Mike said he didn't want the players going out afterwards. I suggested that would be difficult as we were in London so he came back to me and explained that he'd arranged for us all to go out together. After we'd beaten England through a Leighton James penalty, Mike took us down to a bar in central London where we had a few beers to celebrate and relax. Then, we hopped on the coach and went back to the hotel. He was quite happy for us to let our hair down but he wanted to make sure nobody overstepped the mark.

Mike was only 13 years older than me and I saw him as much as a friend as a manager. He used to be on the phone regularly, he'd come up to my house before internationals and he was prepared to confide in me. We were staying at the Bryn Howell Hotel at Llangollen near Wrexham before a game at the Racecourse when Mike told me he'd been offered a job in the Middle East. We talked for a while and I advised him to take it. When he came back, he said that, even though he'd listened to what I said, he wouldn't be going. He said he'd wait and perhaps look for a job in England. He later managed Hull before coaching the Egypt national team between 1985 and 1988.

Mike's first match in charge was against Austria in Vienna as we began our campaign to qualify for the 1976 European Championship which had been known as the Nations Cup. He didn't make too many changes to the side which had beaten Northern Ireland at the Racecourse – apart from bringing back Wrexham's Arfon Griffiths three years after his debut as a substitute in a 3-1 defeat by Czechoslovakia at the Vetch Field in Swansea. Because he lived near Wrexham, Mike knew Arfon very well and used to watch him play a lot. Arfon had been with Arsenal as a youngster but didn't really settle into the London life so he returned to Wrexham. Arfon repaid Mike's faith in him by scoring our goal in a 2-1 defeat by Austria at the ripe old age of 33! It was my 16th appearance for Wales in Vienna and my next cap was another key moment in my career because Mike decided to make me captain.

If we were going to qualify for the last eight of the European Championship, we knew we had to get some points on the board pretty soon. Our next qualifier nearly two months later saw us take on Hungary at Ninian Park in Cardiff. I replaced Arsenal's John Roberts as captain and my old pal, Leighton Phillips, who'd moved from Cardiff to Aston Villa, took over from him in the centre of defence. John went on to win another five caps before being phased out as Mike began to stamp his mark on the Welsh team. I think Mike felt I'd be a better bet as skipper because John was only getting a few games with Arsenal and I'd established myself in the 1974 League Championship-winning Leeds side. My leadership qualities were starting to show at that time and I'm sure being with such a successful club played a part in Mike's decision in that he thought other players would listen to me as I played for Leeds and occasionally captained their side. I'd been taught by the coaching staff at Elland Road that a captain could do anything on the field and I was prepared to tell team-mates what to do in a game no matter how experienced they were. I thrived on the responsibility and as I was playing in midfield, I was well placed to carry it out. Mike explained to the team what he wanted on the training ground, then I was his man on the field. He made me feel good as a captain and I was delighted to make a winning start in my new job. Leighton James set up both goals for Arfon and John Toshack as we beat Hungary 2-0 and then walloped Luxembourg, the fourth team in our qualifying group, 5-0 at the Vetch Field three weeks later. I broke my duck that night by getting our last goal when a corner from the right was headed out to me on the edge of the box out on the left. I controlled the ball and then fired it into the top left-hand corner. Not the most crucial of goals but it was nice to get off the mark. Arfon popped in another to make it three in three games in his comeback career and Mike England scored his fourth goal in what turned out to be his 44th and last game for Wales. The match also marked the end of the road for another member of the old guard, Gary Sprake. Mike Smith decided that it was time for Wrexham's Dai Davies to make his bow so Sprakey's Welsh career ended with a clean sheet in a 5-0 win in which Brian Flynn, a Burnley team-mate of Leighton's, made his debut as a substitute for John 'Josh' Mahoney.

We then had a five-month break before our next group match

against Hungary in the magnificent Nep Stadium in Budapest. Just as I had been on my first trip abroad with Leeds when we played Ferencvaros in 1968, the players were really impressed by the luxurious oak-panelled dressing rooms. It was great simply to sit down in an armchair and chill out before the game and I felt quite at home there! Apart from Dai making his debut in goal, Malcolm Page and John Roberts returned to the defence as the two Cardiff cousins, Tosh and Josh, scored the goals in a comfortable 2-1 win. I played a part in the first goal, winning the ball in midfield for Arfon to send Leighton away down the right and his low cross was met at the far post by Tosh. For the second, Josh worked a neat one-two with Flynny and, after a good first touch, casually poked the ball home from eight yards. We passed the ball about well and dug in when we needed to – we were very resolute. Two weeks later, we put ourselves well and truly in the driving seat when we won in Luxembourg with Burnley's Leighton James scoring twice in a 3-1 win, one of them a penalty. His other goal was the result of a well-worked free-kick just outside the area. I slid the ball in to Tosh who laid it off first time for Leighton to drive home from about six yards. Two draws and a defeat in the 1975 Home International Championship kept the team ticking over until the crucial return qualifier against Austria at the Racecourse in Wrexham in November.

After our four straight wins, we knew that a draw would take us through to the quarter-finals of the European Championship. The game was rightly billed as one of the most important matches in the history of Welsh football. Of the other British teams, England and Northern Ireland were on their way out of the tournament in Portugal and Yugoslavia respectively and the Scots had already failed to qualify. We all knew that our destiny was in our own hands and so did the capacity crowd who had packed into the Racecourse on that nervous, November night. Three players were making their debuts: Wrexham's Barry Lloyd in goal for the injured Dai Davies, the Crystal Palace centre-half, Ian 'Twiggy' Evans, an 'Anglo' Welshman who qualified because his father had been born in Abercarn, and another local boy, the irrepressible Joey Jones, at left-back. We nicknamed Ian after the 1960s model because he was so thin. As captain, I went round to talk to every player individually as I normally did. If some of the team hadn't been playing for their club for a few weeks, I'd say this was a great chance to put themselves in the shop window. I'd encourage players who'd been injured by talking about the importance of the occasion. But nobody needed pumping up on this particular night. Everyone to a man knew what they had to do and it was my job to make sure they did it.

The former West Germany coach, Helmut Schoen, once described me as 'not a great player but a great leader and the Welsh players respond to him'. For the man who coached such a successful German side to say that about me was fantastic. I suppose it was a bit of a back-handed compliment but I knew my limitations. Leadership was one of my strengths and the players certainly responded to me against Austria.

Tosh was suspended for the game so Wrexham's Dave Smallman played up front alongside his club-mate Arfon who was superb that night. It was wet and windy, there was no score at half-time and in the second half, although we were up against the wind, we started to really play. With three quarters of the match gone, Rod Thomas clipped the ball into space down the right-hand side and when an Austrian defender lunged but missed it, Arfon nipped in and fired home the winning goal. Everything about it was right – from his position to the way he struck it. Arfon was a miniature Peter Osgood in that he was able to balance himself perfectly when running with the ball. I can still see him scoring it now – he took the goal excellently. At the age of 34, it was fairy-tale stuff for Arfon and there was a fantastic feeling for us all at the final whistle because at last we'd really achieved something. It was down to hard work and everyone believing in themselves and the manager – and him believing in us. We all went back to the hotel where John Mahoney, who knew a lot of Welsh songs, decided to sing the national anthem about 25 times. Then Ian Evans started up with 'Maybe it's because I'm a Londoner' – which he was – before Josh threw a pint of beer over him!

The disappointing part of our achievement was that we went straight from our qualifying group into a knockout competition – unlike nowadays when teams go from one group situation to another in a foreign country and then, if they finish in the top two, on to the quarter-finals. We were just unfortunate that we didn't have the chance to go abroad, stay in an hotel and use a training complex so we could really bond together as a team and finish what we'd started. But we were into the last eight against Yugoslavia, one of the top sides in Europe and it was a terrific achievement. To this day, it annoys me when I hear people say that Wales haven't qualified for the finals of a major tournament since 1958. It's not true because we did it in 1976. It was a knockout rather than a round-robin group format but it doesn't alter the fact that we qualified for it by what we had achieved on the pitch. Wales went through the back door to the 1958 World Cup in Sweden while we actually reached the quarter-finals of the European Championship fairly and squarely with no help from anyone. We were a team drawn from all four corners of the Football League and united by a common bond: we all loved playing for our country. It meant the world to me, Dai Davies would have killed to represent Wales and not far behind were people like John Mahoney, Brian Flynn, Malcolm Page, John Toshack, Leighton James and Leighton Phillips. They were fantastic people to be with – not only on the field but off it too. We weren't the greatest side in the world at that time but our tremendous team spirit actually won us games.

Dai Davies was Mr Ultra Serious when it came to anything to do with football. He would do his yoga before a game and always gee me up by telling me I was the greatest living Welshman. He made some mistakes, as all goalkeepers do, but he was a reassuring presence and such a spur to the side. Dai was one of only two Welsh-speakers in the team and he was so proud to play for his country. He replaced Gary Sprake and was succeeded by Neville Southall. Sprakey was a natural goalkeeper and one of the best shot-stoppers I've ever seen but Nev had everything. Dai was, if you like, a journeyman keeper and his greatest attribute was his attitude – he just kept everybody going around him. He was fearless, he'd dive at people's feet without think-ing about it and we were very fortunate in Wales to have three such good goalkeepers one after the other.

John Roberts was a real hard man and a good header of the ball. We never talked about me replacing him as captain. I didn't want to bring up the subject in front of him and he probably felt the same but when I took over, it was good to have John behind me because he was solid as a rock. Rod Thomas was probably my best mate in the team. I roomed with him on most Welsh trips. He was a smashing footballer and he used to make me laugh. Like me, Rod loved his horse racing and he liked to socialise – he'd take to your friends straightaway. He won the first four of his 50 Welsh caps at right-back but later made the left-back position very much his own. As well as helping Swindon to their famous 3-1 League Cup win over Arsenal in 1969, he won a First Division championship with Derby in 1975.

I had a very close relationship too with Leighton Phillips because we were room-mates as we made our way through the international ranks together from Welsh Schoolboys to the national team. I shared many a private moment with Leighton and it was a great comfort that we were able to confide in each other. He was a brilliant reader of the game who had the knack of nipping dangerous situations in the bud. After leaving Cardiff, Leighton played for Aston Villa before returning to South Wales to help Swansea reach the First Division in 1981. Everybody knew Joey Jones as a joker but deep down he was a lot more serious than people thought. He and his Wrexham team-mate and close friend, Mickey Thomas, were unbelievable to be around. They were always playing the fool – little Mickey couldn't sit still and Joey pretended to be his minder. Another member of the full-back club, Malcolm Page, was very versatile. Like me at Leeds, he played in every position for Birmingham apart from goalkeeper and he was one of the most consistent players, winning 28 caps during the 1970s. He had a brilliant game when we beat Hungary 2-1 in the Nep Stadium in 1975.

John Mahoney was a tremendous character. He was born in Cardiff but his father was a rugby player who turned professional and went north to England. John joined Crewe as a youngster before moving on to Stoke, Middlesborough and Swansea and grew up to become a true Welsh Nationalist. Everything about him was Welsh. He sang the national anthem louder than anyone else and like Dai, he'd be a spur to everybody. He loved talking about players and he was always quizzing me about Johnny Giles and Billy Bremner. It was just unfortunate that after becoming manager of Newport County, he got conned by the Canadian businessman, Jerry Sherman, in 1989. He re-mortgaged his house to buy a player but Sherman disappeared, the club folded and Josh lost his money. It's sad that life has been so hard on him – he didn't deserve it.

Like me, Brian Flynn was a South Walian who played a lot of his football in the north of England. Towards the end of my time at Leeds, if I wasn't captain, I'd always be one of the last out on to the pitch. As we were standing in the tunnel at Burnley in 1974, I looked forward and saw this little lad standing at the front of their team – it was Flynny but I thought he was their mascot! He was still a teenager when he got into the Burnley side and it was the first time I'd ever seen him. Flynny may have been small at 5ft 4in but he was so gutsy. And his size didn't stop him winning 66 caps for Wales and marking his full debut with a memorable goal against Scotland in 1975.

Arfon Griffiths will always be remembered as the man who scored the goal that took Wales into the quarter-finals of the European Championship. After being recalled by Mike Smith, he'd scored four times in just seven games before the Austria match. It was being staged on his home ground just round the corner from where he'd grown up so it was fitting for him to score the winner. To have played at Wrexham's level in the lower divisions for so long and then step into an international team and carry it off so well was brilliant. Arfon was an intelligent player who just took it all in his stride. Despite Wrexham's position, he had the respect of the other players straight-away. When I first saw him play, I was surprised that he hadn't been called up again since making his debut in 1971 but then I hadn't seen a lot of him playing for Wrexham.

That Welsh midfield was full of players who worked their socks off for each other and bounced off each other too. Flynny, Josh and I had a very good understanding and the three of us played more than 175 times for Wales with Brian scoring seven goals compared with my two and Josh's solitary one to win us that game in Hungary. But I think we missed a genuine playmaker like Ivor Allchurch who was probably the last Welsh 'midfield general' back in the 1950s and 1960s. The three of us, and later Peter Nicholas, were all pretty similar. We ran about and gave people a good whack every now and then and we had plenty of *hwyl* – spirit – but we never had the one player like Liverpool's Graeme Souness, now Newcastle's manager, who dictated the pace of a match in the middle of the park.

Leighton James was a truly wonderful winger. Two-footed, hard-working and with real pace, he made his debut in a 1-0 defeat by Czechoslovakia in Prague in 1971 after being called up as a late replacement at the age of just 18 years and 238 days. You might have thought that a young lad going into that type of situation would be shy and retiring, happy to listen and learn. Not Leighton! The dinner table at our evening meal was dominated by just one voice and straightaway you knew that he had the confidence to go anywhere and perform. Leighton could not only talk a good game – he had an opinion on almost everything – he could play one too. He was passionate about playing for Wales and he wasn't afraid to let team-mates know what he thought of them – no matter how experienced they were. Against Czechoslovakia, Terry Hennessey, then with Derby and winning his 36th cap, started the match despite having a bad ankle. After about half an hour, he went down and this precocious teenager stood above him and yelled:

'Get up you fucking bastard!'

Terry just looked up at Leighton – if looks could kill – before hobbling off and being replaced by Ronnie Rees. But nothing was said about it afterwards. Leighton has always had a good football brain – he ended up winning 54 caps and it's a pity that he hasn't had the breaks to stay in the full-time game. I think his prickly personality and forthright views on football have tended to upset too many people along the way.

I had a very good relationship with John Toshack because we'd known each other since our Cardiff Schoolboys days. Tosh had a certain arrogance about him that would rub a lot of people up the wrong way but because I'd known him since I was nine, it went over my head and I was able to communicate with him. He was a great player who scored some wonderful goals. He was fabulous in the air but he had a much better touch on the ground than most people gave him credit for. Tosh didn't have huge vision, he wasn't someone who turned and ran at defenders but he was a very good link man. He needed people to play off and for them to play off him. His contribution to Welsh football as a player and a manager with Swansea has been immense and it could have been a lot bigger. Not making use of his experience of working abroad in Spain, Portugal, Turkey and France is nothing short of an indictment of the people who run football in Wales.

Tosh played with a lot of strikers up front and missed quite a few games through injury so it's perhaps not surprising that he didn't develop a partnership at international level like his one with Kevin Keegan at Liverpool. Quite often, we had to make do without him and right at the end of Tosh's career, Ian Walsh, of Crystal Palace and then Swansea, came in for him. When Walshy made his debut against the Republic of Ireland at the Vetch Field in Swansea in 1980, Tosh had a word with the proud rookie outside the dressing room before the game.

'Hey Walshy', he said 'just remember you're only keeping that shirt warm for me!'

Tosh was right because he returned for the next game but after the 5-1 defeat in West Germany a month later, his Welsh career was over. He'd scored 12 goals in 40 appearances and if it hadn't been for injury, he would have won many more caps. Walshy, who scored on his debut, was a useful player who had a bit of pace and could go by people. He was well capable of holding his own in good company and ended up with an impressive scoring record – seven goals in 18 games.

Having had to sit out the Austria game through suspension, Tosh then missed a 2-1 defeat by England at Wrexham when Swansea's Alan Curtis scored on his debut but he was back for the first leg of the European Championship quarter-final against Yugoslavia in Zagreb in April 1976. It turned into a bit of a battle partly because of me as much as anyone else. There were plenty of late tackles flying in, we didn't do anything quietly and although we upset the Yugolsavs, they beat us 2-0. We then lost to Scotland and England but beat Northern Ireland in the Home Internationals before meeting Yugoslavia again in the second leg at Ninian Park in Cardiff. For this game, Mike Smith recalled Tosh in place of Curt and paired him up front with Brian Flynn to create a footballing 'Little and Large', a sort of Welsh version of Keegan and Toshack.

Not surprisingly after the first leg, the Yugoslavs came to Wales expecting it to be another physical game – and we didn't disappoint them. Ninian Park was packed and there was a certain edginess to the whole day – partly because of the importance of the game and partly because of the atmosphere in English football at the time. Hooliganism was at its height so perimeter fencing had been put up by many clubs, including Cardiff City. Supporters were still allowed to take alcohol into grounds and although there was no barbed wire on the top of the fencing, Ninian Park did have the feel of a fortress about it that afternoon. The situation wasn't helped by Rudi Glockner, from East Germany, one of the world's top referees who'd been in charge of the 1970 World Cup Final and the UEFA Cup Final just a week earlier. Before the game, I found him pompous and arrogant and his brylcreemed short back and sides and officious manner made him stand out among the long hair sported by the majority of 1970s footballers – on both sides of the Berlin Wall.

We knew we had a mountain to climb because nobody had put three past Yugoslavia for nearly four years. We need to win by two clear goals to take them to a third match in the San Siro Stadium in Milan a week later. A three-goal victory would see us through to the last four. Once again, the boys didn't need motivating on such a big occasion. Our game plan was pretty simple: we had to keep it tight for the first 20 minutes and then hope we'd get a break. As it happened, the Yugoslavs got one in the 18th minute when Mr Glockner decided to make his mark on the game. Brian Flynn was fouled 10 yards inside the Yugoslav half out on the right. I took the free-kick and when the ball was headed out to the edge of their penalty area, I rushed forward to try to win it back. My foot was no more than a couple of feet off the ground but the referee penalised me for dangerous play. Not only that, the ball was still moving when their free-kick was taken and, a couple of passes later, Popivoda burst through into our penalty area. Malcolm Page had tracked him across from the left to the right-back position and just as he was about to tackle Popivoda, he seemed to stumble as the Yugoslav rode his challenge. Pagey fell to his knees, Popidova went over and the referee pointed to the spot. We couldn't believe it. They'd caught us napping but three dubious decisions – the foul against me, their too-quickly-taken free-kick and then Pagey's challenge – had combined to give them the chance to put the tie beyond us. Katalinski sent Dai the wrong way and we were really up against it from then on.

Straight after the goal, Brian Flynn was lucky not to be sent off off for retaliating after a hefty tackle by Dzemal 'Jimmy' Hadziabdic, who would later join Swansea when John Toshack was in charge. A Tosh knock-down then gave Flynny a chance but his shot from six yards hit a post. The equaliser came seven minutes before half-time from a Flynny corner on the left. Tosh flicked it on and when Arfon Griffiths' shot was blocked by their keeper Maric, he coolly laid the ball back for Ian Evans to fire home from about 12 yards. It was Twiggy's only goal for Wales. He'd been doing a sterling job in the centre of defence alongside Dave Roberts, a fellow 'Anglo' with Hull, but took his goal just like a centre-forward. Game on!

But the second half was a huge anti-climax. I became the fourth player to be booked for going over the top on Hadziabdic. I think it was the result of pure frustration and, to be honest, it could well have been a red card. We then had a 'goal' disallowed when a Leighton James cross from the left was won by Tosh in the area. As the ball came down, John Mahoney launched himself into a bicycle kick and the ball fell to Tosh who drove it home but Rudi Glockner had already blown – again for dangerous play, this time by Josh. The decision led to a mini-pitch invasion with Flynny eventually calming down one very angry supporter who then climbed back over the fence into the crowd. Glockner threatened to abandon the game and added an extra five minutes because of the incident.

As we pushed forward looking for another goal, Arfon Griffiths was replaced by Alan Curtis and full beer cans kept being thrown on to the pitch. We thought we were in business when I crossed from the left for Tosh to head home but the linesman's flag was already up for offside. But then a decision finally went our way just before the end of the game. Leighton James was involved again by providing the initial cross. Tosh challenged as Maric punched the ball to the edge of the area, Josh Mahoney headed it back in, Maric punched it again but this time only straight up in the air and as it came down, he then upended Tosh with his legs about three yards out. Rudi Glockner had no doubts it was a penalty. The only problem I had as captain was finding somebody to take it.

Our regular penalty-taker, Arfon Griffiths, who'd got our only goal from the spot in a 3-1 defeat by Scotland at Hampden Park a fortnight earlier, had been substituted so I couldn't turn to him. Leighton James was next on my list. He'd scored a penalty in our 3-1 win over Luxembourg a year earlier after Arfon had been substituted but he said he didn't want to take it – as did Flynny. I waited for somebody to come forward but nobody did. Leighton was a cocky bugger but I didn't mind him or Flynny turning it down – that was their preroga- tive. I then realised that, as captain, it was going to have to be me – even though I'd never taken a penalty before.

As I prepared myself, Maric went walkabout outside the penalty area to the left of the goal before slowly coming back to his line. I swear to you my knees were knocking. I don't mind admitting that I was petrified. They always say you should never change your mind when taking a penalty. I only wish I'd followed that advice. I put the ball down and walked back to begin my run-up. It was a little longer than usual so it took me just outside the area. As I was about to start, I changed my mind. Instead of putting the ball to the keeper's left, for some unknown reason, I put it to his right. I hit it weakly with the instep of my right foot and Maric just flopped across and gathered the ball at the second attempt. I just sank to my knees, put my head in my hands and, as the BBC commentator, Barry Davies, said at the time, wanted 'the ground to open up.' I felt dreadful. I was captain, we were in the last eight of the European Championship and I'd missed a crucial penalty that would have given us a good chance of getting back into the game. Nobody came up to commiserate with me – I was left to suffer. It ended 1-1 and we went out 3-1 on aggregate. It was one of the lowest points in my career – especially as the game had been played in my home city.

I headed straight for the tunnel and, as I found out when I watched a BBC Wales programme about the game recently, Rudi Glockner needed a police escort to get off the pitch. Naturally enough, the Yugoslavs were full of it – the match coverage showed one of their players, Jerkovic, even having a fight with a fan near the tunnel. We were subdued when we filed back into the home dressing room. There was absolute silence. Lots of people, including Mike Smith, came up to me and said 'never mind' and there were a few tears shed. 'Never mind' is a silly expression because you do mind but it's what everyone says and you know what they mean. I climbed into one of the slipper baths by myself while the rest of the lads were in the big bath. I just wanted to be alone. Eventually, we all drifted upstairs to the players' lounge to see family and friends. It remained very quiet.

I know it was late on in the game but if I'd have put away that penalty perhaps we might have got back into it, won 3-1 and forced a third match with the Yugoslavs. Who knows? What I definitely know is that I'll never forget my miss as long as I live. It was strange because we'd all been practising penalties during the week in training and I'd been putting mine right-footed to the goalkeeper's left in the top right-hand corner. I very rarely missed one. Looking back now nearly 30 years later, I'm glad I had the bottle to take that kick but I also wish I hadn't had to. As captain, I had to lead from the front and it was the only thing I could do. That's the only satisfaction I can take out of it; it was a big occasion and I had the bottle to take the penalty. After the game when I was getting flak for missing it, I'm pleased I didn't go around shouting my mouth off by saying that I wasn't a penalty-taker – it would have been very easy to do have done that.

When I was watching the BBC programme, I picked up on something Barry Davies said twice during the game. After Leighton James had just been cynically brought down by Zungul in the first half, I rushed up to the Yugoslav and indulged in quite a bit of finger-pointing and threatening behaviour. As I read Zungul the riot act, Barry said in his commentary:

'I don't think the Welsh will prosper with this sort of attitude. They're allowing their fire to get in the way of their football.'

On the final whistle, Barry repeated the comment in his match summary and suggested that we'd been our own worst enemies in taking an over-physical approach to the game. In retrospect, I wonder if he was right? Perhaps we were too aggressive – thinking the only way we could win was by roughing up the Yugoslavs and knocking them out of their stride? Were we right in believing that intimidation was the key to beating them? We'd shown in qualifying for the quarter-finals that we could play some decent football but maybe we suppressed that side of our game and concentrated too much on being too competitive? It's easy to be wise after the event but were we too hyped up for that match? Perhaps we had too much Welsh *hwyl* for our own good.

Yugoslavia went home to play in the semi-finals but lost 4-2 to West Germany after extra-time. They were then beaten 3-2 by Holland in the third place play-off while Czechoslovakia beat the Germans 5-3 on penalties in the final.

After the game at Ninian Park, I took my family – including my brother, David, from Margate – out to a restaurant in Cardiff. As we were eating the meal, a man came up, rested his hand on my shoulder and said:

'That was the worst penalty I've ever seen!'

As I turned around, I saw Max Boyce the comedian grinning down at me so I had to laugh. There was nothing else to do. I couldn't do anything about the result so I went home to Leeds and chilled out over the summer as we prepared for the birth of our first son, Daniel.

If that game was a very low point of my Welsh playing career, then one of the highlights was undoubtedly our first and, as it turned out, last win over England at Wembley a year later. We won thanks to a penalty by Leighton James who, running on to a 30-yard pass by our best player – a blond lad in midfield – was brought down by their keeper, Peter Shilton. Now there was only one person who was going to take that penalty – even though Leighton had turned down the chance at Ninian Park. The occasion was different as were the circumstances. Yugoslavia had been a big European game and this was a Home International at Wembley. Leighton had been brought down, he was nearest the ball and he picked it up and put it on the spot. I was very confident he would score and I was delighted when he did because to beat England at Wembley was a massive achievement. John Toshack missed the game through injury but I'll always remember his comment afterwards:

'Don't give away your shirts because we'll never ever do what you've done tonight again'

It made no difference to me that my old boss, Don Revie, was England manager at the time. I was playing for my country and to lead out Wales against the 'Old Enemy' at Wembley and then beat them for the first time was the ultimate. But I do recall a couple of incidents that seemed important when, not long afterwards, Don suddenly resigned. As soon as we'd finished celebrating, we changed and made our way to the tea room behind the Royal Box to see family and friends. I came out of the dressing room on my own and started walking up the tunnel and around the pitch towards the tea room. I was about 20 yards out of the tunnel when I saw Don coming towards me. I knew from experience that he was feeling let down. He would hunch his shoulders, put his hands in his pockets and walk with his eyes trained firmly on the ground.

'Sorry boss,' I said as I approached him.

'It doesn't matter son,' Don replied and just walked past me. Usually, he would have stopped and had a chat. I felt sad at that moment because he looked very depressed. Managing England wasn't working out for him. When I got upstairs to the tea room, we were standing around in small groups when a man aged about 70 with the three lions badge on his blazer came up to us:

'Good win', he said.

'Thanks very much,' we said.

'Now we can sack the manager.'

Those words always stuck with me – mainly because of my loyalty to Don. I'm sure our win played a part in his downfall. Lo and behold, a month later Don walked out and went off to the United Arab Emirates on a super salary. His decision to leave tells me two things: one, that he was ahead of the game in that he knew the knives were out for him and two, when people talk about him being disloyal, they should realise that if he'd waited much longer, the English FA would have sacked him anyway. So I say good luck to him. I don't blame him for taking the money and disappearing off to the Middle East. Don would go to any lengths to try to get the best result on the pitch but this time he was concerned about the best result for himself – for Don Revie. They called him Don Readies and I believe he was obsessed with making himself financially secure. He came from a working-class home in Middlesbrough and was always looking for the best deal for his family.

Money played a key role in another memorable game I played in for Wales at Anfield in Liverpool in October 1977. We were in a World Cup qualifying group of three with Scotland and Czechoslovakia and the winners would go to Argentina the following summer. We'd lost 1-0 at Hampden Park but beaten the Czechs 3-0 at the Racecourse in Wrexham through two goals from Leighton James and one from the PSV Eindhoven striker, Nick Deacy, on his debut. We needed a point against the Scots to stay in with a chance of qualifying via our last match in Prague a month later. Why Liverpool? Well, the crowd trouble against Yugoslavia in 1976 meant that playing the game in Cardiff was out of the question – only 10,000 would have been allowed into Ninian Park. In their infinite wisdom, the Welsh FA decided to cash in on the huge support given to Scotland by the Tartan Army by moving the fixture to a ground with a bigger capacity than Wrexham. So instead of playing the game in Wales, they chose Anfield in England. They made a lot of money but handed the psychological advantage to the opposition because most of the 50,000 crowd that night seemed to be Scottish! I couldn't believe it. We were meant to be playing a home game but when I led out the team, it looked as if the whole ground was covered in tartan and blue. The players weren't very happy about it before the game and when we saw the crowd, we were livid. As one reporter wrote afterwards, we felt 'about as much at home as a leek in a bowl of Scotch broth' but we still felt we could at least get a point – even when Dave Roberts failed a late fitness test and Nowich's Dave Jones came in to win only his third cap. We were in control for most of the match and but for a brilliant save by Alan Rough from a beautiful, dipping shot by John Toshack would have taken the lead after about an hour. I was then booked, Dai Davies kept us in the game with a fantastic save to foil Kenny Dalglish and then 12 minutes from the end, Scotland scored – thanks, of all things, to a blatant piece of gamesmanship by Joe Jordan, godfather to my daughter, Gabby.

When the Scots won a throw on their left almost level with our 18-yard line, the Rangers winger, Willie Johnston, hurled the ball into our penalty area aiming for, among others, my former Leeds team-mates, Joe and Gordon McQueen. Up went the heads and up too went one hand – Joe's. 'Penalty!' shouted the Scottish players along with the whole of the Tartan Army and the referee, Robert Wurtz, from France, amazingly agreed. As soon as he signalled the spot-kick, I went straight over to him.

'Who handled it?' I demanded. The ref pointed at Dave Jones.

'I didn't touch it,' protested a distraught Dave. All our players told the ref that Joe had handled the ball but he wasn't prepared to change his mind and he told me to go away. I didn't say anything to Joe and the Scottish skipper, Don Masson, coolly stuck the penalty away.

As we pushed forward for an equaliser, a large dose of salt was rubbed into a gaping wound when, two minutes from the end, Martin Buchan crossed for Kenny Dalglish to head home a spectacular second goal. Our World Cup campaign was over and the Scots had become the only British team to make it to Argentina. Six months after the disappointment of the defeat by Yugoslavia, it was heartbreaking to be knocked out in a game awash with yet more controversy.

Afterwards, I shed a few tears before going into Scotland's dressing room to wish them all the best for the World Cup. Joe refused to discuss the incident then – as he has done ever since. He won't tell me if he handled the ball but everybody knows he did because the camera never lies. It didn't matter about Kenny's goal – the penalty was the killer. We were playing as well that night as we had done for years and, to be fair, until then the referee had been having an outstanding game. But the decision he made was unbelievable. We were wearing short-sleeved shirts and the television footage clearly shows that the ball was touched by the hand of an arm in a long-sleeved shirt with a white cuff on it.

How do I feel about Gabby's godfather helping to provide me with one of the biggest disappointments of my career? Well...Joe's a former team-mate of my mine and a close family friend and I don't blame him for what he did – not at all. I would blame the referee before him. OK, I accept that if Joe hadn't handled the ball in the first place then the referee wouldn't have had to make a decision. There may have been too many bodies in there for the linesman to see but it was an easy decision for the referee to make because of the difference in the length of the shirt sleeves. I see it as another case of somebody doing all they can to win. Joe did what he did for his team, he meant to do it and it got Scotland through but the referee was the arbitrator. He was the only person who could sort it out and he decided it wasn't cheating. Would I have done it? Probably not. I would have felt even more aggrieved if Joe had tapped the ball into the net with his hand but all he did was try to gain an advantage for his team and, to our cost, he got away with it.

I last saw Joe at the Wales-Scotland game at the Millennium Stadium in Cardiff in February 2004. The incident was mentioned but when I asked him if he handled the ball, he still didn't answer – he just looked at me. But I was very interested to read his recent autobiography in which Joe writes about the most famous handball in the history of Welsh football. He claims he is innocent:

'I denied it then, I deny it today. I will deny it at the moment of my death, which may be necessary if by some cruel fate the sad event should occur in the presence of somebody from Wales.

'For Scotland it was the door swinging open to the great tournaments and for Wales the beginning of the end of another brave but futile campaign. There, every man, woman and child would soon enough believe that I was the guilty party, the most hated foreigner since an English king strung castles across their country. I had touched the ball with an outstretched arm, they claimed. I was the man the Welsh loved to hate. I had cheated them of their rights.'

Let's just say it was handball by person or persons unknown – although Joe was seen to kiss his knuckles straight afterwards!

I still feel unhappy about the way the game was staged in Liverpool in front of at least 30,000 fanatical Scots. It was such an important fixture that the Welsh FA should have made sure it was played somewhere in Wales. Instead, they sold out for the money and we suffered as the Scots took over Anfield. As it happened, we lost 1-0 in Prague in our final qualifying match and we later failed to qualify for the 1980 European Championships. Mike Smith became Hull's manager at the start of that year and was replaced by Mike England. After leaving Spurs, Mike had gone to America to play for Seattle Sounders before returning to help Cardiff City win promotion from the Third Division in 1976. He then went back to Seattle where he was suddenly given the Welsh job. I was a bit surprised because he hadn't served any sort of club apprenticeship and he'd been out of English football for a while. He started using American terms like the 'offense' and the 'defense' that took a bit of getting used to but he made a fantastic start to his career as Welsh manager.

In his very first match in charge, we beat England 4-1 at the Racecourse in Wrexham. It's true that it wasn't a settled England side with Glenn Hoddle winning his second cap, Paul Mariner his sixth and Trevor Cherry his 23rd but we had a couple of people making their debuts in David Giles and Paul Price and Ian Walsh had only played once before. We beat England well on a baking-hot day through goals by Mickey Thomas, Walshy, Leighton James and an own goal. It wasn't the best preparation for England's trip to Euro'80 in Italy and the scoreline suggests that we tanked them – which we did. Mike was obviously overjoyed. He couldn't get enough of it – the Messiah had arrived home!

Mike was always very keen to try out different ways to motivate us. Sometimes, they worked and sometimes they didn't. Before we played the USSR in a World Cup qualifier in 1981, we found some brown envelopes lying on our kit. I was curious about what was in them so I picked up mine.

'Don't open those yet!' Mike shouted, 'I'll tell you when you can.'

So we went out to look at the pitch before returning to the dressing room to get changed. A quarter of an hour before kick-off, Mike said we could open the envelopes. Inside there was a photo of Christine with the kids and Jodie our dog.

'That's who you're playing for,' said Mike rather sombrely.

I'm afraid he was wrong. I've always played for myself, my country and my club. My family may have benefited in that I was earning a living as a player but I never thought of them before a game. In my view, Mike had reversed the priorities of all professional footballers. As it turned out, we weren't inspired on that particular occasion and we drew 0-0. On a lighter note, I remember the time when Mike walked into the Ninian Park dressing room before a World Cup qualifier against Turkey wearing a white stetson hat. He looked like JR Ewing from Dallas and as we all fell about laughing, Joey Jones started humming the TV programme's theme tune.

The best thing Mike did as manager was to bring in Dougie Livermore as his assistant to sort out the tactics. Dougie wasn't much older than us and he'd played with Mike at Cardiff. He'd already been a coach and he took most of the training but Mike had his say – he would come in if he thought something needed attention. I thought they were a good combination.

The draw against the Soviets turned out to be my last internation-al. I'm not being big-headed but I didn't have too many bad games for Wales. I admit that I wasn't at my best against the USSR because I'd just flown in from Vancouver and felt jet-lagged. Afterwards I heard rumours about people complaining about the cost of bringing me over from Canada. I was on the bench for the 2-0 defeat by Czechoslovakia in Prague but didn't come on. We then drew 2-2 with Iceland at Swansea in October and I was named as one of the substitutes again. Mike made me sit between him and Dougie in the dugout and when things started to go badly, he turned to Dougie and said:

'We need somebody in the middle of the park to start playing!'

I wondered if Mike was taking the piss. That was precisely what I did! But I didn't get on and he never gave me any indication that my career was about to finish. It just ended – full stop. One minute I was captain, the next I was on the bench and the next I was out. I had a couple of letters from Mike thanking me for being a great pro but not telling me that my career was over. I would have liked him to have told me that I wasn't going to be picked again – either to my face, on the phone or by letter. I felt I deserved better. I was very upset. I thought I had a good three years left in me at international level and if I was dropped because of my form, then I think Mike made a very hasty decision. He might have felt that I was Mike Smith's boy because he'd made me captain but I still feel the Welsh FA were telling Mike England not to pick me for financial reasons. I was discarded because it was costing them a flight from Canada for every game. I believe it was as simple as that. It was purely financial and had nothing to do with the way I was playing. I wasn't the only one who had an off-day against the USSR but, as the captain, I was the one who was singled out. It seemed odd to me and to the rest of the players. They were astounded that I'd been dropped. I have no evidence to support my theory but I know how the Welsh FA worked and how strapped for cash they were. Their short-sightedness cost me my international career.

Over the last 23 years, I've seen Mike England quite a lot. Like me, he has a place in Spain and I bump into him when I'm there but we've never discussed what happened. That sort of thing normally comes up over a beer but we tend to meet in airport lounges so we've never sat down and discussed it. It's a manager's prerogative to deal with his players as he sees fit but when I was in charge of Wales, I never told anyone in my squad that it might be their last game because I never knew when I might need them. My former skipper, Kevin Ratcliffe, hadn't played for Wales for 11 games when we ran into an injury crisis in 1993. I brought him back for a World Cup qualifier against Belgium at the old Cardiff Arms Park and he played very well in a 2-0 win. It turned out to be his 59th and last appearance.

Having captained Wales a record 43 times, I've been very proud to have had a special place in the history books for so long. I've also been aware of Gary Speed edging closer to the magic figure season by season. He's a smashing lad who I've known since he was a kid. In fact, I gave him his first cap as a substitute in a 1-0 win against Costa Rica in 1990. Gary has been a wonderful servant of Welsh football and I'm delighted that he's developed into such a respected and long-serving skipper. There's no better feeling than leading out your country, especially now at the Millennium Stadium in Cardiff. I just wish my decision to go to Canada hadn't led to me losing the chance to captain Wales a few more times.

Managerial Merry-go-round

I'll never forget the day when we returned to Britain towards the end of 1982. The contrast could hardly have been starker. No disrespect to Coventry but on a grey, dank and drizzly day in the middle of November, there really was no comparison with Vancouver, the beautiful city which I'd dragged my family away from for the sake of my career.

We came back from Canada to live in the apartment we'd bought in Coventry, having rented out our house in the city. Reality hit us as soon as we turned on the television – there were only four channels compared with at least 20 in Vancouver – so I suggested we go into town and buy a video. When we did, the gloom descended even more.

'This is like Poland with lights,' I said to Christine. I felt we had, quite literally, been sent to Coventry. It rained a lot in Vancouver but even when it was wet, you could drive from your home to the shopping mall and back without having a drop of water fall on you. Not so in Coventry and the general air of depression as we looked for a video simply added to my problem of trying to convince Christine and the kids that this – or rather Bradford – was the place to be.

I hadn't told Christine but I'd been thinking about going back to the UK anyway even before Bradford rang up when they did. I told them I'd consider their offer and discuss it with my family. When I did, I wasn't the most popular member of the Yorath household because we'd just spent a terrific 18 months in Vancouver. Christine was absolutely distraught about the prospect of returning permanently to Britain. She and the kids, who were aged nine, eight and six, had made good friends in Canada. They all wanted to go back west – especially as we'd supposedly just returned to Britain for a winter break – so I had everyone against me. I did my best but, in all honesty, it was mission impossible. I tried to explain that if I didn't get back into English football, I had this fear my name would disappear and I wouldn't be able to find a job. I knew my Welsh career was over after the Iceland game and it didn't enter my head that I might play for my country again if I did well for Bradford. The fact was I was nearly 33 and I needed to get back into the swim of things in the Football League. In the end, I wasn't able to sell the idea to the family but they knew I wasn't going back to Canada. They were dead against us coming home to Britain but I was determined to put my career before anything else.

The then Bradford chairman, Bob Martin, had made the initial contact. He'd been left in the lurch by the former England defender, Roy McFarland, who had resigned and joined Derby County in the middle of November. Bob wanted to know if I'd be interested in working with Trevor Cherry who was in the process of moving from Leeds to Bradford for £10,000. Trevor and I had got on well as team-mates at Elland Road but because he lived in Huddersfield and all the other players were based in Leeds, we hardly ever saw him socially. He was a pretty versatile defender who played nearly 500 times for Leeds and had just been voted the club's player of the year. When we spoke on the phone, Trevor told me about his plans for the club and said the people running Bradford seemed alright. So he became player-manager and I took over as player-coach.

Christine then had all the hassle of bringing our furniture back from Vancouver and it was a very traumatic time for everyone. The rest of the family still weren't happy but once I'd made the decision to return, the discussion was over. There was no going back on it. At that stage, we were still living in Coventry but we soon found a home in Leeds on the ring road in Shadwell where Christine and Jordan live today. It's an art deco house with seven bedrooms with an acre of garden. Although it was where Daniel died, 'Valdor' holds so many wonderful memories for me – in fact, Jordan was born there in 1986. The three other children had also been born in Leeds so they had a certain affinity with the city and that slightly softened the blow of having to leave Vancouver. After I agreed to start work at Bradford, my personal finances were starting to cause me a few problems. Vancouver still owed me about £30,000 and Bradford said they'd sort it out – not in a lump sum but over a period of time. But when one of their weekly cheques bounced, I realised something was wrong and I soon discovered that they were in dire trouble.

When Leeds slapped a winding-up order on the club because they hadn't received their £10,000 for Trevor, the board called in the receiver. Luckily, it was Peter Flesher who was a big football fan and later became a Bradford director. He did everything in his power to make sure the club survived after being reconstituted as Bradford City (1983) Ltd and two local businessmen, Stafford Heginbotham and Jack Tordoff, took over. Jack was one of the biggest car dealers in the north, a real down-to-earth Yorkshireman who had his own plane and who always looked around for the cheapest fish and chips he could find.

Having won promotion under Roy McFarland the previous season, Bradford were in the then Third Division, now League One. I made my first-team debut when we were knocked out of the third round of the FA Cup by Barnsley, then managed by a certain Norman Hunter. I was picked for the three straight defeats by Leyton Orient, Reading and Wigan but then didn't play again. We hovered around the middle of the table and eventually finished 12th but in the next season, when I made about 20 appearances, we ended up in seventh place. It all came together in the following year when we won the Third Division championship by four points. I made three appearances before I decided to call it a day as a player. We'd just lost 1-0 away at Leyton Orient in late September and I'd come on as a sub. I remember taking my boots off, throwing them into the corner and telling Trevor, who hadn't played that day, that I was finishing. I just wasn't enjoying all the up-and-under stuff. I was 34 going on 35, I'd been there and done it all around the world and I'd had enough. Trevor carried on playing so there was a slight role reversal as I moved permanently into the dugout. The important thing was that we still had one of the management team on the pitch. Trevor played 20 League games that season but not everyone was happy with him being in the side. It was quite funny...some of the players used to ask me if I could get 'the Gaffer' out! Why? Well, I think they thought we defended too deep and to be fair, Trevor was coming towards the end of his career too – after all, he'd just turned 37!

The side was full of characters with Bobby Campbell being the greatest of them all. He became a legend in Bradford and they actually named a bar after him opposite the ground. He was a rough-as-hell centre-forward who scored and made a lot of goals. When he was with us, he also won a couple of caps for Northern Ireland. Bobby used to smoke and drink and his voice was as rough as his appearance and his style of play. He'd come into the club wearing boots, jeans and a T-shirt, he was always unshaven and nothing frightened him on the pitch. After breaking his leg, he was left with a terrible scar on it. The last time I saw him in the dressing room, he was still squeezing pus out of the wound but he dismissed anyone's concern about the injury – he was as hard as nails. Bobby had played for a few clubs, including Aston Villa, Huddersfield and Sheffield United, before joining Bradford. After scoring 76 goals in only 148 league games for us, we sold him to Derby and then brought him back because he couldn't get on with their manager, Peter Taylor. Bobby played in all 46 League games and hit 23 of the 77 goals that took us up in 1985.

One of our other strikers, John Hawley, had been with Hull, Leeds, Sunderland and Arsenal before coming to Bradford. He was another one who smoked and looked as if he hadn't slept in his life but he could score goals too. Stuart McCall had been a schoolboy with Bradford and got in the first team when he was only 18. He was a great lad to have around the place and chipped in with quite a few goals from midfield. We picked up three players from Coventry – Greg Abbott, John Hendrie and Martin Singleton. Most of the new recruits arrived after the club came out of administration. We had to go out looking for bargains because there was no money available.

Our keeper, Eric McManus, had also begun his career at Coventry before making more than 250 appearances for Notts County. Chris Withe, the brother of the former Aston Villa and England striker, Peter Withe, played at left-back while my boss at Huddersfield now, Peter Jackson, was captain and centre-half. Pete was a fantastic header of a ball who wanted to be a winner. Alongside him we had Dave Evans who began as an apprentice with Aston Villa before we picked him up on a free transfer from Halifax. We were strict with the players – hard but fair – but we wanted them to enjoy playing the game. We sometimes had to curb their social activities because they were great ones for going out partying. I never went with them but I remember the morning after one session, taking one look at Stuart McCall and Greg Abbott and whipping them straight into the office to read the riot act:

'If you two ever come in here in that state again,' I said, 'I'll have you out of this football club!'

It frightened them and although they obviously kept going out, they didn't come in looking like that ever again.

Once we got into our stride, we made pretty rapid progress towards the top of the table during the 1984-85 season. A 1-0 defeat at Leyton Orient in late September left us 12th but from then on we gradually improved until becoming leaders in early December. When we played Derby at home, it was 0-0 at half-time so we stuck Don Goodman on as a substitute. We'd picked him up from local amateur football and he could move like shit off a shovel. The former Nottingham Forest and Scotland defender, Kenny Burns, was playing at the back for Derby and Don just tore past him to set up goals for Bobby Campbell and Stuart McCall and score one himself as we won 3-1. On New Year's Day, we went to Rotherham who were up near the top. I always told the players that it might not be a great volley or a header that wins a game – it might just be a tackle. Rotherham had this big centre-half called Nigel Johnson – all 6ft 2in and 12 stone of him. I'll never forget Stuart McCall, a mere 5ft 6in and 10 stone, going into a tackle with Johnson and coming up with the ball. We beat Rotherham 2-1 and I said to Peter Jackson afterwards that Stuart's tackle had won us the game – it was the turning point.

By the time we played Derby at the Baseball Ground in late April, we were still top and Derby were one of a number of clubs chasing us. We drew 0-0 and after shaking hands with their manager, Arthur Cox, he came out with this prediction.

'You might be top now,' he said, 'but I don't think you'll be there at the end of the season.'

'Why not?' I asked.

'You haven't got enough experience.'

But Arthur was wrong and we used his comments to keep geeing up the players during the last seven games. We clinched promotion with a 4-0 win at Cambridge before amazingly losing 4-1 at Bournemouth and then 5-2 at home to Reading. But a 2-0 win at Bolton with goals from Bobby and Stuart gave us the title and among the supporters who ran on to the pitch at the end of the game were two Davids – my father and brother. It was a fantastic turnaround bearing in mind that a year earlier, we'd been in administration. After finishing 7th in the previous season, we knew we had a team capable of mounting a decent promotion challenge if we could only strengthen the side. I think we were lucky in choosing new players like John Hendrie, Don Goodman and Eric McManus. We had no money, we brought in every player on a pittance and fortunately it paid off. And, of course, it was a bonus having Bobby back from Derby at the start of the season. It's nice to hear players like John Hendrie, who went on to play at Newcastle and Leeds, say that his time at Valley Parade was the best period of his career. The Bradford lads were very like the lot Peter and I have at Huddersfield now. They enjoyed each other's company and there was a very good team spirit. They respected Trevor and me because of what we'd done – likewise, the younger lads at Huddersfield have been made aware of our playing careers by their fathers!

After the Bolton result, everything was set up for our last game of the season against Lincoln at Valley Parade. It was to be a celebration of nine months' hard work, a joyous occasion on a sunny day to mark the end of a successful season and the end of an era. Our promotion to the Second Division meant the antiquated main stand needed upgrading for safety reasons and the chairman, Stafford Heginbotham, had agreed to replace its old wooden roof. The shiny new steel was actually lying in the club car park waiting for the job to begin two days later. The TV cameras were there to record our skipper, Peter Jackson, receive the Third Division championship trophy from the Football League's life president Dick Wragg before the game and the players would be given their medals afterwards. Two years after nearly going bust, Bradford City were on their way back and more than 11,000 people had gathered to pay tribute to the club. But instead, Saturday 11th May 1985 put Bradford on the map for all the wrong reasons. It became known as the worst day in the club's history when 56 people died and more than 200 were injured as fire swept through the main stand, engulfing it in a little under five minutes.

That morning, I had gone to the ground as usual by myself. My mother and father were up from Cardiff for the game and they squeezed into the family car along with Christine, Gabby, Louise and Daniel. They were all sitting in the directors' box right in the centre of the main stand. The club's offices and dressing rooms were underneath the south west corner of the stand which had been built in 1909. There were flaps underneath the seats that you could open up and see piles of litter that had accumulated over the years below. Right at the back of the stand was a tunnel or pathway about 10 feet wide. The crowd would leave their seats and walk along that tunnel to get out past the turnstiles and through gates at the opposite end. It was the only route to the directors' box and was used by everyone else queuing for refreshments. Just before half-time when it was 0-0, a policeman walked down in front of me near the home dugout and asked where he could get some water. I was completely unaware of what was happening behind me. I pointed him in the direction of a tap in the far corner of the ground which had a groundsman's yellow hose stuck to it. When the policeman came back past me, I noticed that he didn't have the hose in his hand. Then I saw that two or three people had jumped over the perimeter wall on to the pitch. The game kept going but more people started to spill on to the grass. A linesman then told the referee what was going on and he blew his whistle with three minutes to go to half-time and when I looked around again, smoke was starting to rise from the main stand. By the time I'd walked quickly from the half-way line to the corner of the pitch on my way to the dressing rooms, I could see the flames shooting up. I immediately recalled a fire in the main stand of the City Ground in Nottingham when Leeds were playing Forest in August 1968. As Don Revie was giving us a half-time bollocking, smoke started coming underneath the door of the changing room.

'Boss!' we'd cried.

'Never mind Boss!', said Don.

'But Boss – look!'

Don turned around and saw the smoke and somehow we all

managed to get out. Along with the spectators who'd escaped the fire, we watched from the pitch as the stand burnt down and the game was abandoned. Remembering that Nottingham experience, I told the players not to go to the dressing rooms. Then I rushed down there and explained what was happening to Bobby Campbell and Bryan Edwards, the physio. They immediately jumped up and a TV camera-man threw his equipment on the floor and ran out. I dashed upstairs to my office where Daniel usually went at half-time for some sweets. There was no sign of him so I rushed into the directors' room and alerted everybody there. Next stop was the players' lounge where I thought the wives and maybe some of the other players would be. I told them to get out and went back to my office to look for Daniel again. By the time I arrived, the flames were licking up against the window. I rushed back to the directors' room and urged the Lincoln contingent to get moving.

'Get fucking out!' I cried.

'You're swearing at me,' said a woman in their party.

'Get fucking out!' I cried as I saw Christine with the two girls and Daniel near the main door.

'Where's my Mum and Dad?'

'I don't know,' replied Christine. 'They left before us.'

'Are you sure?'

'Yes!'

Christine went off to try to find my parents and make sure that she and kids got out. It was complete confusion. I saw one man with his hands burnt white and he asked me when the ambulances were going to come. I told him to sit down in the gutter and wait for them. By this time, the fire had reached the roof and wood and molten felt were raining down all over the place. Then it hit the tunnel. The fire went whoosh! – right along the tunnel so anyone in its path would have stood no chance. It had taken just four and a half minutes for the whole stand to go up. It was an inferno – the flames had spread faster than a person could run.

I didn't rescue anybody by pulling them out of the fire – I just went around doing all the screaming, raising the alarm and trying to make people who thought they were quite safe jump. I pushed a few people through doors but not windows. In the end, I had to throw a chair at a window in the players' lounge and then jump through it to escape myself. The road outside sloped downwards so I cut open my leg when I landed. I told the players who I found to congregate at a pub at the top of a nearby hill as far away from the ground as possible. Eventually, we all got together and we found my mother and father safe and well. I just thank God they were creatures of habit. Whenever they went to a game, they usually left just before half-time to have a cigarette. So when everything went off, they had already gone out through the directors' box door and along the tunnel. They were still in Valley Parade but away from the fire in the stand. Others weren't so lucky. Having managed to escape from the stand, they rushed towards gates and turnstiles only to find them locked. After checking my parents were alright, I went back into the ground where I saw all sorts of dreadful things. Dead people were lying on the terracing – they had simply been burnt to death – while others who'd been badly injured were being treated. As I was walking along the road outside the ground back up to the pub, I met the chairman.

'They say there are two dead,' Stafford said to me.

'There are many more than that' I said. 'I've seen half of them.' He turned pale.

When we'd rounded up all the players in the pub, they stood and watched live television coverage of the tragedy. The Yorkshire TV commentator, John Helm, a lovely man and a good friend of mine, was working on the match from a gantry in the opposite stand.

'We've actually got a fire in the stand on the far side of the ground,' he'd said when he first saw the smoke. 'And that looks very nasty indeed.'

How right he was. Poor John, who's from Bradford, then had to commentate not on a football match but on a tragedy unfolding right in front of his very eyes. He remarked that 'a day of triumph could turn into a day of disaster' and noted that supporters had come 'to celebrate the club's promotion to the Second Division for the first time in 50 years and now they're running for their lives.' John then commented on his personal position at the ground.

'The heat is now becoming tremendous. I'm sitting immediately opposite the main stand and I can feel the heat. It's almost beginning to burn me over here quite honestly...this was supposed to be a day of utter joy, triumph and celebration and it's turning into a nightmare.'

As the flames tore through the stand and a policeman was spotted running out of it with his hair on fire, John just had to keep going.

'The roof is caving in. The black pall of smoke is riding hundreds of feet in the air and the whole place is scorching. They've been talking about having a new ground at Valley Parade, they might soon have to have one because this is the day that Valley Parade football ground is burning down.'

John couldn't get over his ordeal for up to a year afterwards. He kept breaking down in tears for no apparent reason. He was so traumatised by having to describe the horror of the tragedy that he's never been able to watch the television footage again. Unlike John, some people didn't realise just how serious it was. As most people stood there in amazement, some young supporters sang and danced in front of the flames and, while one or two people tried to help the injured, stones were thrown at John and his two cameramen as they continued to film. In the weeks after the tragedy, he received letters of apology from some of the stone throwers once they'd realised that he and his crew were only doing their job. In fact, the footage is now used by the police and fire services on internal training exercises. No matter how many football matches he works on, I suspect John will always be remembered as the man who commentated on the Bradford fire. Although he's now recovered from the experience, he admits that terrible day will live with him forever.

The players were stunned by what they were seeing on the box but they couldn't turn it off. It was so awful but they felt they had to keep watching. When the fire had finally been dealt with, we had to go back into the ground to collect our personal belongings. Trevor and I were advised not to look through the office window but we just had to. We saw masses of dead bodies – some just a collection of bones – lying out on the terracing.

The next day, we had a meeting with the club directors and I remember being interviewed on local TV. I said that a tragedy like that put everything in perspective. It didn't matter about the stand or where we were going to play next season – more than 50 people had died. During the summer, the players were magnificent as they visited hospitals and went to funerals. A few days after the fire, Stuart McCall took the championship trophy to the special burns unit at Pinderfields Hospital in Wakefield to show his father, Andy, who'd been badly burned in the fire. Stuart was worried that it might seem a little insensitive but the visit actually united the victims and reminded them of the reason they'd been at Valley Parade on that awful day. It was the same whichever hospital ward we went to. The fans, who had bandages all over their heads and hands, used to say to us:

'Great season lads! Well done. We'll be there in August.'

It was fantastic how they were so positive about something so very negative. Once the final death toll had been arrived at and the bodies had been sorted out, there was a stream of funerals – up to eight a week. If Trevor or I couldn't attend, we would delegate a couple of players to represent the playing side instead but they had to go in pairs because we didn't want them going on their own – we weren't sure how they'd cope. I didn't keep a record but I must have gone to about 20 funerals. The tragedy made me question my religious faith at times but it helped that I could go to church and not feel like an outsider. I felt incredibly lucky that my family had escaped when I visited the injured in hospital and attended the funerals. The relatives were so brave by taking over the season tickets of their loved ones who'd died in the fire. I didn't keep in special touch with any of the bereaved families but a couple of the priests at the church where the funerals were held did get in touch with me when Daniel died in 1992. In the days and weeks after the fire, we did what we were asked to do but were advised not to get too involved with the families. All the players responded well. Not one of them said they didn't think they could do it but if they had, of course, we wouldn't have insisted. They all stuck together and carried out their tasks on a rota basis – they were brilliant. We were a very tightly knit bunch anyway but the fire probably brought us all even closer together.

The Popplewell Inquiry into the fire heard that the club had been warned about the rubbish accumulating under the dilapidated stand but most people in Bradford seemed to accept that the tragedy was the result of bad luck. Among the 77 witnesses who gave evidence was a forensic scientist, Dr David Woolley. He said the cause was possibly a match being dropped or a cigarette being stubbed out in a polystyrene cup and then accidentally falling on to some of the rubbish in the stand. A 1968 newspaper and a peanut bar wrapper with a pre-decimal currency price were found in the debris. A staggering £4 million was collected by the disaster fund and some good came out of the tragedy because it led to a complete safety overhaul of all sports grounds and stadia throughout the country.

My overriding concern after the fire was trying to get my head round what had happened: 56 people had died just watching a football match. How could their families ever come to terms with the fact that their loved ones had gone to see a game and would never be coming home? It was terrible. One of the victims was a former girl-friend of Don Goodman, one of our players. She had rung him and asked for tickets for the special occasion. Another was Bradford's oldest supporter, 86-year-old Sam Firth and two Lincoln City fans, Bill Stacey and Jim West, both in their seventies, also died in the fire. They later had a stand named after them at Sincil Bank.

I was reminded of the tragedy just over a fortnight later when, during a dinner party at our home with Peter Flesher, Trevor and their wives, Gabby suddenly came running into the room screaming her head off.

'They're burning each other!', she cried. 'They're burning each other!'

Gabby had been watching the European Cup Final between Liverpool and Juventus in Brussels on television in the lounge. She'd obviously associated the bodies being lifted out at Heysel with the terrible scenes she'd witnessed at Valley Parade. Whenever I smell smoke now, I think of the Bradford fire and that man with his white arms. Twenty years later, I can be driving along in a car past a field where crops are being burnt and immediately my mind goes back to it. The memory of the fire will never ever leave me.

The tragedy had a big impact on the team because with Valley Parade being rebuilt, we had to play all our 'home' games elsewhere for the whole of the next season and half of the following one. The players received their Third Division championship medals in August and then we were off on our travels. We pitched our tents at Huddersfield's ground, Leeds Road, and also at Elland Road, the home of my old club, Leeds, but most of our matches were played at the Odsal Stadium, where the Bradford Northern rugby league team, now the Bradford Bulls, were based. The whole experience was a nightmare. The ground lies near the M62 on the other side of the city and it was famous for holding rugby league cup finals. The old speedway stadium is actually shaped like a bowl and when we played there, the corners used to go upwards – the flags were a foot higher than the rest of the pitch! You had to be pretty clever when you took the corners. It just wasn't a football stadium but there was little alternative and it was good of Bradford Northern to help us out. Footballers can usually adjust to circumstances and, to be fair, our lads had done their duty in the summer. They were relieved to get back to playing football but it wasn't the same at Odsal. They sometimes used the ground as an excuse for a dodgy result by saying it was shocking having to play there. We finished about 13th in the table and bearing everything in mind – the fire and the ground switch – I thought we did reasonably well.

There was a bizarre twist to the tragedy. Although the first team had to move to Odsal, the reserves were able to carry on playing at Valley Parade because only two men and a dog made up the crowd. So I would stand in the stand where all those poor people had perished watching our reserves – it was really eerie.

Over the next five years, I found myself shuttling between Bradford and Swansea – breaking one of football management's golden rules 'never go back' not once, but twice. I walked out of each club and fell foul of a couple of chairmen, one of whom was a real character, Swansea City's Doug Sharpe. You couldn't help but warm to Doug, he was so enthusiastic about his work, the club and his property in Spain. He was the local builder made good – Sharpe by name and sharp by nature. Doug was someone who I respected for what he'd done to keep Swansea afloat but I'm afraid we didn't see eye to eye on the best way to run a football club – especially when I was given the chance to manage Wales at the same time.

I linked up with him in the summer of 1986 after Coventry had expressed an interest in me joining their coaching staff. But after going down to Highfield Road and meeting the manager, Don Mackay, I decided it wasn't for me. At Swansea, Doug had done a grand job in resurrecting the club after they'd been officially wound up just before Christmas in 1985. They were still paying the price for spending too much money in reaching the old First Division in 1981 but Doug put together a rescue package which was eventually accepted by the creditors after the former directors agreed to write off nearly half their debts in May 1986. Swansea survived in the High Court but not in the old Third Division – they were relegated along with Lincoln, Cardiff and Wolves.

When Doug came up to my home in Leeds and offered me the manager's job, the Bradford chairman, Stafford Heginbotham, wasn't too happy. I was on a six-month rolling contract at the time but it wasn't watertight so I was able to walk out. I liked taking the training and organising the tactics at Bradford and I was trying to make sure the club played the same way in all their teams – from the firsts right down to the youth – but I was keen to have a go at being number one. Trevor was the manager, I respected him and although he would listen to my opinion, he'd always make the final decision himself. I wanted to be the man who made that decision. Trevor wished me good luck when I told him about the approach by Swansea. He knew I'd always wanted to be a manager and this was my chance. What I didn't realise then was that Swansea still had financial problems. Doug hadn't told me about them when he came up to Leeds and spent the day drinking lager in my back garden! So for the second time, I'd joined a club without being fully in the picture about their finances, but I didn't hold it against Doug. I'd made the decision to become a manager so I wasn't about to turn around and say he'd been economical with the truth.

I wanted the family to move down to Swansea so I took them to a beach at West Cross in the west of the city on the way down to Mumbles. It's one of the most beautiful areas in the whole of Wales, if not Britain, but Christine made it clear that she wasn't prepared to re-locate down to Swansea so we all had to accept that I would be away from Leeds for a lot of the time. Wherever I've been in my managerial career, it's always been understood that Christine and the children would stay in Yorkshire. I took over from Tommy Hutchison, my old team-mate from Coventry, who, in turn, had replaced the former Manchester City manager, John Bond, at the Vetch Field. Immediately after my first pre-season training session on a Saturday, I asked the players to come and see me if they had any problems: I finally left the ground at about half past four that afternoon. Some complained about certain promises not being kept and others wanted transfers. One of our central defenders, Dudley Lewis, who played once for Wales against Brazil in 1983, came in with his wife.

'Rochdale have approached Dudley,' said Mrs Lewis, 'and he wants to go there.'

'Do you?,' I asked Dudley but he wouldn't answer me.

'He wants to go to Rochdale,' insisted his wife.

'Have you ever been to Rochdale?' I asked her.

'No.'

'Right. I'll give Dudley the day off on Monday. Get in the car tomorrow and let him show you Rochdale.'

'It's just like any other place.'

'It's not. If I were you, I'd stay where you are.'

And Dudley did – after I got him a pay rise. He went on to become an important member of the team which won promotion to the old Third Division in 1988. The combination of money – or rather the lack of it – and Doug Sharpe was nearly always at the root of my problems at Swansea. I felt Doug was a bully who always wanted his own way and he would always be backed up by his sidekick, the club's vice-chairman, Glyn Hammond. Like all managers, I believed we should be left alone to get on with our job without any interference from the board. With my stubborn streak and Doug's very hands-on approach, I suppose it was inevitable that we'd have disagreements. After our first away game, the players didn't have anything to drink or eat on the way home so I went to see Doug to find out why.

'It's not a bottomless pit, you know!,' he replied. 'I'll try and get the sandwiches sponsored!'

We were up near the top of the table for a while in the 1986-87 season before our centre-forward, Ian Love, broke his leg at Cardiff. We didn't bring in anybody to replace him and we finished 12th. But with Dudley, left-back Terry Phelan and Tommy and Gary Emmanuel in midfield providing the backbone of the side, we played some good football. My second season in charge went much better as we took full advantage of the play-offs that had only been introduced during the previous season. A local lad, Mike Hughes, proved a safe pair of hands in goal and we had Chris Harrison at right-back. We'd sold Terry to

Wimbledon for £100,000 but we were fortunate that Chris Coleman, now Fulham's manager, came to us on a free transfer and went straight into the side. He was born in Swansea and, after becoming homesick at Manchester City, returned to South Wales as a 17-year-old. Chris went on to play for Wales, Crystal Palace, Blackburn and Fulham – making Swansea quite a few bob in the process. It's nice to know that he's grateful for the way we brought him through at the Vetch. He says I turned him into a man at Swansea by encouraging him to stand up in the dressing room and say what was on his mind and by hammering home the need to be professional but Chris was always going to make it as a footballer. He turned out to be not only a good player but a good person too.

In central defence, we had Andy Melville, another local boy who also moved on to bigger and better things and who's won more than 50 caps for Wales. Even then, I knew he was going to be a really top-class player. Andy always wanted to learn, he could play the ball out from the back and he could head it well – he was a joy to work with and I'm delighted that he's still going strong at West Ham. Another central defender was big Alan Knill – and at 6ft 3in he was big – who first came to my attention when he was at Southampton and I was at Bradford. He had no League experience and when he was coming up north to have a chat with Halifax, we asked him to call in afterwards at Valley Parade. But after we'd met him, I told Trevor Cherry that I didn't think he was what we we're looking for. I went to see him play for Halifax a few times and he was starting to fill out a little so when I was looking for a centre-half at Swansea I remembered him and brought him to the Vetch Field. With his height, Knilly was a great header of the ball. I was delighted when I was able to give him his only Welsh cap in 1988. An injury crisis meant he had to mark Marco Van Basten in a European Championship qualifying match in Amsterdam! Even though we lost 1-0, Alan did a fantastic job but when our injuries cleared up he was out and I never had to call on him again so he became one of the best known of all the thousands of one-cap wonders!

In midfield, we had Hutchy, Gary and Alan Davies who'd played for Manchester United in the 1983 FA Cup Final against Brighton. Some days, Alan would seem to have the world on his shoulders but other days, he'd be bright and sparky in training and his natural foot-balling talent would come out. He was terrific during the promotion season as was Hutchy who kept rolling back the years by playing on into his forties. Sean McCarthy was scoring goals for us and we bought another bustling centre-forward, Joe Allon, from Newcastle to operate alongside him. Word soon got round that Swansea wanted to play football. We liked to build from the back and when I wanted to sign a player, I told him this was the way we played. As long as the financial package was OK, they'd come.

To be fair, Doug usually backed my judgement on buying players but I think he felt that meant he could have a say in choosing the team. He couldn't help putting his oar in. We were always near the play-off positions during the 1987-88 season and Ian Love's recovery from his broken leg and the return of Robbie James to Swansea from Leicester as skipper in January gave us a big boost. Towards the end of February, we travelled to Cambridge. Before the game, the chairman and one of the directors, Mal Griffiths, asked me for the team. Foolishly, I told them and they then questioned my ability to pick a side! As it happened, we won 3-0 with Lovey scoring two and Chris Harrison getting the other. We then played Wrexham a fortnight later at the Racecourse and while we were in the hotel near Chester, Doug asked me for the team again. This time, I wasn't so forthcoming.

'You'll see it when the players walk out,' I growled, obviously not endearing myself to Doug and his fellow board members, but they weren't endearing themselves to me by poking their noses in. We won 2-1 with Lovey and Robbie James getting the goals but Doug didn't apologise afterwards – he probably told people that he'd picked the team anyway! His attitude was typical of football club directors – they think they know best. As well as choosing the team, they think they can tell you which tactics to use. But usually they're just glori-fied supporters.

We knew it was going to be touch and go whether we made the play-offs and with two games left, we picked up a lucky point in a 1-1 home draw against Scunthorpe thanks to a goal from our top scorer, Sean McCarthy. I still had my home base in Leeds so I went home for the weekend and then drove up to Carlisle for the pre-match meal before our game on the Monday. When I arrived at the hotel, I noticed the players all had their heads down. They told me that the chairman had just called them a bunch of wankers to their faces. I immediately confronted Doug and he more or less said it was true. I don't know whether his remark got the players going but we won 1-0 – Alan Knill scoring the goal – and it now all depended on the last game of the season. In the early days of the play-offs, the team that finished fourth from bottom in the old Third Division would go into a group with the sides in fourth, fifth and sixth place in the Fourth. Scunthorpe and Torquay were already there but the last spot was between Leyton Orient, Swansea and Peterborough. We had a better goal difference than Peterborough and we knew that if we beat Darlington at the Vetch Field and Orient lost to champions-elect Wolves then we'd be into the play-offs.

Darlington were just below half way in the table and we hammered them 3-0 with two goals from Sean and another by Alan Davies. When we heard that Wolves had beaten Orient to win the title by five points from runners-up Cardiff, we knew we'd done it – but only by the skin of our teeth as we'd edged out Peterborough on goal difference. After the final whistle, Doug brought a crate of beer into the dressing room. At most clubs, it would have been champagne but with Doug it was only beer!

We had just over a week to prepare for the semi-finals. Another goal from Sean helped us beat Rotherham 1-0 at the Vetch in front of a crowd of just under 10,000 and when he popped up with another one in the 1-1 draw at Millmoor, we were through to the two-legged final against Torquay who'd beaten Scunthorpe 3-2 on aggregate. A week later, Sean and Lovey scored the goals at the Vetch that gave us a 2-1 lead to take down to Plainmoor where we drew 3-3 to clinch promotion 4-3 on aggregate. Paul Raynor, Sean and Alan Davies were each on target – all before half-time.

Bearing in mind the club's recent financial problems, I thought it was a marvellous achievement. Obviously, everybody was ecstatic about going up but the players didn't want to be at the hotel in Torquay where the club hierarchy were staying. After such a long season, they wanted to let their hair down by themselves so I asked the secretary, George Taylor, if I could have a couple of hundred quid to take them to a pub on the way home. He went to see Doug who

thought it was a good idea – he seemed happy that the players celebrated their success in their own company. But two weeks later, I was
called into George's office and told that the money was coming out of
my wages! On the way home from Torquay back to Swansea, I was
sitting opposite Hutchy.

'What are you feeling?' I asked.

'Nothing,' he said. I felt exactly the same because of the way Doug
had treated us – especially with his penny-pinching attitude. I was very
pleased for the players but not for myself. I felt really deflated even
though we'd done so well in winning promotion. I was dropped off at
my mother's home in Cardiff as the coach went on down the M4 to
Swansea and I remember phoning Christine to tell her all about it.

'You don't exactly sound ecstatic!' she said.

'I'm not,' I said.

'There's something wrong with you,' she said and she was right.
Here I was, having just proved myself as a manager in my own right,
feeling like someone who's just drunk a glass of flat champagne. I
should have been on top of the world but I just couldn't get enthusiastic about the biggest achievement of my managerial career so far.

Throughout the summer break, I was in dispute with Doug about
my promotion bonus. When I took over as manager, we hadn't discussed a figure but he said he would see me right if I took Swansea up.
But after we'd been promoted, he said there was no bonus – it wasn't
in my contract. And then he told me that although he was happy to
extend the length of my contract, the wages would stay the same. I
stormed off home to Leeds where three weeks later, I was asked to go
for an interview at Hull. I did but when the story broke, for some
reason their chairman denied he'd ever spoken with me. So back to
Swansea I went for the start of the new season.

Doug and I also fell out over my involvement with the Welsh team
as part-time manager. Mike England had been in charge for nearly
eight years when he was sacked in February 1988 after we failed to
qualify for that year's European Championships – the third major
tournament in a row that we'd narrowly missed out on. I'd never forgotten that Mike had ended my international career in 1981 – in my
view prematurely. I must be honest and sadly admit that every time
Wales played towards the end of his spell in charge, I was hoping

they'd get a bad result because I wanted my chance to do the job. I don't think I wished any ill on Mike personally but I didn't want them to win. I was fed up with Wales always falling at the final hurdle and I wanted it to be my time. I wanted the chance to put things right and eventually it happened. But before I took over in March 1988, Wales played Yugoslavia at the Vetch and David Williams, who was then coaching at Norwich, was put in charge for that one game. He'd won five caps under Mike and was a well-respected coach. I rang him up at the Seabank Hotel in Porthcawl where the team were staying and offered him the services of my kit man. When we met later, he complained about the terrible set-up and the bunch of players he was dealing with. I was astounded because someone like Dave would have been good for Welsh football. I thought to myself then that he wouldn't be in the job for long. As it happened, I took over for the next three games. I'd made it clear through the media that I'd be interested in doing the job on a part-time basis but when I told Doug, he said I wouldn't be able to do it.

'How can you stop or stand in the way of someone who wants to manager their country?' I asked him.

'You've got a big enough job to do here,' he replied.

While I thought that was fair enough, by then the wheels were already in motion. I met with the three-man Welsh FA sub-committee – including Doug – who were trying to find a successor to Mike England. I was a little disappointed with the FAW's attitude – especially those councillors who were unhappy about the way Mike had been sacked. They weren't sure about me so I was put on trial while an abortive attempt was made to recruit my former manager at Leeds, Brian Clough.

My first match as a stop-gap manager was a classic baptism of fire – we lost 4-1 in Sweden – but we then beat Malta 3-2 in Valetta before pulling off a great result by winning 1-0 in Italy in June. That was the turning point because a month later, I was officially appointed part-time manager with the aim of taking Wales to the 1990 World Cup finals in Italy. In the end, Doug agreed to the job-share but only after negotiating a compensation package that saw Swansea being paid £12,000 a year – a third of my club salary.

The best thing I ever did was to bring in Peter Shreeves as my assistant. He had a lot of experience and was very confident. He'd been born in Llanelli but had left Wales quite soon afterwards and played for Finchley, Reading, Chelmsford City and Wimbledon before filling various coaching jobs at Charlton and Spurs. When I'd arrived at White Hart Lane in 1976, Peter was youth-team coach there and I noticed he was wearing a Welsh tracksuit – even though everybody else was dressed in blue and white. When I asked him why, he said – in a pronounced Welsh accent – that he'd been born in Llanelli. He soon told the Welsh boys where he was from and although they all respected him for his Tottenham connections, he soon went up even more in their estimation through his work on the training ground. We were unlucky to lose to Holland 1-0 in our first World Cup qualifier in September 1988 and we then drew with Finland, who were also in our group, and Israel in a friendly.

I was quite happy to leave Tommy Hutchison in charge at the Vetch and the job-share seemed to be working out quite well. But my relationship with Doug worsened during the first half of the 1988-89 season. We hadn't been able to push on from our promotion success and we seemed to be standing still. Doug wanted me to sign a new two-year contract at the Vetch but I just didn't get round to it and then just before Christmas I was linked with a move to Walsall.

Two months later, I was on my way back to Bradford as a replacement for Terry Dolan who'd been sacked. Jack Tordoff had succeeded Stafford Heginbotham as chairman and I told Doug as soon as he came in for me. Jack then rang Doug who refused to let me go. I phoned my lawyer for the first of many conversations over the next few days and he advised me to get out. So I walked. I resigned with five months left on my contract. Swansea were going nowhere at the time and I'm afraid the emotional pull of Valley Parade and the family in Leeds proved too much. Christine and the children were obviously pleased that I'd be spending more time with them. It was always difficult being away for such long periods, only managing to come home after games on a Saturday or perhaps in midweek if Swansea had been playing somewhere not too far from Leeds. I was worried that my life on the motorways between Yorkshire and South Wales meant I was missing the children growing up. There was always that dilemma but I had to make decisions based on football rather than domestic circumstances. Christine's decision not to disrupt family life by staying put in Leeds didn't make any difference to me. We had a lovely house and a nice lifestyle and I wanted to make sure we were able to maintain it. If Christine wouldn't follow me, I had to decide for myself where I could earn a living. I had to be prepared to go where the work was – even if it meant travelling backwards and forwards to Swansea as I had done for the last three years. Around that time, Christine set up her property firm, First Homes, after buying a house, doing it up and then selling it at a profit. It was the start of her career as a property developer. It didn't bother me because she'd always worked through her various companies and this was just something new for her to become involved in.

After I left for Bradford, Tommy Hutchison took over the reins for a while before Ian Evans became my permanent replacement. When I arrived back at Valley Parade, I discovered that Swansea had slapped an injunction on me. I couldn't work as a manager so I had to walk out and attend the game at Blackburn on the Saturday as a spectator while our physio, Bryan Edwards, filled in for me. Bradford lost and I officially took over on the Monday and everything settled down for a while. The Football League later upheld Swansea's claim that I'd been poached by Bradford and fined them £10,000 and I had to repay a personal liability of £18,000 that was written into my contract. At the end of the season, Bradford finished 14th in the old Division Two while Swansea ended up in 12th place in Division Three.

Unfortunately for me, Jack decided to sell the club a year after I'd gone back. The head of the consortium that bought his 81 per cent holding for £800,000 in February 1990 was Dave Simpson, a travel agent who'd been in charge of Keighley Rugby League Club. It was pretty obvious that Bradford City were going to be run in a very different way. Jack's board meetings were held in the secretary's office and lasted five minutes but the new lot wanted me there all afternoon. At my first board meeting under the new regime, eight of them were sitting around the table. I gave a report on the football side and then one of the men slipped me a card with the names of two players from Scotland on it.

'Do you know them?' he said to me.

'Of course I do', I replied.

'They're available.'

'Right.' I turned the card over to find the name of a Chinese tailor in Hong Kong. 'Is he available too?', I asked.

Matters came to a head before one home game when I was giving my team talk in the dressing room. I could see the players looking past me as I spoke and I turned round to find Dave Simpson standing there.

'Can we go outside?' I said.

When we got outside I turned on him.

'Don't you ever do that to me again! That's my domain in there – I don't need you in the dressing room before a game.'

It was pretty obvious that we weren't going to get on but results went against me and I was sacked 24 hours after we'd lost at Swindon in the second week in March. We were third from bottom of the Second Division and hadn't won in nine League matches so I didn't really have a leg to stand on. The next day, I said goodbye to the players and the following day Christine asked me to clean the windows and mow the lawn. I'd never been sacked before, it wasn't nice but neither was the prospect of helping round the house with the chores so I was desperate to get back into football. A couple of days later, the phone rang. It was Doug Sharpe. He'd been away and had only just heard the news. He asked if I would be interested in going back to the Vetch Field. So, not long after I'd been replaced by John Docherty at Bradford, I was taking over from Ian Evans. He was sacked by Doug as Swansea headed towards the bottom of the table.

I didn't feel guilty about replacing a former playing colleague of mine because once you come into football management, you know the score. Nobody is trying to get you the sack – it's not exactly dog eat dog – but people do step into dead man's shoes. If you're out of work, you're always waiting to take somebody else's job if they lose it. In retrospect, I should have remembered the sort of man Doug was and thought it through a little more – instead of being a bit naive and wanting a job just to work. But I didn't so I found myself back at the Vetch and it wasn't a very nice period of my life. In the short term, Swansea managed to stay up – we finished four points off the relegation zone – but I'm afraid Bradford went down and the two teams found themselves playing each other in the Third Division in the

1990-91 season.

I was still managing Wales part-time and although we hadn't been able to stop Holland and West Germany qualifying for the 1990 World Cup finals, we'd made a good start to the new European Championship qualifying campaign. We beat Belgium 3-1 at the old Cardiff Arms Park before Ian Rush scored the only goal in a 1-0 win in Luxembourg in the middle of November. Four days later, Doug went public on his worries about me doing the two jobs. He described our recent defeat at Mansfield as the worst performance he'd seen for 10 years and said that I should have been geeing up the players before the next game – an FA Cup tie against non-League Welling – but instead I was in Luxembourg with the Welsh team. Basically, Doug felt Swansea were suffering because of my involvement with Wales and he had a point. Despite spending more than £650,000 on bringing strikers like Terry Connor and Jimmy Gilligan to the Vetch, we'd won only four of our first 15 games and we were the lowest scorers in Division Three. Doug was understandably looking for some return on his investment in terms of results. As the pressure started to mount, I was stopped by the police in Swansea as I made my way home to Cardiff three weeks later. They followed me out of a petrol station near the city centre and I failed a roadside breath test.

We only lost twice in 14 League and cup games between late November and the start of January but by the beginning of March, we were in the middle of another slump. Rotherham knocked us out of the FA Cup in a third round replay, we kept losing in the League and crowds started to fall away. Doug and I agreed that I should have a few days break but we then lost 2-0 at Birmingham to continue the dismal run.

Doug then gave me the dreaded public vote of confidence after the game, but I hadn't spoken to him for a week. It came to a head just over a fortnight later after we lost 3-0 at Crewe in a midweek match to set a club record of nine successive League defeats that still stands today. The next night, I was sitting in my office waiting to watch a Welsh Under-21 game with Hutchy and our youth-team coach, Ron Walton, when Doug asked if he could see me outside.

'You're sacked,' he said. 'You're finished and I'm not paying you what it says in your contract because of the drink-driving business.'

'I'll see my solicitor about that.'

'Right then – see your solicitor.'

My solicitor told me to walk out so the next morning I went down to the ground to collect my stuff and say goodbye to the players. I was putting everything into a box when Doug appeared with Glyn Hammond who hadn't been with him the night before when he sacked me.

'I want you to resign,' he said.

'Resign from what?'

'Your job.'

'But I haven't got a job – you sacked me last night.'

Doug then started to get a bit tetchy but I reminded him that he'd sacked both me and Hutchy without Glyn being there.

'Now you know you've made a mistake.'

Then it all turned a bit nasty with the club sending me a letter ordering me to report to the Vetch at three o'clock on the following Saturday to take the first team for our game against Grimsby. I ignored it and later discovered that Frank Burrows had been at the match. Frank had just resigned as manager of Portsmouth and he was soon appointed as my replacement. After the players stopped the rot with a point against Grimsby, Frank kept Swansea up – again by just four points.

Being sacked for the second time in a year left me feeling pretty depressed but my season ended with a good personal result when I was cleared of the drink-driving offence a month after I'd left the Vetch. Two policemen had stopped me as I drove along Fabian Way on the way to Cardiff and when I was put in the back of their car after failing the breathalyser test, I noticed my lights were still on. One of the officers had locked my car but he couldn't switch off the lights. When I suggested that I should do it instead, they both agreed. Down at the police station, a machine aborted and the officers on duty didn't follow the proper procedure when giving either a blood or urine test. They just called for a doctor who took a blood test. I explained all this to my barrister and because the police knew that he knew about it, the case was adjourned. I was later charged with driving while unfit through drink. When it came to court, I explained that I'd drunk two or three glasses of whiskey with lemonade after a 13-hour day having driven down from Chester. My eyes were glazed through tiredness not through drink. My barrister let the two policemen read out their statements and then asked one of them to read out the charge. My barrister then homed in on the word 'unfit', asked one of them to explain the lights incident and then posed the killer question:

'So you were sober and you couldn't turn the lights off and Mr Yorath, who was supposedly drunk, could?'

The magistrates took about five minutes to find me not guilty. But I hold my hands up to the charge of not respecting that old football saying 'never go back.' It didn't work out twice for me when I returned to the scene of a previous triumph – first at Bradford and then at Swansea. I'm sure my second spell at Valley Parade would have been OK if Jack Tordoff had stayed. He wanted me to go back and my relationship with him was quite good because I understood his foibles. But had he told me he was going to sell the club, I wouldn't have gone. I should have done better when I returned to the Vetch and it was sad the way it all ended. For a while, I fought to get some compensation out of Doug but when we weren't making much progress, my solicitor advised me to jack it in because it was costing me so much money. Like most self-made businessmen, Doug was financially driven but I know he also had a real affection for Swansea City and he put his money where his mouth was to keep the club going when other so-called fans weren't prepared to.

Looking back, perhaps Doug was right about me not being able to manage my club and my country at the same time. The arrangement worked fine in my first spell at the Vetch but not the second so who knows? Being sacked by Swansea was a blow but I was lucky. Less than a week later, I was in charge of the Welsh team that picked up a very useful point in a European Championship qualifying game against Belgium in Brussels. And what do they say about every cloud having a silver lining? Well...it's true. Leaving Swansea led to me landing my dream job as full-time manager of Wales.

Triple Tragedy

Without doubt, it was the high point of my time in charge of the national side; perhaps not quite a once-in-a-lifetime experience but a very special occasion all the same.

Wales 1 Germany 0. The victory over the reigning world champions at Cardiff Arms Park on 5th June 1991 was a remarkable result that took us to the top of our European Championship qualifying group and shattered Germany's 16-month unbeaten run. It still stands as one of the most defining moments in the history of Welsh football on a night when everything went right at the cathedral of Welsh rugby.

The famous old ground may have been transformed into the magnificent Millennium Stadium but I can still clearly recall Ian Rush's decisive goal with a quarter of the match left. The years simply roll back as I close my eyes and re-live Liverpool's most prolific striker scoring the most famous of his 28 goals for his country. It was a true moment to savour.

There was still no score but we were starting to get on top. Germany's inspirational captain, Lothar Matthäus, had retired hurt at half-time and their right-back, Thomas Berthold had just been sent off for stamping on our skipper, Everton's Kevin Ratcliffe. When a cross was swung over from the German left into our penalty area, the ball was headed clear to Paul Bodin about five yards outside the D. Our trusty left-back, then with Crystal Palace, took one touch before launching a long ball over the top for Rushie to chase with his marker, Guido Buchwald, in hot pursuit.

When it finally came down, the ball bounced midway between the half-way line and the German penalty area. Rushie's first touch took him into the box. As Buchwald vainly attempted a challenge near the penalty spot and keeper Bodo Illgner rushed out desperately from his line, Rushie fired a low shot into the bottom right-hand corner of the net. With his great pace, Ian had become so much of a lone striker at that particular moment that he had to wait a while for his ecstatic team-mates to catch up with him. We were up from the bench as soon as the net started to ripple – as were most of the 38,000 crowd. Sixty-six minutes gone and Wales were in front!

History shows that we hung on to our slender lead for a victory that not only confirmed we could live with the best in the world but helped me to achieve one of my greatest ambitions in life. The win gave us a three-point lead at the top of our group with two games to go. Three weeks later, I became full-time Welsh manager.

The Welsh FA held a special meeting and agreed to more than double my money to £40,000 for the remaining 12 months of my existing contract. They actually admitted to bowing to public pressure after the Germany result and I knew that if we could reach the European Championships in Sweden, the next World Cup qualifying campaign would be my oyster. For once, everyone was singing from the same hymn sheet – the supporters, the players, the Welsh FA and me. To their credit, the Welsh FA had grasped the nettle by appointing a full-time manager and my decision not to apply for any club jobs since the end of the previous season had been vindicated. I heard the news when I was in Cardiff for the wedding of my nephew, the boxer Carl Stephens, and it made the weekend back in my home city even more enjoyable. It was a wonderful feeling to finally have the job on a permanent basis but sadly it didn't prove to be a long-term arrange-ment for gradually, over the next two and a half years, my personal and professional life fell apart. Despite beating Germany in Cardiff and picking up three points out of four against Belgium, we weren't good enough to make it to Sweden and I was left devastated by three tragic deaths before being sacked when our campaign to reach the 1994 World Cup in America failed at the final hurdle.

It had all began so well with another impressive win against another team who regularly won the World Cup. After the summer break, we beat Brazil 1-0 at Cardiff Arms Park in September thanks to a goal by Rushie's fellow Liverpool striker, Dean Saunders, but all the time I was trying to dampen down the post-Germany euphoria and expectation. OK, we'd beaten the world champions at home but playing on their patch would be a very different matter. We knew the hardest hurdle was yet to come. In the middle of October, we travelled to Nuremberg needing at least a point to stay in with a chance of winning our group. Germany were favourites to beat Belgium and Luxembourg while our last game was at home against Luxembourg.

We were doing OK until the last 10 minutes of the first half during which Germany scored three goals. Andreas Moeller set them on their way and then a horrendous back-pass by Gavin McGuire five minutes later put the game beyond us and soon it was 3-0 at the break. My assistant, Peter Shreeves, had found out that Gavin's mother came from the Rhondda Valley when the two were at Queens Park Rangers together but through other family connections, Gavin could also have played for England or Ireland. He chose Wales and because I didn't really have a regular right-back in the squad, I decided to give him his seventh cap against Germany. Some journalists later called it a monumental gamble but I knew Gavin could play there because I'd seen him in that position for QPR. In one of the books about Welsh international footballers, the then Portsmouth player is described as being 'adept at creating attacks by long and accurate passes out of defence'. But it was a German rather than a Welsh attack he created when he didn't spot Rudi Voeller and allowed him to intercept the back pass and easily beat Neville Southall. I felt let down by Gavin – not so much for his actions on the field as his words off it. To be fair, he held his hands up by admitting he hadn't seen Voeller before saying the ball had bobbled as he was about to play it to Nev. He then told the press that he couldn't understand why he'd been picked at right-back because he hadn't played there for a long, long time! Gavin tried to shift the blame for his terrible mistake – talk about players dropping their managers in it! – as he was understandably concerned that he'd be made the scapegoat for the defeat. After being replaced by Gary Speed, of Leeds, at half-time, he never figured in any of my squads again. Someone who can make an excuse like that can make an excuse for anything.

We ended up losing the match 4-1 with Paul Bodin scoring a late penalty and an up and coming Manchester United winger, Ryan Giggs, making his debut as a substitute for Crystal Palace's Eric

Young. It was only a matter of time before I would have picked Giggsy but he was only 17 and just making his way into the United first team so we had to tread carefully. I knew all about and understood his manager, Alex Ferguson's determination to shield him from the media but I was under pressure from the Welsh FA to pick Ryan so I rang Alex. He agreed that he could make his debut but asked me to be careful with him and maintain the Old Trafford policy of keeping him away from the media. When it was 4-1 in Nuremberg, Peter Shreeves suggested we put Ryan on for the last six minutes to give him some experience. We did and he enjoyed it but that didn't stop me getting a right bollocking from Alex as soon as we arrived back in England. I was driving home to Leeds from Heathrow Airport when my mobile phone rang. As I picked it up, I could almost feel the steam coming out of it!

'Do you realise what you've done?', he said.

'But you agreed we could give Ryan his debut,' I replied.

'He's now become the youngest person to ever play for Wales so you've put him under even more pressure! The press will want to make even more of him now!'

I swallowed hard and let the rant continue but, until that phone call, I honestly didn't realise that we'd inadvertently given Giggsy a place in the record books. I had no idea that he'd taken over from the great John Charles and I told Alex so. But Ryan later revealed that as soon as he'd arrived back at Old Trafford, Manchester United's commercial department had got on to him straightaway. They wanted to put his first Welsh shirt on display in their Theatre of Dreams museum! Now come on. You can't have it both ways. Sure, there was new pressure on Ryan but his club were very proud and more than willing to make some money out of his achievement. It was all about picking the right time to put him in. International football is such a high-pressure business that his first game could have gone badly. His career could have been spoiled for ever but I think we handled it well.

That defeat in Germany all but ended our campaign to reach Sweden. A month later, another Paul Bodin penalty kept alive our slim hopes as we beat Luxembourg in Cardiff in our final group match but Germany then won 1-0 in Belgium. I watched the game in Brussels with the Luxembourg manager, Paul Phillipp, who later reminded me that we had to rely on his team if we were going to qualify. As I expected, they couldn't help us and were thumped 4-0 in Leverkeusen. Germany finished top of the group by a point and our dream was over. It was no consolation to me that they eventually reached the final in Sweden before losing 2-0 to Denmark. Once again, we had done well but not well enough. My predecessor, Mike England, had narrowly failed to lead us to two World Cups and two European Championships; now it was my turn to experience a frustrating near miss. But that campaign had restored both confidence and pride in Welsh football and it made me even more determined to reach the 1994 World Cup finals – the first time the tournament had been held in the United States.

As I was preparing for our next game – a friendly against the Republic of Ireland in Dublin towards the end of February – I was given the shock of my life when I received a phone call from one of my old Swansea players, Steve Thornber, then still at the Vetch Field and now coaching at Rotherham.

'The little fella's taken his life,' he said.

'Who?' I asked, not knowing who Steve was talking about.

'Al,' he said.

I just couldn't believe it. Al – or 'Little Al' as we also knew him – was Alan Davies, a very skilful midfield player-cum-winger who I'd signed three times as I moved between Swansea and Bradford in the 1980s. His father was from Corwen in North Wales but lived in Manchester and Alan had joined Manchester United as an apprentice in 1978. He'd made just one League appearance when he replaced the injured Steve Coppell in two of the team's last three First Division games in May 1983. He then found himself in the 20-man party for the FA Cup Final against Brighton but thought he was just making up the numbers until an another injury crisis led to him being picked in the starting line-up.

Al played well in the first game – a 2-2 draw at Wembley – and even better in the replay when he had a hand in two of United's goals in their 4-0 win. He won the first of 13 caps against Northern Ireland five days later but then broke his leg in a pre-season friendly and was never the same after that. Even so, he moved on to Newcastle before joining me at Swansea, Bradford and then Swansea again. He won eight caps under Mike England up until 1985 before I brought him back into the fold in my second game in charge against Malta in 1988. As Peter Shreeves soon remarked, the lad could play and he was a joy to work with. When I was sacked by Swansea in 1991, Frank Burrows took over and Alan started to pick up a few injuries. After scoring against Stoke in October, he'd been in and out of the first team and was still playing in the reserves over the Christmas period. He made his last appearance at West Bromwich Albion at the end of January 1992 when he was substituted and replaced by his best friend at the Vetch Field, Steve Thornber. Ironically, Steve went on to score an amazing hat-trick in 13 minutes as Swansea won 3-2. Alan knew his contract would run out at the end of the season and, with his wife, Deborah, expecting their second child, I think it all became too much for him.

The day before he died, Alan burst into tears in the kitchen of his home in Gowerton – telling Deborah he was fed up with himself – and in the evening he sat around watching his Manchester United videos – including the one of the 1983 Cup Final. The next morning, he took their four-year-old daughter, Kate, to school and then drove to a beauty spot on Gower where his body was later found in the fume-filled car by a local farmer. A hose pipe led from the exhaust into a window of the car and a suicide note was found scrawled on the back of an envelope. Alan was just 30 years old. Steve Thornber, everyone at Swansea and anyone in football who knew Little Al just couldn't believe what had happened. His dumbstruck team-mates rightly voted not to play in a Welsh Cup quarter-final tie against Cardiff City as a mark of respect.

I attended his funeral in Manchester along with former United players like Mark Hughes, Clayton Blackmore and Frank Stapleton and the then assistant manager at Old Trafford, Brian Kidd. Deborah left a handwritten message on Alan's coffin saying she would never understand why he had killed himself and it's something that's always puzzled me. I had a very good relationship with Alan. He was a prankster, he liked to have a gamble on the horses and he'd always join a card school if there was one going. There was never any hint of a depressive side of his character. I always talked to Al and if I thought he was looking a bit gloomy, I'd ask him what was wrong. He always said he was fine. He seemed so laid back but obviously not. When he was with me at Swansea and Bradford, Al was also playing for Wales but when I left the Vetch Field, he couldn't get in the Swansea first team so I couldn't pick him for his country. I think his fall from grace – from Manchester United to Swansea's reserves – was too much for him and watching his videos probably tipped him over the edge.

A week after the funeral, we beat the Republic of Ireland 1-0 and then I went on a spying mission to Bucharest to see Romania beat Latvia. I also wanted to sort out our accommodation for the first World Cup qualifier in Bucharest in May. The most difficult part of the trip was getting in and out of the country. It took me ages to pass through customs and passport control and the standard of my hotel left a lot to be desired. The television didn't work properly and it took hours to get through on the phone but I managed to find a better hotel where we could base ourselves. Even without their inspirational play-maker, Gheorghe Hagi, Romania easily won what was the Latvians' first game after the break-up of the USSR. I knew that their new manager, Cornel Dinu, had fielded an experimental side against Latvia but it was a worthwhile trip and I felt we'd done everything possible to prepare for the opening match of our World Cup campaign. In our final warm-up game, we had a very useful workout in a 1-1 draw with Austria in Vienna.

By this time, I felt a lot happier in the job of Welsh manager. We took a real hammering in the 4-1 defeat by Sweden in my first game but I then enjoyed a brief honeymoon when we beat Malta and Italy on the road. We then had to wait for another 11 matches before we won again – Dean Saunders scoring the only goal against Costa Rica in Cardiff when, along with Gary Speed, Paul Bodin and Eric Young made their debuts. True, four of those matches were World Cup qualifiers against West Germany and Holland but I admit I was finding it difficult to make the transition from club management to international football. I had a dilemma knowing how to play things as I moved from running Swansea, where I was able to dictate everything, to suddenly being in charge of world-class players like Neville Southall, Ian Rush, Kevin Ratcliffe and Mark Hughes. Should I blow my top when things went wrong or speak to them quietly? I chose the latter. I felt it was the best way to go about it. I respected the players and I wanted to earn their respect. Those who'd been my team-mates could remember me as being pretty tough and always shouting and screaming during games. After one of my early matches as manager, I was very disappointed with our performance but I didn't rant and rave. Kevin Ratcliffe said the lads had been expecting a bollocking.

'I'll do that in my own time,' I replied.

In the early days, I was getting advice from all over the place. On one away trip, our former keeper, Dai Davies, who was working for the media, rang up to ask me to come to his hotel room. When I arrived, he gave it to me straight:

'You've got to start bollocking these bloody players! Give them hell!'

At first, I thought there were certain individuals in the squad who would test me – like Ian Rush for one. I'm keen on people I'm working with being punctual and on that Malta-Italy trip, Rushie turned up late for a couple of team meetings. Having won 36 caps, he was one of the bigger players and I think he did it on purpose just to prove a point. But instead of confronting him in front of all the other players, I went up to him quietly and had a word in his ear.

'Ian,' I said, 'I've got the utmost respect for you. All I want you to do is to turn up on time. I understand your point but if you're here on time, then everybody else will be here on time.'

Rushie was never late again. The Everton contingent – Nev and Kevin Ratcliffe – had talked me into taking along their team-mate, Pat Van Den Hauwe, on that trip even though he wasn't fully fit. Despite being born in Belgium, Pat qualified for any of the four Home countries and had been given his debut by Mike England against Spain in 1985 when Mark Hughes scored with that spectacular bicycle kick at the Racecourse in Wrexham. Pat did nothing on the trip except drink and be a bit of a problem – although he did win his 11th cap against Italy and turned in his usual tough-tackling performance at full-back. He played in two of the next three matches against Finland and Sweden but didn't turn up with the rest of the squad before the World Cup qualifier against West Germany at Cardiff Arms Park in May 1989. Everton had just been beaten 3-2 by Liverpool in the FA Cup Final. Nev said he didn't know where Pat was so I phoned up Everton the next morning. I was put through to the physio who told me Pat was having treatment. I asked to speak to him but he wasn't there. I then went through to the manager, Colin Harvey, and told him I didn't want Pat in the squad any more. I asked him to tell Pat that he was finished with Wales. He never played for us again. The rest of the squad were on my side. They realised they could go so far but no further.

The turning point in my relationship with the players came once they'd got used to me and my assistant, Peter Shreeves and we'd got used to them. Managing Wales wasn't like running a club team where you can get to know your whole squad within a week. At international level, you only have them for a few days at a time. Some players come across as arrogant, others as friendly and it takes time to work out how to treat each individual. We changed the system to play three at the back – two marking and one as sweeper – and then things started to look brighter. I couldn't always pick my strongest team because of the usual crop of injuries and suspensions and the domestic fixture list. The international dates used to do my head in because they came at the worst time. Round about Easter, the old First Division and then the Premiership was getting down to the business end involving League titles and possible relegation in some cases so I had club managers asking me not to pick their players. It was a difficult time then but once we had a settled team and the lads adapted to the way we wanted to play, we started to make progress.

What I loved about the squad was that they were all so keen to play for Wales. I'd go to watch Premiership and First Division matches and see them talking to each other out on the pitch before the game – and I'd know what they were talking about. They gelled very well as a group and although it may be frowned upon today, we gave them a certain amount of freedom. We would meet up on a Saturday night and let them have a drink and go out if they wanted to. We trained on Sunday morning, they could play golf in the afternoon and then go out in the evening. The routine was exactly the same on the Monday but they knew that Monday night was the cut-off point before the game on Wednesday night. I probably couldn't do the same thing today but they were responsible lads who enjoyed playing and being together. Ten of them would go and play golf and occasionally Nev asked if he could go to the theatre. They had a fantastic camaraderie –

almost a club spirit at international level in the end.

Neville's only flaw as a goalkeeper was off the field. Everybody else would be eating steak, potatoes and pasta and he would sit down to a plate of bacon and eggs! Sometimes I wondered if he was just doing it to be awkward or if that was simply the way he was. Eventually I realised it was the latter because Nev was a one-off. I believe he was the best goalkeeper in the world at the time. The way he trained was absolutely spot-on. Our second and third-choice keepers would get fed up with him because they weren't used to training so thoroughly. Nev would really put himself – and them – through the mill with his routines and I'm sure they learned a lot off him.

I made use of a few 'Anglo' players – people like Jeremy Goss and Eric Young who were with teams in English football but opted to play for Wales. With such a small pool to choose from, we had to take advantage of the rules and these players all contributed immensely to the Welsh cause and indeed felt Welsh. We followed the lead taken by Jack Charlton when he was the Republic of Ireland's manager. We went through the Football Association's list of players to find out where they were born, sort out some stats on those who seemed suitable and then rang them up to see if they were interested. Eric said he was straightaway. His parents were West Indian, he was born in Singapore and because he had a British passport, he was eligible to play for any of the four Home countries. He was a stopper who had pace and wore a distinctive headband. I remember we played the Republic of Ireland at Wrexham in February 1991 when there were about two inches of snow on the ground. Eric was like Bambi on ice. His long legs were going everywhere. I took him off at half-time and christened him after the Disney cartoon character – he just started laughing and enjoyed the joke at his expense. Eric was a very intelligent lad who won 21 caps while he was with Crystal Palace, Wimbledon and Wolves. It was said that he didn't drink before he became one of the team. It certainly wasn't true afterwards!

I gave the Portsmouth defender, Kit Symons, his debut against the Republic and Chris Coleman, having left Swansea and joined Crystal Palace, played his first match in the next game against Austria. Those two – along with Andy Melville, who'd moved from Swansea to Oxford – provided me with valuable cover in case any of the first-choice central defenders were missing.

At his peak, my first skipper, Kevin Ratcliffe, was probably one of the best defenders in British football. He had pace, a great left foot and he very rarely missed a tackle. Radders wasn't the biggest player in the world but he was good in the air and read the game very well. He didn't let me down when I brought him back for the World Cup qualifier against Belgium at Cardiff Arms Park in 1993 when Giggsy made his full Welsh debut. After the game, Rats told the press, a little tongue-in-cheek, that he could now tell his grandchildren that he'd played with Ryan Giggs! He thought a lot about the game and I'm surprised that he's not back in football after leaving Shrewsbury at the end of the 2002-03 season. Mark Aizlewood was another of our central defenders who had a good left foot, was excellent in the air and read the game well – but he wasn't as quick as Kevin. I bought him from Leeds for £200,000 when I was at Bradford in 1989 but instead of following me to Swansea, Mark joined Bristol City a year later. We linked up again at Cardiff in 1994 – the year he won the last of his 39 Welsh caps. He was a key member of the defence, someone whose commitment and fiercely competitive streak meant you'd always want him in your side. After retiring, he developed into a fine media pundit and I'm delighted that he's now back in football as Ian Rush's number two at Chester.

We were spoilt for choice at full-back or wing-back. Two versatile Neath boys, Mark Bowen and Clayton Blackmore, played quite a few games in those positions – in fact, I gave Mark his first full cap in a 3-3 draw with Israel in 1989 after he'd moved from Tottenham to Norwich. He could always been relied upon in whichever position he played during his 41-cap career as he showed when I recalled him for the 4-1 defeat in Nuremberg. His performance in his first start for 18 months was one of few plus points from that match. Having established himself in Manchester United's first team in the 1988-89 season, Clayton was another important member of the squad, slotting in all over the place – mainly at full-back and sometimes in central defence. He won 39 caps and played his last game in a 2-1 defeat by Belgium in 1997.

Dave Phillips had been born in West Germany to RAF parents but his father came from Caerphilly, just north of Cardiff. He made his debut at full-back in the 1-0 win over England at Wrexham in 1984 and was unluckily involved in the controversial handball incident against Scotland at Ninian Park in Cardiff which ended our hopes of reaching the 1986 World Cup finals. Dave played in midfield for Manchester City, Coventry and Norwich and I used that experience by picking him at wing-back for Wales. When I became assistant manager at Huddersfield in 1997, Dave was one of the players we brought in to turn the club around after he'd won the last of 62 caps against Italy the year before.

After playing for both Newport and Cardiff, Paul Bodin's career really blossomed when he helped Swindon reach the old First Division, now the Premiership, via the play-offs in May 1990. A long-running inquiry into alleged irregular payments led to Sunderland being promoted in their place as Swindon were relegated back to Division Two, now the Championship, but later that same month, I gave Paul his first cap against Costa Rica. He was a whole-hearted defender with a sweet left foot who became our regular left wing-back and penalty-taker. As well as helping to set up Ian Rush's goal against Germany in 1991, he was to become one of the most famous – or should that be infamous? – players in Welsh football history in my last match in charge.

Peter Nicholas was one of the squad who I knew from my playing days and he won another 19 caps while I was manager. 'Nico' was a combative midfielder who could get stuck in but then still pass the ball. He enjoyed a long club career with Crystal Palace (twice), Arsenal, Aberdeen, Chelsea and Watford and his 73rd and last cap against Luxembourg in 1991 meant he held the record for the most Welsh appearances for an outfield player. Ian Rush, and later Mark Hughes, equalled it before Dean Saunders overtook everyone. The record is now held by Gary Speed. My second skipper, Barry Horne, was probably more like me as a player than anyone else in the squad. Like his predecessor, Kevin Ratcliffe, he won the same number of caps as me as well. It must be something to do with the honour of leading your country – 59 and no more! Barry was a very intelligent boy with a university degree who, after a career with Wrexham, Portsmouth, Southampton, Everton, Birmingham and Kidderminster, worked for the Professional Footballers' Association before becoming a science teacher at a school in Chester. I felt my captain should be somebody who was going to be a regular in the team. Instead of picking a player like Rushie or Mark Hughes – which would have been easy – I chose Barry. I think it went down well. He always had something to say, he'd come to see me if there was a problem and nobody ever questioned the decision to make his captain. He was a grafter who put his foot in when it counted – and a good player at giving the easy ball. Gary Speed has been so keen to play for Wales over the last 14 years, that he's willing to turn out in any position – apart from, I suspect, in goal! He's led the team very well from left-back recently but I think his best position is central midfield where he can dictate the game. He's had a marvellous career and he's never changed – he's the same Gary Speed I knew when he was 17 or 18. He's now moved on to Bolton and it's a tribute to his professionalism that he's made the most appearances in the Premiership since it was formed in 1992.

We had an embarrassment of riches up front with three top-class strikers in Ian Rush, Mark Hughes and Dean Saunders. My view was that I had to accommodate all three of them in the team otherwise it would be a waste of their talent. I remembered 'Sparky' being a midfield player when he first started off at Manchester United so I decided I would put him there for Wales.

'As long as I play somewhere,' he said, 'I don't mind.'

That summed up his attitude and made my decision easier. He relished being more involved in games in midfield. Despite the stick he took – and gave out! – Mark kept himself incredibly fit and won 72 caps before ending his international career and taking over as national team manager. 'Deano' was the life and soul of the dressing room, a real livewire who took all his energy out on to the pitch with him. He had great pace and his 22 goals make him the third highest Welsh scorer behind Ivor Allchurch (23) and Ian Rush, out on his own with 28. Rushie was so cool it was unbelievable. His goal against Germany at the old Cardiff Arms Park summed him up. He had it all – speed, the most uncanny positional awareness, tremendous work-rate and superb finishing. Having done so well at Liverpool, it was sad to see his career go into decline at Leeds, Newcastle and then Wrexham but he remains the most lethal goalscorer ever produced by Wales. After being in charge of the Welsh Under-17s team, it's quite fitting that his club managerial career should begin at Chester, the place where it all started for him.

With so many world-class players reaching their peak and confidence pretty high after our narrow failure to qualify for the European Championship, we really felt we were in with a great chance of making it to the 1994 World Cup finals. We were in a group with Romania, Belgium, Cyprus, the Faeroe Islands and Czechoslovakia who, after the country split in January 1993, became known as the RCS – the Republic of Czechs and Slovaks. The top two teams would go through to America. As it turned out, we couldn't have got off to a worst start in our first match against Romania in Bucharest in May 1992. With Eric Young missing, I tinkered with the team. We'd watched Romania quite a lot and we'd noticed they only played with one man up front and out wide. So we decided not to bother with a sweeper. Instead, one central defender would mark their striker with the other tucking in around the back. What's that famous saying about 'the best laid plans of mice and men'? Our decision sounded fine in theory but turned into a nightmare in practice. We were losing 5-0 at half-time! Shreevesy and I couldn't believe it as the goals – including two from Hagi – kept flying in. How could we have watched Romania so many times and be 5-0 down at the break? I stood up from the bench and as I headed towards the tunnel, I turned to my trusty assistant for some inspiration.

'What do I say to them?' I asked Peter in desperation.

He looked at me, paused for a second and then uttered the words I will never forget.

'You're the manager!'

Thanks Peter. We had a word with the boys about the defending and to be fair to them, they turned it around in the second half with Rushie scoring to make it 5-1 at the end of a partially successful exercise in damage limitation.

That defeat really hurt. Not only did it mean that we were immediately on the back foot having to play catch up for one of the qualification places but my professional pride had taken a knock. Six months of careful planning had been blown away by Romania's first-half performance and I now had to pick up the pieces before our next qualifier against the Faeroe Islands in September. I was very depressed on the flight back to Wales and I drove home to Leeds determined to make sure the result in Bucharest would remain just a bad night at the office.

Five days later, on Monday 25th May 1992, my whole world collapsed when our son, Daniel, died in my arms while we were playing football together in the back garden of our home in Leeds. He was just 15 years old. My life has never been the same since. More than 12 years later, I'm still trying to come to terms with my grief. Nothing I do seems to make it go away. Daniel's death obviously cast a long shadow over the whole family but while Christine, Gabby, Louise and Jordan have been able to move on, I'm stuck in a time warp. It's just me and Daniel and I just can't let go of the pain that I've felt for every single day since he was taken from us.

Daniel was a typical lad – intelligent, popular with the girls and sports-mad. He had a brilliant relationship with his two sisters and, even though he was nine years older than him, like any elder brother, he would always kept an eye out for Jordan. The four of us would play doubles at tennis – Daniel and me against the two girls – and I'd often take him golfing with me. But the big passion in his life was football. He loved being around the game and we'd go together to matches involving Wales as well as Football League teams. Daniel was always going to be a footballer and just before he died, he'd signed associate schoolboy forms with Leeds, the club where I'd begun my career nearly 30 years earlier. Like me, he'd always been the player who ran everything from midfield and then got forward to score goals – but he hit the back of the net a little more often than I did at his age! When Daniel was about 10, I remember going to watch him play in a match. He showed great skill in chesting a ball down and then volleying it towards goal. It didn't go in but he did score twice in the game. When he got into the car afterwards, I gave him 50 pence.

'That's not for the goals,' I said. 'It's for the chest-down and the volley.'

He was obviously delighted. Even at that young age, he knew why I'd rewarded him. He could also be very hard on himself. Sometimes after a game, he'd climb into the car and wouldn't speak.

'What's the matter?' I'd ask.

'Oh...I was crap!'

'No you weren't.'

'Yes I was. I was rubbish!'

The truth was Daniel was a perfectionist. He always wanted to be the best. He was determined that he'd be able to kick with both feet so he'd spend hours practising on his own. He was lucky because our house in Leeds had a big garden with two five-a-side goals as well as a normal-sized one. He was in his element kicking a ball around and often I'd be out there with him. We were really like a couple of brothers, we were so close. Daniel was a chip off the old block in that I had captained teams ever since I became involved in sport and he enjoyed the responsibility of being skipper of the Leeds City Boys and the West Yorkshire Under-15s teams. Despite my connections with Elland Road, I didn't use any influence I might have had with the club. It didn't matter that Daniel had the Yorath name. If he was going to make it, he would make it because of the sort of player and person he was – not because of a family connection. Whenever I went to see him play, I would stand by myself and not say a word to anyone. Daniel was spotted by the Leeds scouts and attended their academy because they thought he showed real promise. Just before they announced they'd be signing him as an associate schoolboy, I rang the academy to ask about his chances. We were going on holiday to the Far East in February and he would be at home by himself. I was told it was 99.9 per cent certain that he'd be taken on. When he received the letter from Leeds, Daniel rang us with the good news. He was so excited because he'd always dreamt of joining Leeds and now his dream had come true.

On the day he died, Daniel had been told by Christine that if he wanted to go out, he would have to tidy his room so he spent some time sorting that out. About half past six at the end of a sweltering Bank Holiday Monday, we were sitting on the settee watching golf on TV. Daniel said he fancied a game on the course just over the road from our house. I said it was too hot so he then started pestering me to play football in the garden. He kept running his hands through my thinning hair – taking the mickey out of me going bald – and trying to rile me into action. In the end it worked because I gave in and we went out into the garden. We'd been out there for about an hour and we were playing a game called two-touch – where you have one touch to stop the ball and the second to score. I'd had a shot at goal and the ball disappeared into some long grass at the top of the garden. Daniel went to get it. As he came back on to the lawn, he just keeled over. I thought he was taking the mickey because he was always playing the practical joker but when he didn't respond, I rushed over to him. The nightmare had begun. Jordan came running out. Poor boy. He just stood there obviously not knowing what to do so I told him to go and get his mother. When Christine appeared, she couldn't believe what was happening and ran inside to phone for an ambulance. Our next-door neighbour, Maurice, came over and we tried to give Daniel mouth-to-mouth resuscitation but I think he knew it wouldn't work. The ambulance arrived about 20 minutes later and I travelled with Daniel to St James's Hospital. During the quarter-of-an-hour journey, I just kept pressing on his heart, hoping against hope that I could get it going again.

'You'll have to sit down,' said the paramedic.

'Why?'

'Because of the insurance...if you fall over.'

'That's my son there!' I cried and stayed standing by Daniel's side.

When we arrived at the hospital, they rushed him inside but I knew it was too late. As it happened, Ian Adams, the doctor who'd brought Gabby into the world, was on duty at the time. Some of Christine's family had arrived and everybody was completely numb. Nobody screamed or shouted as Ian took us all into a room and told us there was nothing they could do – Daniel was dead.

An hour later, we were back at home, ringing around family and friends to tell them the terrible news. Both the girls became hysterical when Christine phoned them. Gabby, who was just about to start studying at Durham University, was in London and Louise was modelling in Tokyo. Gabby came home straightaway to look after us – she was marvellous – and Louise flew back as soon as she could on what must have been a horrible journey for her. I had a whiskey or two to try and blot out the pain. Later, we popped into Daniel's room. It was immaculate. He'd done what his mother had asked by cleaning, hoovering and polishing – it was out of character for him to have such a tidy bedroom. When I finally went upstairs, I couldn't sleep but eventually dropped off and woke up at about half past five. It was a beautiful day and after putting on my dressing gown, I went down into the garden. I could hear the traffic going by on the ring road and I remember thinking to myself: 'don't they know that my son's dead?'

As we tried to come to terms with what had happened, we couldn't work out how such a healthy boy could go so suddenly – without warning and with no history of any medical problem. It was tearing us up that we didn't know why Daniel had died but we found out a couple of days later when a reporter from a national newspaper knocked on the front door. He said the cause of death was hypertrophic cardio-myopathy – a medical term we'd not heard of. He told us it was hereditary so other people in the family could have it.

I felt so strongly about the crass and insensitive way the reporter had broken the news to us that I wrote to his editor to complain about his behaviour. I later received an apology. On the other side of the coin, we had sympathy letters from loads of people trying to give us support – from Daniel's friends, who looked up to him so much, and his teachers. We also had one from Elton John that we put on display in the house with the hundreds of others. It was a very personal letter in which he told us about his own problems, including his addictions, but, can you believe it, inexcusably, someone stole it on the day of the funeral the following Friday.

Christine took the lead in organising everything and we gained great comfort from our Catholic faith. The priest came around to the house and Daniel's friends were terrific too. They told us lots of things that we didn't know about him – like parties he'd held in the house when we weren't there. In fact, after one session, Daniel realised that his friends had drunk so much beer from the fridge that they'd have to replace it so he organised a whip-round of all the lads! He knew how to entertain his friends on our beer but they said he didn't drink at all himself.

Louise arrived home from Tokyo the day before the funeral which was held at The Immaculate Heart of Mary Church, about a 10-minute drive from the house. It was a lovely and very emotional service with about 500 mourners inside the church and another 300 gathering outside. Daniel's coffin was carried in by six of his team-mates from the Cardinal Heenan School and we'd asked for the Elton John song, 'Daniel', to be played by a small guitar band. It was a par-ticular favourite of mine and I'd chosen it as one of my eight records on a recent edition of the BBC programme, Desert Island Discs. Gabby and Louise read poems and one of the hymns was Daniel's favourite called 'Majesty'. I'd never heard of it but he apparently loved singing the word 'Majesty' at the top of his voice.

The girls had wanted to say something but neither Christine nor I could manage that – and unfortunately the occasion proved too much for one of Daniel's teachers, John Flanagan. He was very involved with the football side and he and Daniel used to go cross-country running after school. John broke down during his moving tribute to Daniel in which he said that in 25 years he'd never taught such a charismatic and cheerful boy. He said Daniel was a joy to work with and he told a story about the way he'd behaved when Cardinal Heenan had won the Under-16s Leeds Schools Final in April 1992. John said he remembered three things about that game which summed up Daniel. In the heat of the match, he'd taken time out to advise and encourage a new defender who was having a difficult time and he then scored an 'extraordinary' solo goal that won the cup.

'But at the end of the game,' John said, 'He came to me, not to talk about the goal but to ask after a player who'd fallen and broken his ankle and to say what a good game that player had had.'

Quite soon after Daniel's funeral, we went to see one of the top heart specialists in Leeds to find out more about hypertrophic cardiomyopathy. He told us the main feature of the disease is an excessive thickening of the heart muscle without an obvious cause. Hypertrophy literally means to thicken. Hypertrophic cardiomyopathy is the biggest single cause of sudden death in the under 25s and one in 500 people in the UK are thought to have the disease. It's been likened to a car engine suddenly cutting out – it can happen to anyone. It often affects young people who are physically active and in extreme cases they can die while exerting themselves, perhaps playing sport, if the problem isn't picked up. The specialist advised us to have the whole family tested. We discussed it and although the girls weren't sure whether they wanted to know, we said it was best that they did. We felt they ought to be aware of a possible problem if they were going to get married and have children. So we went along to a private clinic about three weeks later and luckily the tests showed we were all OK. We had the usual ECG – an electrocardiogram – but we were then put on a sort of video machine and checked with ultrasound around the heart.

We could hear our hearts beating and see them on the screen and various measurements were taken. It was a huge weight off our minds when nothing was found. I was obviously concerned that I might have passed on the disease to Daniel and I would have been devastated if Christine had because she'd given birth to him and there would have been nothing she could have done about it.

As a result of Daniel's death, the family became involved with the Cardiomyopathy Association through one of the leading experts into the illness, Professor William McKenna, from St George's Hospital in London. He thought their campaign would receive more publicity via myself and Gabby and our family name. We helped in whatever way we could to raise awareness of the problem and the Daniel Yorath Appeal Fund was set up. In 2002, the fund and the Cardiomyopathy Association produced the first CD-ROM on the condition which was sent free to more than 20,000 GPs as well as to coroners. In the old days, the disease was masked by the phrase 'death by natural causes' but it can't be natural for any child of any age to die. There has to be something wrong. I became very emotional when I went down to London to speak about Daniel but I felt I had to do my bit to highlight the cruel way the disease can strike. The association started to lobby MPs, the Football Association and the Professional Footballers' Association. I'll always remember one MP who said that not enough people died from the condition for them to do anything about it. How cruel and uncaring.

Since Daniel's death, a number of other people have become victims of hypertrophic cardiomyopathy. They include David Longhurst, a 25-year-old York City player who died during a televised match, Adrian Hawkins, aged 22, who was shortlisted for the British Olympic cycling team before dying after a race and Marc-Vivien Fo, the Manchester City midfielder who collapsed and died while playing for Cameroon against Colombia at the age of 28. They were all apparently very fit but the disease was like a time bomb just waiting to go off. We're still involved with the association but linking up with them didn't help me cope with losing Daniel.

Looking back, I'm just relieved that Daniel died playing football with me in our back garden. His condition meant that he could have collapsed anywhere at any time and at least he was with the people who loved him most. I dread to think about what might have happened an hour and a half later on that Bank Holiday Monday. Christine and I would have been out and Daniel would have been in the garden with Jordan. In the months following his death, we inevitably kept asking ourselves: why him? Daniel had everything going for him. He was about to take his GCSEs and he'd already gained an A in his course work in business studies. Although he was about to join Leeds as an associate schoolboy, he wanted to continue his schoolwork and had arranged to go on day release to study business and finance. It all seemed such a waste – an intelligent boy, on the verge of a career in football, cut down by a genetic disorder that we were all unaware of and helpless to do anything about. I noticed that a lot of the lads who Daniel grew up with – like Andrew Couzens and Mark Ford – did go on to play in the Leeds first team, but only managed a handful of games. When I saw they hadn't done as well as expected, I clung to the thought that perhaps Daniel wasn't meant to be a great footballer and his death was God's way of saying 'I'm not going to disappoint you.'

By staying in the house with the garden where he died, we made a statement as a family. We could quite easily have sold up and moved – if it had been up to me then we probably would have done – but we didn't. Christine and I tried to deal our grief in different ways. She underwent counselling and went to see mediums while I thought I could cope with it myself. I buried my head in the sand. I did go to see two mediums but they only told me things I already knew, some things that were, if you like, regular. They didn't give me anything to think about and they didn't tell me anything I thought would help me. If they had, then maybe I would have been OK. Christine suggested that I went with her for counselling but I didn't want to share my grief with anyone. I didn't want to go and talk to a stranger about Daniel. I felt I could handle it but I was wrong. I now realise I should have gone with her. But that stubborn streak that's been in me all my life wouldn't let me. Instead, in the early months after the funeral, I would drive to Killingbeck cemetery and spend hours lying on Daniel's grave, during the day and at night, crying my eyes out. My life was shattered but I knew that somehow, I had to keep going. Life has gone on but I haven't moved on. I've never been able to get over Daniel's death – and I never will.

I took leave of absence from the Welsh job over the summer so Peter Shreeves was in charge for the next three matches. The day after the funeral, the team lost 4-0 in Holland where the players wore black armbands as a mark of respect for Daniel. They then travelled for two games in the Kirin Cup in Japan – losing 1-0 to Argentina and then beating our hosts 1-0. I decided to go back to work when our campaign to qualify for the 1994 World Cup re-started in September. Although I found it difficult to motivate myself, I knew that keeping busy, trying to make my life as normal as possible, was the only way to help me cope with Daniel's death.

After our nightmare in Nuremberg, we hit the Faeroes Islands for six at Cardiff Arms Park with Ian Rush scoring a hat-trick and our campaign was really up and running when we beat Cyprus 1-0 in Limassol a month later. It was very hot and despite a dreadful pitch and a very vociferous crowd, Mark Hughes scored the winning goal. I'm afraid we then took a step backwards when some poor defending let us down in our next game – a 2-0 defeat by Belgium in Brussels. Frankly, we were shambolic and we deserved to be beaten. After a three-month break, I organised a friendly against the Republic of Ireland – Sparky scored again as we lost 2-1 – and then we played Belgium in the return qualifier at Cardiff Arms Park. Ryan Giggs had made five appearances for the team, all of them as substitute, and we decided it was time to give him his first full cap. We were playing at home, supporters had been calling for him to start a game and we felt he would rise to such an important occasion. The most excited person in the Welsh camp was Peter Shreeves. He adored Ryan's talent and made it clear in training that Giggsy would be a key player for us.

'Corners on the right,' said Peter. 'Giggsy will take them with his left foot. Corners on the left, Giggsy will take them also with his left foot. One swinging in, the other swinging out. He'll also take free-kicks on the edge of the box.'

It got to the ridiculous situation where Peter even came up with this very simple game plan:

'Right. From the kick-off, we pass the ball to Giggsy and he'll go running through.'

He was deadly serious! Ryan was loving all the attention but he was embarrassed when the boys started calling him 'Georgie' because of all the comparisons that were being made with George Best.

I was convinced the time had come to give Ryan his first start – and he proved me right. He had a great game and topped it off with a fantastic free-kick out on our right just outside the box to put us on our way. Rushie scored the other and the 2-0 win was a turning point because it kick-started our campaign.

Sparky was back on the scoresheet a month later when we drew 1-1 with the RCS in Ostrava. We should have won that game but we didn't take any of the other chances we created. We then beat the Faeroes 3-0 in Toftir in our last match before the summer break. Eric Young scored his only goal for Wales with Deano and Rushie getting the others. But we blew it against the RCS in our next match at Cardiff Arms Park in early September. Giggsy and Rushie scored the goals and, like the game in Ostrava, we drew when we should have won. If we'd beaten the RCS in one of those two games, then our last match against Romania wouldn't have been so crucial. We picked up two points when we should have had at least four. We now knew that we had to beat Cyprus in the penultimate game if we were to have a chance of reaching America via the Romania game. There were 30,000 people at the Arms Park that night and they gave us some terrific support. It took us a while to break the deadlock but the crowd stayed behind us. When we couldn't score for so long, I started to see all the old headlines being written about how we'd failed again. When Rushie missed a very good chance, I thought if he wasn't going to score from there then we were finished again. But the crowd didn't get frustrated and their patience was rewarded when Deano and then Rushie popped in a goal each. We'd done it! Romania had beaten Belgium on the same night so it would all depend on our showdown with Gheorghe Hagi and Co. Group 4 would end in exactly the way we'd been predicting. I'd always said that the team who finished fourth could just as easily finish first and four teams were still in with a chance of grabbing one of the two qualifying places. Belgium had 14 points while Romania, Wales and the RCS all had 12. On the night we played Romania, Belgium would meet the RCS so the race was wide open. The Belgians needed a draw to qualify but it was a case of winner takes all at Cardiff Arms Park on Wednesday 17th November 1993.

As the game drew nearer, I kept recalling something Daniel had said to me after we'd been hammered by Romania in our opening group match. A journalist had posed the question in his paper: what is Terry Yorath going to do for the next 18 months? A few days later, Daniel had simply said to me: 'we'll show him' and we had. He wasn't with me anymore but he'd been my inspiration as we had gradually repaired the damage. I was delighted for Daniel that we were back in contention with just one game to go.

It's not an excuse because injuries and suspensions are part and parcel of every manager's life but we weren't helped by having to do without the two Marks, Aizlewood and Hughes, for one of the most important game in the history of Welsh football. They were both missing through suspension and I was particularly annoyed that Sparky was out after he'd picked up a second-half booking against Cyprus. I know Mark was a physical player but the Cypriot guy was yards away from Sparky when he fell. Andy Melville and Paul Bodin came into the defence as Barry Horne moved from wing-back to his normal place in the heart of midfield.

I was convinced we would win but I remember on the morning of the game, Peter Shreeves and I went for a walk near the team hotel on the outskirts of Newport.

'We've got to play at 120 per cent,' he said, 'and Romania have got to play at 90 per cent for us to have any chance at all.'

He was right of course. Although we'd done our homework on Romania, we knew we'd have to be at the top of our form to beat them. Their danger man was Hagi who eventually won 125 caps – 65 of them as captain – and scored 35 goals – one of them in this match. He had a great left foot and just after the half-hour mark, he picked up the ball on our right wing in front of the Welsh bench. At the moment he pulled it inside Paul Bodin with his right foot, a horrible thought flashed through my mind:

'Shit! I forgot to tell Bods that Hagi would come inside every time!'

With the ball on his left foot, Hagi decided to have a shot. To my horror, the ball skidded under Neville Southall's body and ended up in the back of the net. Nev should have saved it, but as manager, I looked at what happened and I blamed myself. I felt that I hadn't briefed Paul Bodin well enough. Of course, he would have known that

Hagi could easily drift out to the right and cut inside but I still felt that I should have told him. Hagi played anywhere but he hardly ran anywhere – he preferred to walk or occasionally jog and somehow the ball would always end up at his feet. It did on that occasion and we paid for it.

We equalised after about an hour of the match through a scrappy goal from Dean Saunders. The ball went into their box, they failed to clear it and all of a sudden, there was Deano to put us level from close range. Knowing the Romanians as I did, I thought they were going to fold. Sure enough, within a minute, Gary Speed was brought down by Dan Petrescu in the area. When the referee pointed to the spot, I felt that we'd score and we'd be going to America. I had no qualms at all about Bods taking it. He hadn't had to take a penalty for Wales for two years – having scored the winner in our 1-0 win defeat of Luxembourg in Cardiff – and I had complete faith in him. He struck it well, as usual left-footed, and although he beat their keeper, Florin Prunea, the ball crashed against the bar and was cleared to safety. Memories of my miss in 1976 didn't come back to me in that moment. I was just thinking about the situation in 1993. With nearly half an hour left, there was still time for us to score again and I still felt we would go on and win. Ryan Giggs had a half-chance soon after but everything went pearshaped when Florin Raducioiu scored what turned out to be the winner eight minutes from time. That was it. I knew we were gone then. For the first time as Welsh manager, I went and stood next to the tunnel for the rest of the game. I'd been in football long enough to know that we weren't going to get back into it but at the final whistle, it didn't occur to me that the defeat would mean I'd eventually be out of a job. That night was all about the penalty and, sadly for Paul, he'll always be remembered for that miss.

As the Romanians understandably started to celebrate, I tried to console the lads one by one as they came off. Back in the dressing room, there was nothing but silence – utter silence. All the players were comforting Paul. I made a beeline for him, put my arms around him and told him to forget it – just like people had done with me in 1976. It's easy to say but harder to do. I still wasn't thinking about my miss – thankfully I'd managed to remove it from my memory bank! Everybody was devastated. After we'd lost 5-1 to Romania in our very first qualifier, we were delighted to be still in with a chance at the end but we hadn't taken it. We soon found out that the Belgians had drawn 0-0 with the RCS so they topped the group and Romania were runners-up. They'd both be off to America and once again Wales had fallen at the final hurdle. Sadly our reputation as the nearly men of international football remained intact.

It was obviously a very disappointing night but the result was soon put into perspective by news of a real tragedy. It took the players over half an hour to take off their kit and have a shower. As I made my way across the pitch from the dressing room in the South Stand to the hospitality area in the opposite stand, I noticed there were a lot of policemen standing around. I could sense something had happened. I asked one of them what was going on and he told me a man had been killed by a rocket in the North Stand. For a moment, I couldn't take it in. It was the Bradford fire all over again if on a smaller scale. How could a man go to watch a football match and not come home afterwards? I know the Romania game meant a hell of a lot to everybody but after someone had died, the result paled into significance. What did it matter after such a waste, the complete and utter destruction of a life? I thought whoever had fired the missile must have been stark raving mad because they must have known the rocket was going to hit somebody over the other side of the stadium as soon as they set it off. Later, I found out what precisely had happened. The distress rocket caused nothing but distress after hitting 67-year-old John Hill in the throat and killing him instantly. Travelling at 240 miles an hour, it took just two seconds to cross the Cardiff Arms Park pitch. John was partially blind and a life-long supporter of Merthyr Tydfil Football Club. For the last two years of his life, he'd been looking after his invalid wife, Jean, at their home in the town near the club ground. She was housebound and suffered from a heart condition. His son, also called John, had bought his father a ticket for the match. The two men who fired the rocket, Kerry Still and Andrew McAllister, brothers from Wrexham with different fathers, denied murder but admitted manslaughter. In their defence, Still said he'd given the rocket to McAllister thinking it was a hand-held flare. Before sentencing them to three years in prison, the judge described their behaviour as 'mindless and crass stupidity' and 11 years later, I think it's difficult to describe the cause of the tragedy as anything else.

Later, I went back to the hotel and had a drink with a few of the players, family and friends and one or two members of the press. At two o'clock in the morning, I was sitting on a stairwell crying. The whole evening had been horrible. We'd lost a game and a man had lost his life. This was the third death to have affected me in a little under two years. First, Alan Davies had committed suicide, then Daniel had died and now John Hill had been killed at a football match. Could things get any worse?

Obviously, John's death completely overshadowed the fact that we hadn't managed to make it to America but gradually, the implications of the result for me and the team started to sink in and people started asking where our failure to qualify left me as manager. My contract only ran until the end of the year and before the Romania game, Jack Evans, the chairman of the Welsh FA's senior international committee, had made it clear that I should carry on. So when I was invited to a hotel in Caersws in Mid Wales for contract talks at the beginning of December, I was pretty hopeful that my career as an international manager wasn't about to be ended by the width of a crossbar.

The Welsh FA's negotiating team was made up of a three-man sub-committee – including the president, the late Elfed Ellis – and chief executive Alun Evans, who'd been recently promoted from secretary. I was earning £45,000 a year as Welsh manager – about half as much as my Scottish counterpart, Craig Brown, who'd just taken over from Andy Roxburgh. The Welsh FA offered me a new two-year contract on the same terms. I rejected it and asked for a figure of £60,000 – roughly half way between my salary and Craig's. Elfed then said to me:

'You do realise that if we'd beaten Romania, you could have come in here and asked for anything? If that penalty had gone in, you would be a God in Wales now.'

The talks lasted for about half an hour and I returned to my home in Leeds to await developments. I then started to hear rumours coming out of Cardiff that I'd insisted that my wage demands were 'non-negotiable'. I'd been in the game more than 25 years and I hadn't come across anyone who'd gone into contract negotiations and used that term – unless they'd won the World Cup! I'd also been involved in enough negotiations as a manager to know that if a player came in and said that to me, I'd tell him that he could go. I'd definitely not used the phrase 'non-negotiable' but Alun Evans later said I had.

A couple of weeks later, I heard that a press conference about the manager's job was about to be held. I knew nothing about it. That was the first inkling I had that my contract wasn't going to be renewed. When I met him on the day of the announcement, Alun Evans confirmed my worst fears. He was leaning back in his chair in his office.

'You should have talked to me about it,' he said, meaning the job.

Although my contract wasn't being renewed, he said I could apply for my old job. He put the blame fairly and squarely on the shoulders of the president, Elfed Ellis, who, Evans claimed, was against giving me a new contract. The stumbling block was money so, because I wanted the job so much, I said I'd accept a £5,000 rather than a £15,000 pay increase. Alun Evans said he'd have to take the matter back to the councillors on the sub-committee set up to make the manager's appointment. That was the last time I spoke with him face to face. On Christmas Eve, I received a letter confirming what he'd told me verbally. It was a huge blow to actually see my sacking spelt out in black and white. I'd lost my son 18 months earlier, I thought I'd done a decent job as manager and I knew that the majority of the Welsh supporters and all the players were behind me. It wasn't very pleasant receiving such a stark letter a day before Christmas although I was told that one of the legal requirements when a contract isn't renewed is that the decision has to be put in writing.

Once the story broke, there was a lot of speculation about who might take over. The runners and riders included John Toshack, who was coaching Real Sociedad in Spain, Terry Venables, in charge at Spurs, and the then Norwich City manager, Mike Walker. As the debate continued about the job and my request for more money, I was heartened by the amount of public support I received. People wrote letters to the editor of the *South Wales Echo* to complain about my treatment and the *Wales on Sunday* carried out a telephone poll of their readers. Who did they want to see as the next manager of Wales? Well...it may not have been the most scientific of barometers but I received 861 votes out of a total of just over 1,500. Tosh came second with 573 votes ahead of the then Wrexham manager, Brian Flynn (39), the former England manager, Bobby Robson (35) and David

Williams, who'd been in charge of Wales for one game in 1988, who received just five votes. Journalists like Rob Phillips, of the *South Wales Echo*, and Paul Abbandonato, from the *Wales on Sunday*, were fighting my corner with Rob in particular laying into the Welsh FA with a scathing article under the headline 'What a shabby way to treat the best man for the job'. I was regularly talking to members of the sub-committee who assured me I was still in the running. I spoke again to Alun Evans in the middle of January when he told me that the councillors couldn't get together because of the recent death of FAW president Elfed Ellis on his way to Manchester Airport. I had no contact with the Welsh FA after that.

Towards the end of January, a journalist friend of mine, Des Kelly, who was then working for the *Today* newspaper, began investigating Alun Evans' recent movements. The chief executive had cancelled an FAW meeting because he was supposedly suffering from a migraine. In fact, he flew to Spain to see Tosh about doing the Welsh job on a part-time basis. On his return, he refused to admit that he'd been to San Sebastian but when a hotel in the town faxed a copy of his bill to the *Today* sports desk, all was revealed. Room 204 in the Hotel Londres had been booked by Tosh himself and Alun Evans had stayed there for two nights – a fact confirmed by Tosh when he rang me while I was having a drink in a pub in Leeds. He said if the former Welsh manager, Mike Smith, would help him, then he'd take the job. I was a bit numb at first. It was very much a 'yes' and 'no' conversation from my point of view. I wasn't really listening to Tosh because I didn't want to hear what he was saying about my job – stupidly, I still regarded it as my job. The next day, he phoned me at home to say that Mike Smith had agreed to help – they were going to go ahead.

'Don't think you can ride in like a knight in shining armour,' I warned him. 'If you don't get it right, the public will have you.'

'If there's any trouble,' Tosh said, 'I'll walk out.'

And that's precisely what he did after his one and only match in charge of Wales at Ninian Park in Cardiff, the ground where he'd begun his career in the 1960s. The press conference in the Marriott Hotel in Cardiff to unveil Tosh as the FAW's new technical director in early February was a complete shambles. The start was delayed for 20 minutes because the room they'd booked was too small. It only had 19 chairs and more than a 100 journalists turned up so the press conference was actually held in the hotel bar with the overspill having to make do with standing room in the foyer. It was typical of the Welsh FA and an insult to Tosh, who'd been a top manager with big clubs all over Europe. It didn't get much better for him. About a month later, his team weren't only beaten 3-1 by Norway at Ninian Park but the crowd kept shouting for me during the game. Tosh didn't like it and he immediately walked out after barely 40 days in charge. While I was proved right, he was true to his word.

I was so annoyed about the way that I'd been treated that I decided to take legal action against the Welsh FA for unfair dismissal. It was the only way I could let out some of the huge amount of frustration and disappointment I felt about being sacked. I was particularly saddened about having to apply for my job – calculated or not, this was a humiliation beyond reason. At the time, my behaviour was calm and, I hope, dignified. I urged the Welsh players not to carry out a threat to end their international careers. Quite a few of them had rung me to sympathise and I know that feelings were running high within the squad. Before he quit, I'd wished Tosh all the best in his new job and I made it clear that there hadn't been a clash of personalities with Alun Evans. We'd had our disagreements over certain things but I said that I'd never really had an argument with him. It just seemed that he and the sub-committee had gone down a certain path. If they'd let me know what was going on, I'd have been a lot happier. I also said that I felt no bitterness towards them whatsoever. But more than a decade later, it's time to explain my true feelings at the time.

Despite my public comments, I was indeed hurting. Deep inside, I did feel bitter because nobody could give me a reason why my contract wasn't being renewed – apart from this 'non-negotiable' stuff. I was heartbroken about losing my job and I could have slaughtered some people over the way I'd been treated but I didn't think I needed to because everybody could see it for themselves. I still wonder precisely why I was sacked having taken Wales to the brink of the World Cup finals for the first time 1958. Was it my record over the last six years, my wage demands, which I later scaled down, or something more sinister? I don't think it was anything to do with my ability as a manger or with us losing the Romania game. As for the financial argument...I was on a pittance compared with other candidates like Mike Walker, who was reportedly earning £70,000 a year at Norwich and Terry Venables, who was said to be on £250,000 with Spurs. I believe I was sacked purely because I was too popular. I was the people's choice but the Welsh FA – guided by their chief executive – were so jealous that they refused to choose me. The men who ran Welsh football refused to make room for the man running the team. They lost sight of the really important issue: the future of the game in Wales. As Rob Phillips wrote in one of his articles at the time 'if this is the Football Association of Wales' idea of showing just how powerful they can be, then they are being extremely irresponsible.'

After returning from his trip to San Sebastian, Alun Evans refused to accept that he'd done anything wrong. 'I personally do not feel that I have anything to reproach myself for' he said at the press conference to announce Tosh's appointment. 'I have done nothing to be ashamed of and have not misled anybody, but others might have.' I took that as a reference to me and my very good relationship with the press. In the end, the backing I received from people like Paul Abbandonato and Rob Phillips worked against me because it antagonised the Welsh FA. I was very grateful for the widespread media support but I think it drummed up so much anti-Alun Evans feeling that the Welsh FA dug their heels in even more and they refused to reappoint me. They were stubborn – a bit like me. I've still got some fabulous cartoons that were produced about the whole business at the time and I was very touched by the groundswell of public feeling that came my way but, in the end, I think it was too much for the powers that be. Maybe I made a mistake in letting the Welsh FA know I wanted to continue in the job so badly. I held on and held on until it all ended in tears when they appointed Tosh. I should have walked away and just let them do what they had to do.

My treatment also generated some furious reaction in the national press with one journalist calling Alun Evans 'an autocrat, a dictator, a one-man band and an ogre.' I don't go in for professional or personal insults but it saddens me to think that petty jealousy rather than poor results ended my career as manager of Wales. Soon after Tosh went back to his day job in Spain, there were calls for Alun Evans to resign. He then wrote to all the organisations affiliated to the Welsh FA to explain his actions. He repeated the claim about my demands being 'non-negotiable' and revealed details of a previously denied meeting of the special sub-committee on 31st December 1993. A letter containing my view of the negotiations had been considered and it was agreed that it 'would impair any future relationship between the association and Mr Yorath.' Alun Evans also maintained that I had been treated 'entirely fairly and properly.' We must agree to disagree. He has since admitted that not renewing my contract was one of the biggest mistakes ever made by the Welsh FA – an example of the faults in Welsh football politics. Well, Alun Evans was closely involved in that decision and those councillors who actually made it should be embarrassed by what happened. But I'm afraid some people have got such thick skins that they never realise what they've done. You have to be a very small-minded person to be jealous of somebody else. I think the Welsh FA were very badly advised and I think events during the rest of the 1990s bore that out.

I've only seen Alun Evans once in the last 10 years. He's now an FAW councillor rather than chief executive and he was with some other people from the Welsh FA at a game in Barry. I could tell by the look on their faces that they were really hoping I wasn't going to speak to him. I didn't embarrass them because I blanked him – just walked straight past him. I had nothing to say to Alun Evans and I still don't. It would be a complete waste of energy.

When Mike Smith and David Williams were appointed to lead Wales into the Euro '96 qualifying campaign in the middle of March, I was so relieved. I could finally get on with the rest of my life. I had really enjoyed my time as Welsh manager but I was getting fed up with being asked if I was still interested in the job. I think the game in Wales was in much better shape when I left than when I took over in 1988. We'd been promoted to second seeds in the European Championship rankings as a result of our performances and the fans were flocking to see the team play at Cardiff Arms Park. I was particularly pleased that we'd re-introduced the Under-21 side – even though the youngsters have been going through a bit of a barren pitch until just recently. Ten years on, I'd like to put on record my thanks to my assistant, Peter Shreeves, for all the help he gave me during my spell as Welsh manager. As soon as I was appointed, the first thing I did was ring

Peter – even though I hadn't spoken to him for six years. I knew he had a lot of experience with Spurs in Europe and he was great with the players because he treated them as men. He was invaluable as my assistant and it's only sad that, after I was sacked, nobody from the Welsh FA bothered to tell Peter he was out of a job too. Typical!

In early August, I reluctantly decided to withdraw my claim for unfair dismissal against the Welsh FA. My solicitor, Peter Levine, expected me to win the case but he said that even if I did, my earnings since Christmas – mainly as a pundit with the media – would mean I'd end up with virtually no money and there would be costs to pay. It was through Peter that I became involved with the consortium who wanted to take over Cardiff City from the Australia-based multi-millionaire businessman, Rick Wright. As well as being a solicitor, Peter also ran a phone company based in Cambridge and he was trying to interest football clubs in using his service for their talk lines – providing supporters with up-to-date news and commentaries. My job was to visit clubs to see if they'd switch to his company and through my work I met Jim Cadman and other members of his consortium. Cadman was a marketing consultant whose company specialised in developing commercial activities at football clubs. He said they were looking to buy a club and I told them Cardiff was the best one on the market. They put the wheels in motion and began talking to Rick Wright while I was coaching in Japan. Rick opted for them rather than the other bidding parties, boxer Frank Maloney and Samesh Kumar, a West Midlands businessman with interests in clothing and property.

When I came to Cardiff, I was told the deal was done and dusted. I was really excited about returning to the city where I'd grown up. It looked like the perfect opportunity to get my life back on track after the turmoil of the last nine months. I insisted that I didn't want anything to do with the football side of the club – I wanted a break from coaching – but I was prepared to let the consortium use my name. I saw it as a chance to work on both sides of the fence – helping the directors and making the manager Eddie May's life a bit simpler – but, not for the first time, I was a little naive. Two months later, I found out the consortium hadn't actually bought the club – they were just leasing it from Rick. I felt I'd been hoodwinked. I wasn't doing anything but living with my parents in Cardiff and I should have taken Christine's advice and walked away from it. But I stayed and the next five months turned into a nightmare. The team were struggling in the old Second Division and the directors started talking about getting rid of Eddie, who's now manager of Llanelli in the Welsh Premier League. I fought his corner so they gave him a very brief stay of execution but he was sacked three days later and I ran the team with Mark Aizlewood as my coach. Eddie probably thinks I got him the sack but I swear on my son Jordan's life that I had nothing at all to do with it. Looking back though, I feel I let him down. Although they had some good ideas – like building a sports hall under the Grange End Stand – none of the consortium had any cash. They wanted somebody else to put in the money. I felt very uncomfortable and in the end, I decided to resign. Eddie returned but he couldn't stop the rot and Cardiff were relegated to the Third Division. Fortunately, Rick Wright came back and kicked Cadman and his colleagues out before selling the club to Samesh Kumar.

My time at Cardiff was one of most frustrating periods of my managerial career. Having been rejected by my country, I'd now suffered a very bad experience with my home-town club. I was floundering about, wondering what do next at the end of a very traumatic three years following Daniel's death. Although it was a relief to have some coaching work in Malaya and Japan over the early summer of 1995, I really wanted to be back in the English game. But when the new season started in August, I wasn't working in the Football League, but in the Middle East.

Rebuilding in Beirut

I became national coach of Lebanon because I was out of work and I was offered the job – simple as that.

After being sacked by Wales and spending a very unhappy eight months at Cardiff, I wasn't feeling very good about myself. In fact, my self-esteem had hit rock bottom. I didn't have the confidence to apply for any top jobs when I returned from an enjoyable spell of club coaching in the Far East. I thought my experience would count for something with lower league clubs but I was wrong. I unsuccessfully put in for a few jobs and when Notts County, who were struggling in the old Second Division, now League One, couldn't even be bothered to reply to my letter about their vacancy, that was the final straw. I did receive phone calls about coaching the Nigerian national team but nothing was ever put in writing. Then a business contact running a construction company in Beirut rang me. Would I be interested in working in the Middle East? He started telling me about the job but, after five minutes, he still hadn't mentioned precisely where in the Middle East it was. When he revealed it was Lebanon, I think he was expecting me to turn him down. But I liked the sound of it and I agreed to go and have a look. I knew it would be difficult because the facilities weren't great but I sensed the job had potential and the money was good so two weeks later, I signed the contract and in June 1995 I was Beirut-bound.

I have to say that although finding work was my main motivation, I was really running away from the whole Daniel situation. When I look back at it now, Daniel's death and losing the Welsh job all in the space of 18 months had taken their emotional toll and I saw Lebanon as a way out. It was a chance for me to start afresh, an opportunity to rebuild my career and my self-confidence away from the spotlight. I appreciated that moving to Lebanon would be a culture shock, but it was a challenge I was really looking forward to.

Once again, there was no question of the family moving with me. It had become a standing joke in the Yorath household – they'd been playing catch up with me ever since I left Elland Road. I moved and they eventually followed – to Coventry, Spurs and then Vancouver. To be fair, by this time, we weren't really a family as such because the two girls had left home. Gabby was just finishing her law degree at Durham University before starting out on a television career and Louise was modelling in America. Jordan was the only one still living with us. Christine's various sports goods, skin care and property businesses were thriving and understandably she wasn't prepared to move to a country that was in the process of being reconstructed after 17 years of civil war. We decided that she would fly out with Jordan whenever she found the time. Being self-employed, she could do that quite easily and it would be business as usual for both of us – Christine running her companies in Leeds and me running the national football team of Lebanon.

Life in Beirut couldn't have been more different from Leeds. From the moment I arrived in the country, the Lebanese Football Federation looked after me very well. They fixed me up with a flat with a veranda on the coast overlooking the beach where the first major battle of the Israeli invasion in 1982 took place but it wasn't the sound of gunfire that disrupted my sleep. Soon after I arrived, the religious festival of Ramadan began and the ritual fasting took place from dawn to dusk. Every day for a month, I was woken up by drumming at four o'clock each morning and there were bugles and singing – the lot – during that period. It was a pretty rude awakening to life in a foreign country and I was determined to find out more about my temporary home while I was there.

Lebanon is half the size of Wales with roughly the same population – about three million people – and many ethnic groups. Since the civil war ended in 1991, a fragile peace had existed although there were still regular border clashes in the south of the country between Israel and the Iranian-backed Hizbullah militia. Hizbullah was the only militia group not to be disarmed after the ceasefire because they continued to resist the Israeli occupation with behind-the-scenes support from the Government. Hizbullah were also heavily involved in the rebuilding of Beirut by financing schools, hospitals and low-cost housing and they sponsored Raia Football Club. The *Sunday Times* journalist, Richard Johnson, wrote an article about my time in Beirut in which he described the city as 'the world's biggest building site'. It couldn't have been put better. The civil war had left a legacy of bombed-out buildings, streets and pavements but when I was there hotels and apartment blocks were springing up all over the place and a network of new roads was being built as part of a massive reconstruction job. As life started to return to normal, people who lived in the city had to begun to pay taxes, gas, electricity and water bills and parking tickets again – some even passed their driving tests! Of course, I knew that the British journalist, John McCarthy, had been kidnapped in West Beirut and when the Israelis attacked Lebanon in 1996, I was forced to move from the coast into Beirut but I can honestly say that during all the time I was there I never feared for my life.

I only worried about my safety when the Israelis flexed their military muscles. Once, after spending a week visiting me, Christine and Jordan were returning to England on a flight at half past seven in the morning. They had to be at the airport an hour before departure so my driver and bodyguard, Hussein, dropped them off and took me back to my apartment. He was due to return for me about midday when we would go training. As I sat on the veranda with a cup of tea, I watched the plane take off and within five minutes, all I could hear was gunfire. I'd never heard this before. I looked about a mile down the road towards the airport and saw a couple of Israeli helicopters firing down into Beirut and the Lebanese army shooting up at them. The Israelis knew the army didn't have enough fire power to hit them so they just hovered there. And that went on for a week!

Even though most of the real fighting was taking place on the Lebanon-Israel border, the Israelis seemed determined to make their presence felt in other parts of the country too. One Saturday, after I'd been to a game in Beirut, we were told the Israelis were going to shoot at any car on the main road going south to Israel. Because my flat lay off that road, Hussein said I couldn't go back and the federation agreed to put me up in a hotel for the night. The Lebanese Cup Final was being held the next day in Tripoli, north of Beirut, and Hussein was going to pick me up around one o'clock. As I prepared to leave, I could hear gunfire as the bullets ricocheted off the narrow street walls. I peeped out of my hotel window and saw two Israeli helicopters going over the city. They then flew down to the stadium where the game was being played and just hovered above the pitch. They wouldn't let the match start so the cup final was called off.

On one of her visits, Christine wanted to wander around the city by herself so she told Hussein he wasn't needed and left Jordan with me for the day. She walked down the street where John McCarthy had been kidnapped and visited the hotel from where the BBC news reporter, Kate Adie, had filed her reports. Although Christine felt perfectly safe on her own, I took Hussein with me wherever I went. He was a former Amal militia gunman in his early thirties who was by my side whenever I wasn't sleeping. He was 90 per cent my translator and driver and 10 per cent my bodyguard. He spoke only broken English but he understood enough of my Welsh accent to get by. He drove too fast and smoked too much but I wouldn't have been without him. I paid Hussein out of my salary and whenever I wanted him, he'd be there. He'd come for a drink or a meal and if anybody touched me, he'd go ballistic – like he did when a guy once took my mobile phone and used it without asking. Another time, I was sitting in a bar when a rugby crowd came in and one of them nudged me in the back. He soon sorted them out.

'He's the coach of Lebanon,' he shouted at them. 'Shut up!'

Hussein was very protective of me and we became firm friends. Because there was no reliable public transport in Beirut, I was totally dependent on him to get around. It was a nightmare. At that time traffic lights were being introduced but most people viewed them as an inconvenience rather than a help. They just drove wherever they wanted to – on the right and on the left. The roads were covered in craters so the main objective was to avoid them – and other cars too! In the West, we look in the mirror, signal and then make a move but in Beirut it was all about honking your horn. The first car I was driven around in blew up and after less than a year, the replacement looked like it had been used in the dodgems!

Apart from the traffic, my other main problem in Beirut was keeping in touch with home. I was allowed five flights back to Britain every year and my letters took seven days to reach Leeds with Christine's replies not arriving for anything up to a month. I tried to ring home as often as possible but it was very frustrating being cut off after about a minute of the call because there were so few phone lines – only 20 per cent of those that had been there before the war were back in working order. In the end, we decided that fax was the best means of communication so I'd use a machine in the Lebanese Football Federation's offices. One Monday, I called in to find a fax from Leeds complaining that my messages were becoming a bit boring!

That evening, Hussein drove me home where I made myself a meal before sitting down to watch the Monday night football programme on Sky. All of a sudden, I felt the room shaking! I couldn't believe what was happening – it was an earthquake! Then I heard a loud bang outside. I rushed to the veranda and saw a man lying in the road. A crowd started to form and another man came out of some nearby flats. Apparently, two Syrians had come round the corner in a car and hit another car. After being stopped by local people, one of the Syrians had got out and shot the man. I then saw the Lebanese man who'd come out from the flats suddenly shoot the Syrian gunman! It was like the Wild West in the Middle East! It certainly made my next message home a little more interesting. From what I remember, it went something like 'Sorry you think my faxes are boring. Hope this livens up your life – I've just had an earthquake and two shootings in one night!'

There was a British community in Beirut but I tended to stay away from most of them. They all stuck together and it got on my nerves a bit. I much preferred to mix with the Arab people and I liked their food – especially their fried fish. I used to watch the Lebanese version of Family Fortunes to improve my Arabic and I loved the contrasts that existed in the country. One day when we were driving to the stadium, we came across a guy with 150 goats in the middle of the road. He was wearing a traditional headdress and it was like stepping back in time – until I saw his mobile phone in one holster and a gun in the other!

When I arrived in Beirut, Lebanese football was in a shambolic state – mainly because of the sectarian divisions. So the main obstacle I had to overcome as coach of the national team was trying to persuade the footballers of such a divided country to identify with their nation rather than with their tribe. The top two teams in Lebanon were Ansar and Nejmeh – fierce local rivals, both Muslim, but from different sects. Almost all the Ansar players were Sunni Muslims while at Nejmeh they were Shia. In my first season, our side to play Egypt contained quite a few players from both clubs and unfortunately, the national team paid the price. They played for their clubs first and Lebanon second so they just wouldn't pass the ball to each other! I soon put a stop to that. Two-thirds of the national team used to come from Ansar, who were supported by the Lebanese Prime Minister and the secretary of the Lebanese Football Federation, but there were only two in my side a year after I took over. I made it clear I would pick the team solely on ability – irrespective of which team they played for and what religion they followed. That was my rule and everyone respected that.

Despite all the different denominations, I couldn't afford to tread too carefully if I wanted to produce a winning team and I found myself indulging in a slightly different form of banter with my players. Jamal Taha, our captain, was a Muslim and he once kept complaining that the other players were fouling him during a practice match. It was obvious he was trying it on.

'Hey!' I said. 'Don't tell me lies. I'm a Christian, You're a Christian. Oops! Sorry. You're not are you?'

He knew what I meant. I could joke about religion but only up to a point. When I threatened to crucify the team if they didn't work harder, I got some funny looks.

During the civil war, players had refused to cross the green line that divided the Christian east of the city and the Muslim west. Teams like Racing Club, Sagesse, Homentmen and Homenmen played in the east with Safa, Ansar and Nejmeh playing in the west. It was a case of never the twain shall meet so standards inevitably dropped. After the war, all denominations played each other but there was still no tackling when I arrived because of the risk of something kicking off after a bad challenge. The players were worried in case their opponents over-reacted. At the slightest hint of a foul, the referee would blow his whistle and there was no spirit of just getting on with the game and letting it flow.

In my first year, facilities were awful. No ground had proper changing rooms and 14 First Division teams shared only four grass pitches. As no games were ever postponed, they turned into mud flats with pitch markings in the winter so we had to play on sand. When it was really wet, big puddles would form while in the summer, the sun was so hot that it baked the sand so hard that passing became very difficult. While I was there, a 65,000 all-seater stadium was built in the Armenian quarter of Beirut but I was always pressing for somewhere less palatial where enthusiastic kids could play. Sometimes, a group of players would turn up at one stadium just as another group were arriving at a stadium on the other side of the city and we'd have to wait for an hour before we could start training.

Communication with the players wasn't easy at first but most of them spoke a little English and I learned a few essential words of Arabic – like 'how are you?', 'straight on' and 'fuck off.' The official team interpreter, Mazzen, was educated in Russia and he spoke English as well as I spoke Arabic. After two days of pestering him to do something, I realised he hadn't understood what I'd asked him to do in the first place. He just wanted to please me and he was too proud to admit he didn't understand. I then had to start drawing everything on a blackboard.

I noticed straightway that, in tandem with the Lebanese Football Federation, the army played a key role in running the game. I watched my first match at Nejmeh in the company of 200 soldiers, two tanks and a very vociferous crowd of about 5,000. During the game, I felt something cold on the back of my neck. It turned out to be a gun with a soldier on the end of it. After I'd asked the person who I was with to ask for it to be moved, the soldier just laughed but then pulled his gun away. But, as I found later, that was par for the course in Beirut and indeed the whole of Lebanon. At every game, there were tanks and soldiers policing the terraces with bayoneted rifles basically because controlling the crowds was the only thing the army had left to do in those days. When someone scored a goal, the supporters went absolutely crazy, trying to climb over the fences. They just loved seeing their side winning – it's all part of the Arab temperament and culture and the Lebanese are a particularly volatile race. There was always the potential of fighting breaking out among supporters either because of disputed line calls, unpopular refereeing decisions and even a photographer kicking a dead ball back into play. If a club's supporters behaved really badly, the team were heavily fined, their ground was closed and they had to play their games at another stadium. Ansar were punished by being forced to move to Tripoli and nobody was allowed inside the ground apart from journalists, Hussein and me – and, of course, the usual complement of soldiers and tanks.

As well as refusing to tolerate hooliganism, the football authorities also cracked down hard on verbal abuse. When one player's friend started bad-mouthing the Lebanese Football Federation from the terraces, the player was suspended. And they were very strict on casual wear. I found out from personal experience because I was once refused entry to their offices in a seventh-floor apartment for wearing shorts. The authorities didn't like Coach – or Mr Terry as they called me – doing things that were part of any manager's daily training routine in Britain. They thought putting balls in bags or laying out cones or moving goalposts was beneath me. I just wanted to get on with things but whenever I became frustrated with my lot, everyone's enthusiasm for the game kept me going. After being abandoned during the civil war, football had only recently been re-introduced and the country was crying out for something to cheer about again.

Despite their rather heavy-handed approach to discipline, the Lebanese Football Federation wasn't too hot on rooting out corruption. It was rife in the league with referees favouring the Prime Minister's team, Ansar, by awarding a tactical penalty if they looked like losing. After watching just a handful of games, I wasn't surprised to hear that Ansar had been champions for the last eight years. Linesmen gave wrong decisions and referees sent off players for nothing. After two decisions by the ref, you knew who was going to win a match. It was a different world to anything I'd known before. At Christmas in 1995, I was told just after the start of a game that a club near the bottom of the league was going to beat another at the top 3-1. And they did. The bigger club owed the struggling one a favour. But I had to rise above all that and concentrate on knocking the national team into shape by picking the best players available to me.

The match-fixing scandal came to a head in 2001 after an official inquiry led to Tadamon Sur being stripped of the league title and being replaced as champions by Nejmeh. The results of games played by seven teams were annulled because of alleged irregularities and those teams were relegated. The incident led to trouble on the streets of Beirut with Tadamon supporters threatening the life of the Lebanese Football Federation's general secretary, Rahif Alameh. So the Lebanese Government stepped in, dissolved the federation and removed Alameh. FIFA objected to such government interference and suspended Lebanon until new elections were held and Alameh was voted out after 16 years in the job. Ansar turned out to have won the head-to-head table among the five teams not involved in the match-rigging but, in the end, the whole 2000-01 season was declared null and void – there were no champions and no teams were relegated.

The corruption wasn't confined just to Lebanon. From what I could see, it was going on all over the place. We'd been drawn in a three-team Asian Cup qualifying group with Kuwait and Turkmenistan, a former Soviet republic that lies between Iran and Kazakhstan. I decided to go and see them play each other in Kuwait City and about two o'clock on the day of the game, I went for a meal. Quite by chance, I found myself in the same restaurant as the Turkmenistan party. It was a five o'clock kick-off but they were still eating at three o'clock! They had one corner in the whole game and were beaten 2-0. The next day, I was sitting outside my hotel having a coffee when their coach rolled up. All the players got off carrying televisions, radios and other electrical equipment – I don't know for sure but it looked very much like they'd been bribed. Six months later in the summer of 1996, having already beaten Turkmenistan 3-1 in Beirut, we travelled to Ashkhabad for the return match which we won 1-0. During that trip, I found out that a third of the population lived below the poverty line so perhaps the gifts in Kuwait weren't totally surprising.

In my first game as coach, we beat Jordan 3-1 in the late summer of 1995 and we then picked up wins over countries like Slovakia (2-1) Cyprus (1-0) and Ecuador (1-0) as we only lost once in 10 games. When everything was going well, I could do no wrong. Slovakia were then ranked midway between England and Wales in the FIFA world rankings and supporters were hanging off telegraph poles and standing on roofs to watch the game. The next day, one of the papers carried a cartoon of me – not a very flattering one I might add – with the caption 'Come on! who's next then?' But when our hopes of reaching the finals of the Asian Cup were dashed by a shattering defeat by Kuwait in Beirut in the game after our win in Turkmenistan, I experienced the down side to being Lebanon's football coach.

In front of 22,000 spectators – our biggest crowd since I'd taken over – we'd started well by going 2-0 up after 10 minutes. But Kuwait hit back to lead 3-2 at the break and although we equalised straight after half-time, they scored twice in the last quarter of the game to win 5-3. Hussein dropped me off at home and I rang him the next day to ask for a lift to a fantastic delicatessen in Beirut. Usually whenever I walked into the place, all the young assistants in their sparkling white coats would come rushing over to ask me what I wanted. They'd then run about collecting my food and putting it in my trolley.

'Coach,' said Hussein, when he came to pick me up. 'I don't think we should go in today.'

'But I need some food,' I replied. 'I've got to go in.'

He shrugged his shoulders and off we went. As soon as I walked into the delicatessen, all backs were immediately turned. Nobody would do anything for me and they started calling me a male prostitute in Arabic – not too loudly but just enough for me to hear. They would normally carry my shopping bags to the car and I'd slip them a tip but not this day. I was Terry No Mates. One of the lads had just helped someone else with their bags and was coming back into the shop as I went out. Just as we were about to pass each other, he spat on the floor. Hussein and I just looked at each other. He'd been right to warn me about going. I tried to laugh it off because if I hadn't they would have slaughtered me. The Lebanese were very free with the stick when they handed it out.

We drew 0-0 in Kuwait City a fortnight later so we were out of the Asian Cup but my contract was extended because the team had made good progress. While we continued to play friendlies – beating Georgia twice, drawing with New Zealand but losing to Bahrain and Oman – our main focus was the 1998 World Cup in France. Again, we found ourselves in a qualifying group with Kuwait. Although we drew 1-1 at home with Singapore before beating them 3-1 away, two defeats by Kuwait (2-0 and 3-1) meant we'd missed out again. But in the other competition we entered, the Pan-Arab Games, we went all the way to the semi-finals. After a 1-1 draw against Jordan in front of 65,000 supporters in the new Beirut International Stadium, we drew by the same score with Oman in our old Municipality Stadium where we then beat Libya 2-1 by scoring two goals in the last 10 minutes. In the semi-finals at the new stadium five days later, we faced Syria in front of another full house.

After falling behind, we were leading 2-1 with 10 minutes to go before Syria equalised through an own goal six minutes from the end. It was still 2-2 at the end of extra-time so it went to golden goals. We hit the bar, Syria scored in the 100th minute and we were out. We gained some consolation by beating our World Cup and Asian Cup conquerors, Kuwait, 3-1 in the third place play-off game but the crowd in the new stadium told its own story. Only 20,000 supporters turned up and I sensed it was time for me to pack my bags. I felt I'd done everything I could and I was missing my family in Britain. I went to see the Lebanese Football Federation's secretary, Rahif Alameh.

'I think it's time for a fresh coach to come in here,' I said.

'Mr Terry,' he replied, 'You're very honest and I think you're right.'

They owed me two months wages and 15,000 dollars in bonuses which they paid me in full the next morning. I booked a flight home and on the night before I left, they threw a farewell party for me, Hussein and all my coaches. It was a wonderful gesture, they gave me some lovely presents and a much-appreciated vote of thanks from the top man.

'If we didn't like you and you hadn't been respectable and honest,' Rahif said, 'you'd have got nothing'.

By that he meant, no money, no party and no presents. Apparently, all the last coach was given when he left was a plane ticket.

Overall, I was pretty pleased with my record of 21 wins and 13 draws in 47 games. I took Lebanon from 145th to 87th in the FIFA world rankings and I felt I'd laid the foundations for some talented players to come through after I'd left. Some of the players from the Armenian quarter of Beirut were excellent footballers and I was pleased to have pointed them in the right direction. It was sad to see that as we made our way up, Lebanon passed Wales on their way down – they'd gone from an all-time high of 27th to 98th in just four years. I know the FIFA rankings aren't necessarily a true reflection of a country's strength – they depend to some extent on your geographical position in the world – but, at the same time, you have to win games. Just after I went to Lebanon, Bobby Gould replaced Mike Smith as Welsh manager and began with a 1-0 win over Moldova at Cardiff Arms Park but then won only one of his next six games – a 6-0 hammering of San Marino in Cardiff. He showed he was prepared to experiment and left out Ian Rush, Mark Hughes and Neville Southall for various reasons during his time in charge. But it was hard to take the two defeats by Holland (3-1 and 7-1) in the 1998 World Cup qualifiers which I watched on television in Beirut. I didn't know whether the decline in Welsh football was down to tactics or team selection because I didn't see Bobby working with the squad at close hand. I was on the outside listening to the players and other people talking about the situation. From what I heard, it sounded farcical and I just couldn't believe some of the stories – like the bizarre teams Bobby picked and the time he changed the captain from Gary Speed to Mark Hughes and back to Gary Speed all within one training session.

I'm pleased that things improved so much under 'Sparky'. To go from being a player to a reasonably successful international coach takes some doing but I'm not surprised Mark achieved it because he was always a thinker when I was in charge. Like everyone else in Wales, I was very disappointed that we missed out on Euro 2004. It's all very well being wise after the event but I have to say I would have played Robert Earnshaw in the second play-off tie against Russia. He should have been included alongside John Hartson instead of one of the five players strung across midfield – probably West Brom's Andy Johnson – and I said so publicly the day before the game. The kid's international record was superb and pure pace is a wonderful thing. It was a one-off game – like a Cup Final – and we were at home. I felt we should have kept something up our sleeves to surprise the Russians. Earnie was our secret weapon but I'm afraid he wasn't used properly. Although it was very frustrating, I still think real progress was made under Mark. It was inevitable he would take the Blackburn job when

The Yorath family...Gabby, Daniel, Jordan and Christine – Louise was away on a modelling assignment

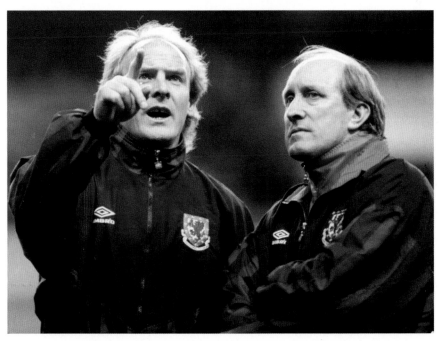

My Welsh right-hand man...Llanelli-born Peter Shreeves

The Welsh wonderkid weaving his way
through the Cypriot defence
as USA '94 beckons

Well done, Giggsy...after Ryan scored
on his full debut against
Belgium in 1993

Fall from grace...after tasting FA Cup glory with Manchester United,
Alan Davies couldn't cope with life in Swansea's reserves

Dear Daniel...my son and my best mate

If only...the penalty miss against Romania at Cardiff Arms Park set the ball rolling

A big hug for Big Nev as our
World Cup dream disappeared

At loggerheads with Alun Evans over
my contract negotiations

The Welsh FA showed me the door...

...and John Toshack and Mike Smith took my place

Bombed-out Beirut...the perfect place to rebuild my career

Peter Jackson cracks open the bubbly
as we keep Huddersfield up...

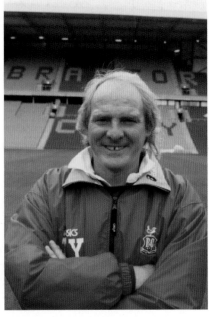

...and I then help Bradford to stay
in the Premiership

Lee Fowler scores the winning penalty on his home patch
in the play-off final against Mansfield...

...and the Terriers begin to party – from administration
to promotion in just over a year!

A proud father and his three children...
Gabby, Louise and Jordan

Graeme Souness moved to Newcastle in September 2004 – especially after the disappointing results against Azerbaijan and Northern Ireland in the first two World Cup qualifiers. Sparky probably thought he'd taken the team as far as he could and the chance to manage a big Premiership club was too good to turn down.

Back in the summer of 1997, as Wales continued on their downward spiral, I returned to Britain with very fond memories of my two years in Lebanon. I had enjoyed both the job and the people. I'd become used to their explosive temperament and I think, through football, I'd played my part in helping to rebuild Lebanese national identity. I identified with the people because, like them, I had experienced tragedy – not on the scale of a war but through the Bradford fire and Daniel's death. They never spoke about what happened to them as a result of the conflict or how Lebanon needed to free itself from Syrian control and Israeli occupation. It was the same when they saw a picture of Daniel. They'd ask Hussein who he was.

'That's Coach's son,' he'd say. 'He died.'

And that would be it. Nothing else. They wouldn't say sorry to me even though I wanted them to open up. Perhaps it would have been better for both of us if they had. Certainly, I felt more capable of coping with Daniel's death when I came back from Lebanon than I had done before I left for the Middle East. My experience there helped me become more patient and I was able to put football into perspective. I realised the game wasn't the be-all and end-all. I learnt that doing my best didn't necessarily mean having to go to war with my employers, colleagues or players. I didn't have to be rude to people or scream and shout at them. And it also made me realise that what I had wasn't so bad after all.

At the same time, the greatest thing to come out of my time in Lebanon was that I rediscovered my passion for football by returning to coaching. By working with players from the national side down to the Under-16s, I'd realised that coaching, rather than managing, was what I did best – and what I wanted to do in the future. I felt rejuvenated, refreshed and my batteries had been well and truly re-charged. My confidence and self-esteem had returned and I was ready for action. Now it was just a case of finding someone who was prepared to give me a job back in the English game.

Trouble at t'Mill

In football, you live and die by results. It's a fact of life that every manager must learn to accept. You know on the day you take over at a club that it's almost certain you'll end up being handed your P45 and I'm afraid that's what happened to Brian Horton at Huddersfield on 6th October 1997. Four points from nine League games wasn't considered good enough by the board so they fired him and I found myself back in the English game as assistant manager to Peter Jackson at the McAlpine Stadium.

When I'd come home from Beirut for a few days in June, I'd told Christine that I'd be back permanently later in the year but I had no job to go to or even one in mind. When you're not actually in the game, you always worry that you won't be able to find a way back in. You can often be forgotten and there are always other managers making names for themselves. On my return to England, as the 1997-98 season got underway, I went to watch a few of Huddersfield's games because their stadium is only 20 miles away from Leeds. Then my old managerial partner at Bradford, Trevor Cherry, who was associate director at Huddersfield, rang to tell me about the board's concern at the team's poor results. Would I be interested in taking the manager's job because they were thinking of pairing me with Peter Jackson? Peter had been our captain at Bradford and he was a former Huddersfield defender. He was then playing for Halifax in the GM Vauxhall Conference and had never managed before. I told Trevor I'd like to be involved but not as manager. I then met Peter at a 2-0 home defeat by Nottingham Forest on a Friday night and I went to the chairman's house for my interview with the board and the secretary, Alan

Sykes, on the Sunday. They said they understood that I didn't really want the number one job.

'That's quite correct,' I replied.

'Why?'

'Because people like you would lie to me.'

They looked at me in amazement. But it was how I felt. I didn't want to be the manager because of everything that went with it – negotiating contracts, wheeling and dealing for new players on the phone all day. After my experience in Lebanon, I just wanted to coach. I didn't want to end up fighting the board so I told them I'd be quite happy to be Peter's number two. I then hopped in my car and drove off to do some coaching at Rochdale. As I went along the M62, I started thinking about the salary they'd offered me. It was really derisory so I rang them up and said I didn't want the job. Almost immediately, the vice-chairman, Geoff Headey, was on the phone wanting to know what the problem was. After I'd explained the situation, he rang me back in the evening with an improved offer and Peter Jackson, instead of landing the youth-team job that he'd applied for, was appointed the new manager with me as his first-team coach. We began work on 8th October with the sole aim of keeping the club up.

The Terriers may have been bottom of the First Division, now the Championship, but I knew they were a club with a fantastic tradition. Rugby League had been born in the town and the round-ball game had struggled to gain a foothold until after the First World War when the club reached the FA Cup Final for the first time. In the 1920s, they'd come under the revolutionary influence of Herbert Chapman whose strict disciplinary regime helped turn the club around. Players weren't allowed to smoke and they could drink only a glass of sherry at bedtime to help them sleep. On match day, Chapman would give them a glycerine tablet and a pat on the back as they ran out on to the pitch. They never looked back. Huddersfield won the FA Cup in 1922 and three successive League championships although Chapman had left for Arsenal by the third one in 1926. They were League runners-up in 1927, 1928 and 1934 and losing FA Cup finalists in 1928, 1930 and 1939 – a sort of forerunner of the Leeds team of the 1960s and 1970s! I knew that when the legendary Bill Shankly had managed the club, he'd given one of the greatest British goalscorers, Denis Law, his

League debut on Christmas Eve 1956. In fact, at 16 years and 303 days, Denis still remains Huddersfield's youngest League player. When I was on the fringes of the first team at Leeds, there was huge interest generated by the four local derbies we had against Huddersfield during their two-year spell in the old First Division, now the Premiership, after being promoted as champions under manager Ian Greaves in 1970. I was also aware that Huddersfield had experienced life in the Football League's lowest division but Peter and I were determined that the club wouldn't be relegated at the end of the 1997-98 season.

When we were arrived in early October, we were odds-on favourites for relegation. The place was in turmoil. I don't want to criticise everything that had gone on before but the players were really down – they wouldn't even look at us when we called them into the office for a chat. Even the physio, John Dickens, who was a highly qualified and very intelligent man, was nearly in tears when we spoke to him. In their words, the players had been hammered. They'd been told they were bad and the more results went against them, the more they'd been told it. Like all footballers, they had made mistakes – the team wouldn't have been in such a desperate position if they hadn't – so we had to cut down on those mistakes and sweeten up the players – a little like trainers have to do with racehorses. We spent the first month rebuilding confidence. We worked very hard on getting the players to smile again and enjoy their training.

I wasn't worried by Huddersfield's position in the table because if you've got belief in your ability, you just get on with the job but we hadn't realised how little depth there was in the squad. The 30 professionals were all much of a muchness and we could have played the first team against the reserves and not known which was which. What we did know was that we had to bring in new players – perhaps four or five in a first-team squad of about 15 or 16.

We began with a hat-trick of defeats before picking up our first point in a 1-1 draw with Portsmouth at the McAlpine Stadium. Our gates had dropped from just over 14,000 for a Yorkshire derby against Sheffield United to just under 9,000 but they started to pick up as we beat Stoke 3-1 at the beginning of November for our first win of the season.

As we set about trying to strengthen the squad, we found ourselves in a bit of a corner. We were still bottom of the table and other clubs, their players and their agents all knew we were looking for new blood so they'd throw all kinds of things at us – like special payments if this or that player helped to keep us up. All this was new to me after being out of the English game for a couple of years so it proved a real eye-opener. At that time, players more or less got what they asked for in terms of wages and if you couldn't pay it, then some other club would. That said, by using our contacts, we managed to bring in midfielders Lee Richardson for £65,000 from Oldham and my former Welsh captain, Barry Horne, on a free transfer from Birmingham. Three quarters of our £800,000 transfer budget went on buying Wayne Allison from Swindon in the middle of November and then another former Welsh international, Dave Phillips, arrived from Nottingham Forest. When we recruited Neville Southall as a goalkeeping coach, I was sent a very sarcastic letter saying there were so many Welshmen in the side that the river running alongside the stadium was going to be re-named the River Taff! Barry and Dave were great influences and all the new players contributed to us gradually climbing the table to safety. Barry was a good leader and big Wayne was terrific – a centre-forward who shook up opposition defenders and chipped in with six goals in 27 appearances behind Paul Dalton with 13 goals and Marcus Stewart who scored 15 times in 41 appearances. Wayne scored the winner when we beat Stockport in early February to go 18th in the table. He got another goal in a 3-0 win over Tranmere as we moved to 17th and another one as we beat Crewe in early April and rose to the dizzy heights of 14th. Three defeats and a win in our last four games meant that we finished 16th after nearly 16,000 supporters had watched us lose 4-0 to Port Vale in our last game of the season! Even though I say it myself, it was a mammoth achievement to keep the club up.

I was particularly proud of my part in the revival because I felt my management career was now back on track. I'd proved myself in English football again and I was very pleased to have helped a club with so much history stay up. OK, Huddersfield weren't back in the top flight but at least they hadn't dropped into the bottom half of the Football League. The move from Leeds Road to the McAlpine

Stadium in 1994 had gone pretty well with the club sharing the ground with Huddersfield's rugby league side and Peter and I had proved a winning combination. I was quite happy to play second fiddle to Peter. I didn't mind him picking the team. As first-team coach, my job was to make sure the players who Peter picked could play the game to the required standard. From the start, I'd told him he must do things his way and during our first season, he'd done a couple of things that maybe I wouldn't have done but he had to stand on his own two feet. By keeping Huddersfield in the First Division, he'd shown that he was one of the brightest young managers around.

At the end of the season, the board were very honest with us. They said they didn't have any more money to put into the club so we knew we would have to make do and mend. After losing two of our first three games, we settled down by winning five of the next six and going top after a 2-1 win over Wolves at the McAlpine Stadium in mid September as Marcus, Paul and Wayne carried on knocking in the goals. During our month at the top of the table, a millionaire businessman, Barry Rubery, who had made his money in digital TV set-top box technology, became interested in taking over the club. While negotiations were going on, his people asked us how much it would take to get Huddersfield into the Premiership. We said about £3 million, they went away and we didn't hear from them again until we were sixth in the table in early December. Barry didn't actually take over control of the club until late January when we'd slipped to 10th and by then it was too late.

I got on OK with Barry but I noticed he was one for testing out people. After a 2-1 midweek home defeat by Swindon, I was about to drive down to Cardiff to see my father who was very ill at the time. As soon as the final whistle went, I felt a hand on my shoulder – it was Barry. Would I like the use of his private jet to go down to South Wales? It was a nice gesture but I declined because I would need my car in Cardiff. After the game, when I was taking the warm-down with the players, Peter came over.

'Barry's just offered me his jet to fly down to the South of France for a few days,' he said. 'I can spend a few days on his yacht.'

'Don't you think that's a test?' I asked Peter.

'No. It'll be alright!'

206

'Peter...remember, we've just been beaten.'

Despite my words of advice, Peter decided to go and while he was away, Barry told me they were thinking of changing the manager but they wanted me to stay.

'Peter is a very popular figure in Huddersfield,' I warned him. 'I think you'd be making a big mistake if you got rid of him.'

He said they had somebody in mind, I mentioned the rumour I'd heard that it was Steve Bruce, then at Sheffield United. Barry looked at me and half smiled.

'If you get Steve Bruce,' I said, 'he'll bring John Deehan with him as his coach and he won't want me.'

'We'll make sure he does,' insisted Barry.

'It sounds to me that you're going to sack Peter,' I said, 'But I've got to tell you I'm his man – he brought me here.'

The defeat by Swindon left us ninth and we only won once in our last five games to finish a respectable but disappointing 10th. At the end of the season, Ian Ayre, who'd been brought in as chairman by Barry, held a review meeting. We talked about things like new facilities and a new coach – not to replace me but to drive the players from the McAlpine Stadium to the training ground! – and when we went back to our office, Peter said he was going to ask the board about his contract. Again, I tried to offer some advice.

'I don't think now is a good time to do it.'

But Peter insisted and up he went to see Ian Ayre – only to return a few moments later in tears.

'I've been sacked,' he said.

After what we'd done at the club, I thought it was a shocking decision. OK, we'd not been able to maintain our position in the table after a good first quarter of the season but we'd made progress after keeping Huddersfield up in very difficult circumstances the previous year. As I've said, results get managers the sack but I felt we were badly treated – our results weren't that bad. Peter was in bits and we all went round to his house to try to comfort him but he was inconsolable. We could tell from his face that he couldn't believe what had happened. The board said they wanted to see me about two weeks after the end of the season but, in the meantime, I had a phone call from the Bradford manager, Paul Jewell, who'd played for me at Valley Parade when I was manager there in the late 1980s. After spending a decade as a player with Bradford, Paul had become first-team coach and then replaced Chris Kamara as manager when he was sacked in 1998. A 3-2 win at Wolves on the last day of the season meant they'd just been promoted to the top division as runners-up in the First Division, now the Championship, and he wanted me to join him as coach. I was very interested because of my connections with Bradford and the chance to be involved with a club in the Premiership.

I met the Huddersfield board at a hotel in Wetherby not far from Leeds and they confirmed that Steve Bruce would be joining as manager after spending only 10 months with Sheffield United. Barry Rubery obviously felt that an equally inexperienced but more high-profile manager would be more successful but it didn't quite work out that way. As I'd predicted when they first broached the subject, Steve would be bringing in his own staff but the board still wanted me to stay. I told them it was impossible.

'Football must be the only game in the world,' said Barry, 'where the owners of the club can't keep the people they want to. Somebody who's employed by us is telling us who he wants to employ.'

I politely explained to Barry that I had to be taken on by the manager and not the chairman – it was the way football worked. To be fair to Huddersfield, they were very good to me and paid me everything I was owed. Being sacked wasn't that much of a shock to me because I could see it coming but Peter was unfortunate – he didn't have a job in football to go to. While he went into the football agents' business, I returned to Bradford for the third time in my career as coach under Paul and his assistant, Chris Hutchings. I think Paul just wanted another senior person there. Even though the training facilities were still the same, the ground had been improved, the whole club had been upgraded and it great being back with the Bantams in the Premier League. My relationship with Paul had always been good even though when we were at Bradford, he'd come to see me to ask why he wasn't in the team.

'Because I don't think you'll score goals in this division.'

The record books show he netted one in every four games while at Wigan and one in every five in nearly 300 games for Bradford. Paul always remembered my remark and threw it in from time to time! The

1999-2000 season turned out to be a terrific year for me and for Bradford. Although I knew all about the First Division, it was the first time I'd been involved since it had been transformed into the Premiership in 1992. The best part of it was seeing all the great players performing at places like Highbury and Old Trafford. What an eye-turner that was! It was wonderful watching people like Patrick Vieira and David Beckham who, first hand, was bigger than I'd imagined. I marvelled at the players' athleticism, how quick and how strong they were. It was amazing season for me but not for Paul I'm afraid.

The root of his problem was his relationship with the chairman, Geoffrey Richmond, who had acquired a controlling interest in the club in 1994. To be fair, the chairman had immediately announced a five-year plan to get Bradford into the Premiership and he'd pulled it off. But then he overreached himself and his dealings in the transfer market – especially by signing the Italian, Benito Carbone, on a £40,000-a-week salary – led, following the collapse of ITV Digital, to the club going into administration in May 2002. The trouble was that Richmond thought having a controlling interest meant he could control everything – including team affairs. Paul is a bubbly, lively character who knows his football, having been brought up in the right school at Liverpool but Richmond tried to dominate him by telling him who he should and shouldn't pick and buy. Richmond made his life a misery by interfering all the time. Paul and I were very close and he'd tell me all about the chairman's shenanigans. Before we were due to meet Manchester United, Paul was given a sheet of A4 with the chairman's thoughts on how we should play against the champions. We were on a mini-roll after beating Watford (3-2) and Arsenal (2-1) in successive games before travelling to West Ham in early February. It was a cracking game and at one stage we were 4-2 up with Jamie Lawrence having scored two goals in four minutes. As usual, Paul would ask 'Hutchy' and myself for our opinions and I made my position pretty clear.

'I think we should throw on another defender now and play with a sweeper.'

'No,' said Paul. 'I'm not going to change it now.'

Unfortunately, we got beaten 5-4 with Frank Lampard scoring the winner seven minutes from time. As he had to after every away game,

Paul phoned the chairman to discuss the team's performance – even though Richmond had been at the game and it could have waited until the Monday. On this particular day, Paul made the fatal mistake of recounting our conversation on the touchline.

'Taff told me to play a sweeper when we were 4-2 up,' I heard him say to Richmond.

The air turned blue as the chairman went ballistic.

'Why do you employ fucking staff,' he cried, 'if you don't fucking listen to them?'

He made that comment to Paul loads of times over the rest of the season. The chairman also thought he was a good judge of a player. In our next game after the West Ham defeat against Aston Villa, Jorge Cadete made the first of seven appearances for the first team. The Portuguese striker, who'd played for Celtic, had pitched up at Valley Parade after negotiations with Benfica involving the chairman but nobody on the coaching staff. So I rang a contact at Celtic and was told that Jorge was a 'box player' who didn't do anything outside the area. We all realised that Bradford were a workingmen's club playing against the Savoy and the Ritz. We'd never be in the same league as Arsenal, Liverpool or Leeds but we always had a solid work ethic. The players all knew they had to bust a gut to survive in the Premiership and they were prepared to roll up their sleeves and get on with it. All of a sudden, the chairman was throwing Jorge Cadete at us! I'm afraid Jorge was a lazy bastard who we just didn't rate. We drew 1-1 with Villa and after he'd been a substitute for the next three games, it was intimated by the chairman that Jorge had to start our home match against Manchester United at the end of March. Richmond was paying him thousands of pounds a week in wages and he was looking for some return on his investment. So we left him on for half an hour and then took him off. The chairman didn't like it but what else could we do? We'd started with Jorge, we felt he he wasn't up to the job so we had to make a change. It was 2-0 at half-time and 4-0 at the end. Jorge was on the bench when we lost 2-0 at Newcastle, then started in a 2-1 defeat by Southampton at Valley Parade before being substituted again and that was the end of him. The penny had dropped and, with six games to go, he was out of the club and on his way back to Portugal.

With just three games left, Paul was feeling very down. We'd spent virtually the whole season in or just outside the bottom three and it was going to be touch and go whether we'd go straight back down. We had beaten Sunderland 1-0 to move up to 18th and we knew the race to stay up was going to go right down to the wire. The chairman had been on at Paul so I suggested that he didn't go training as we prepared for the game at home to Wimbledon. They were one of our relegation rivals and I didn't want the players to see him in such a depressed state. He stayed away but he was still pretty down on the day of the game. As we were getting changed, Paul actually said to me that he wished the season was over – he was that fed up.

Before the game, I was speaking to the Wales striker, John Hartson, in the tunnel and I could see he was really hyped up for such an important match. The Bradford tunnel is very small and as the players were leaving the dressing room, John tried to unsettle Stuart McCall by putting his head right in Stuart's face and giving him a lot of abuse. The referee came out and warned John that he'd send him off before the game if he didn't stop so John cooled down.

There was no score in the match until just before half-time when Peter Beagrie scored with a penalty. Five minutes after the break, we were 2-0 up – thanks to a blatant handball that the officials missed. The ball was crossed in and Peter scored his second. The whole Wimbledon team rushed up to the linesman shouting and swearing – the lot – and the referee picked out John Hartson and sent him off. I always felt that John had too much to offer to get involved in stuff like that but the referee had obviously marked his card. After the fracas in the tunnel, it was pretty obvious that the next time John put a foot wrong, he was going to be sent off and that's what happened. We went on to win 3-0 – with Dean Windass scoring his 10th goal of the season – and we moved up to 17th.

After beating Wimbledon, we then slipped back to 18th after a 3-0 defeat at Leicester so everything rested on our last game of the season against Liverpool at Valley Parade. They needed to win to go into the Champions League and we had to win to stay up. We took an early lead through a David Wetherall header in the 13th minute and, after doing the business at one end, David played his part in a fantastic rearguard action as we hung on for the three points. The scenes at Valley Parade will stay with me forever. As it turned out, a draw would have been good enough because Wimbledon lost 2-0 at Southampton and went down with Sheffield Wednesday and Watford. We finished three points clear of the Dons who had joined the Football League on the same day 23 years earlier. Remarkably, when the fixtures for the season had come out, Paul said to me before a ball had been kicked that he'd be delighted if we needed to beat Liverpool to stay up. He had his wish and we rounded off a very good season by defying the odds – and all the pundits who thought we'd go straight back down.

Unfortunately, that was as good as it got at Valley Parade. Paul had been unhappy for a while and the following Tuesday, the chairman rang him and said he wanted to take him out to lunch. I could hear Paul making excuses – like he'd only got his tracksuit on – because he really didn't want to be in Richmond's company but, in the end, he said he had to go.

'Just be careful,' I replied.

When he came back, Paul told me what had happened. He was just on the second mouthful of his main course when the chairman came out with the immortal phrase:

'Paul...I think you've had a bad season.'

This was just after we'd managed to keep Bradford in the Premier League! It was a miracle that we were there in the first place and we'd performed another miracle in staying up! That was the final nail in the coffin for Paul – he'd had enough. We both went off on holiday and when Paul came back, he handed in his resignation. Richmond refused to accept it but Paul was determined to escape his clutches and he signed a three-year contract to manage Sheffield Wednesday towards the end of June. They'd seen how he'd helped Bradford reach the Premiership and then stay there for a season and they saw him as the man to lead them back to the big time at the first attempt. Chris Hutchings was given Paul's job at Valley Parade straightaway and Stuart McCall was made assistant manager/coach. I was lying on a beach in Spain when Hutchy rang to tell me the news. I asked about my position and he said I was staying where I was but the chairman wouldn't give me a pay rise. I thought about it for a bit and then Paul rang to tell me he'd was moving to Hillsborough. Would I like to join him? I went to see Richmond when I came back and told him I'd had enough and I wanted to resign.

'But you still got a year left on your contract,' was his reply.

He then became very obstructive, knowing that, having been brought to Bradford by Paul, I was his man and would probably be going with him to Sheffield. We then discussed why I hadn't been promoted to assistant manager.

'Having coached the Welsh national team,' I said, 'I think it's a bit of a snub when you appoint a player to be assistant manager above me.'

In the end, I agreed not to speak about what had been happening at Valley Parade as long as Richmond let me go. As it turned out, Chris Hutchings only lasted 12 games before being sacked, Bradford were relegated at the end of the season and a year later they went into administration. At least, Richmond had the decency to admit his mistakes – 'I will never ever forgive myself for spending the money we did' – but to be fair to him, Bradford and all the other non-Premiership clubs weren't helped by the collapse of ITV Digital in March 2002. Richmond re-surfaced as an adviser to Gerald Krasner, whose consortium eventually took over Leeds to save it from liquidation in March 2004, but a month later the former Bradford chairman was declared bankrupt and severed his connections with Elland Road. His son, David, later resigned as managing director of Leeds.

When I moved to Hillsborough in the summer of 2000, I was delighted to be joining another Yorkshire footballing institution. Wednesday were the fifth oldest League club, they'd won the League title four times, the FA Cup three times and the League Cup a decade earlier. Their ground had staged some memorable FA Cup and World Cup matches over the years. I was disappointed to be leaving the Premiership but I was working again with two people I knew very well and respected a lot. Paul was the manager and his assistant was Peter Shreeves, my old number two with Wales. Shreevesy had taken over when Danny Wilson was sacked in the previous March as Wednesday started on the slippery slope towards their current position in League One. But he couldn't turn it around in their last nine matches and they were relegated after finishing second from bottom.

One of the first things I noticed was the split in the camp between the British players and the foreign legion. During the 1999 close season, high-profile signings like Gilles De Bilde (PSV Eindhoven) and Gerald Sibon (Ajax) had joined other foreigners like Petter Rudi and Wim Jonk at Hillsborough. Some of them were earning more than £750,000 pounds a year and although they were happy to pick up the money, they didn't seem to care too much about Sheffield Wednesday. The club received a Premiership parachute payment of more than £1 million to soften the blow of relegation but it was a drop in the ocean compared with the money being spent on wages. It was so infuriating to have so many big earners who didn't appear interested in playing for such a big club.

On the first day of training, I became aware of the split in the ranks because the two groups wouldn't talk to each other! All the foreigners – Jonk, Sibon, De Bilde and Rudi – were at the back while the home-grown players like the former England defender, Des Walker and goalkeeper Kevin Pressman were at the front – along with the two Scots, Phil O'Donnell and Simon Donnelly, who'd been signed from Celtic. We couldn't hold a training session and know for sure that it was going to go OK. The British lads didn't like the foreign players because of their poor work ethic. They were the archetypal Fancy Dans. Lots of tricks but little hard work. Because of the bad feeling, we had to knock the two dressing rooms at the training ground into one. The foreigners would change in one and the British-based players in the other and if we hadn't carried out those alterations, they wouldn't have mixed. I'd never come across anything like this in all my time in football.

'We've got the piano players and the piano carriers,' Peter Shreeves once said. 'Unfortunately, we've got too many piano players.'

Everybody knew the club's financial problems were growing all the time and that people being paid an awful lot of money weren't prepared to put their necks on the line.

Gerald Sibon had a certain arrogance about him. He felt he was too good for Sheffield Wednesday yet sometimes he couldn't get into the team. He was so inconsistent – one week he could be brilliant, the next absolutely disastrous so you never knew what you were getting with him. Gilles De Bilde came to the club with a big reputation. He was a Belgian international and had scored a goal in every two games for Anderlecht and PSV. He was told that some big names were going to be joining him and then the Scottish players arrived. He would later

214

tell me that one of the reasons that he couldn't perform was because his team-mates weren't good enough! In November 2000, I was sitting in the office when the Aston Villa manager, John Gregory, rang to ask about De Bilde. He wanted to take him on a month's loan. Paul couldn't believe it but we were delighted to get him off the pay roll. De Bilde went down to Villa Park and then John rang again. He wanted to take him for three months! It was party time at Hillsborough and Paul asked John why he'd extended the loan. Apparently, De Bilde had said he needed a month to get himself right – physically and mentally. That gives you an insight into the type of people – and, more importantly, their temperaments – who we were having to deal with. For the record, De Bilde played four games for Villa without scoring before returning to us. While he was at Sheffield Wednesday, the mollycoddling even extended to his two dogs. It was written into his contract that the club would pay for the animals to be put into quarantine when he came over. The situation was so out of control that one of the foreigners was paid £5,000 appearance money – even if he didn't play! If the manager dropped him, then he would-n't get the bonus. He made two appearances before injury put him out for the rest of the season but every time the team played, he picked up the £5,000 – on top of his astronomical wages. It was far-cical. We used to call it the 'disappearance money.'

A month after De Bilde had returned from his spell in the West Midlands, Paul Jewell was on his way. On the Monday morning after a 4-1 defeat at Wimbledon, he was called into the office and sacked because of poor results. We'd only won once in the last 10 games and we were bottom of the table. Peter was promoted in his place and our relationship worked fine. He was a very good coach but we were dealing with the same group of players. They weren't battle-hardened so we had the same scenario as at Leeds now – we brought in players from lower divisions. They were all we could afford but at least they were prepared to work. A key signing was Trond Soltvedt, a Norwegian who we got on a free transfer from Coventry. He made his debut in the game after the Wimbledon defeat – a 1-0 win over Tranmere – and we made him captain because he was a good pro. He was completely different to the other foreigners. His work ethic was brilliant and his former Coventry team-mate, Carlton Palmer, came back to Hillsborough to play alongside him in midfield from the Tranmere match until the end of the season. We won eight of our last 15 games with everyone pulling in the same direction. Gerald Sibon finished top scorer with 13 goals – including five in seven games – while Gilles De Bilde picked up three in eight starts as we finished 17th in the First Division.

With Peter being handed the manager's job permanently, we were hoping to build on our promising finish when the 2001-02 season got underway. We'd managed to unload a few of our high-earning but low-achieving foreign players like De Bilde and Wim Jonk and there was a good team spirit about the place but it all went wrong – virtually from the off. We only won one of our first 13 games and after a 2-1 home defeat by Preston in the middle of October, Peter decided it was time to go. He said it just wasn't happening and he would be seeing the chairman the next day. I was promoted from assistant manager and my salary was doubled to £180,000. Was I being hypocritical in accepting such a big increase having criticised some of the players for negotiating ridiculously high wages? No. While I accept it was a huge hike, I felt that, unlike them, I would actually be earning my money in trying to keep the team up. I was being paid to deal with the pressure and I had no qualms about accepting such a massive pay rise.

I have to be honest, I didn't really want to be manager but it was there on a plate for me and I accepted the chance to run a big club with a great crowd and ground but very poor finances. The money troubles were a millstone around everybody's neck and they meant I couldn't bring in too many new players. As is often the case, a change of manager produces an improvement in results – and we won three of our next four games but then struggled all season. Gerald Sibon was again top scorer in the League with the Nigerian striker, Efan Ekoku, finishing second with seven goals and scoring another five as we reached the semi-finals of the Worthington Cup only to be beaten 6-3 on aggregate by Blackburn. The signing of Shefki Kuqi from Stockport in the middle of January proved decisive. He'd been born in Kosovo, capped by Albania and Finland and at 6ft 2in was a real handful. He scored six goals in 17 games including the equaliser in a 2-2 draw with Wolves on the last day of the season at Hillsborough that confirmed we'd be staying up by a point.

Once again, the 2002-03 season promised much but we made another bad start. I had high hopes of Lloyd Owusu who we'd signed from Brentford in the summer. He had a strike record of about one goal in every three games but he was missing through injury for our first five matches – none of which we won. Our first victory was well worth waiting for though because we beat Sheffield United 2-0 at Hillsborough! Lloyd came off the bench to score with his first touch in an Owls shirt and Shefki sealed the result with his third goal of the season. I have a saying that strikers get you the sack. They miss chances, their heads go down and they lose confidence. The more chances they miss, the more pressure it puts on defenders. Shefki, now at Ipswich, scored in our next game – a 2-2 draw with Preston – but then his goals dried up until early December. Lloyd had a different problem. In his first few games, he kept collapsing. He would fall to the ground and throw up. I'd seen players be sick in the dressing room before a game but never on the pitch. Nobody could explain to me why it was but I think it was nerves. Lloyd couldn't cope with being at such a high-profile club like Sheffield Wednesday. And neither could Leon Knight. He'd been a big success at Huddersfield and later scored the winning penalty for Brighton in the Second Division play-off final in May 2004 but he couldn't hack it either. Maybe it was the big crowds or the aura of the place, the ground itself – again this stage-fright was something I'd never come across before. The worst case was John Beswetherick, a lad we'd bought from Plymouth in the summer of 2002. He was a left-back who I'd had great reports about and he'd made more than 150 appearances in five seasons at Home Park. He had a good left foot on him but he just couldn't play at Hillsborough. Sheffield Wednesday the club was miles too big for John. Martin Hodge, our goalkeeping coach, was part of the three-man coaching team, along with my assistant, Willie Donachie.

'I don't think he'll be able to cope with Sheffield, the club or the city' said Martin soon after John arrived. 'He's a small-town boy.'

And Martin was right. It was pretty obvious from day one when John was playing pre-season friendlies at Hillsborough in front of 8,000 people that he just couldn't cope with it. We wanted to try and help and, in the end, we suggested that he went to see the club doctor. It was all down to nerves – he just couldn't handle it. He played in our first four games of the season but was taken off in the last two of them and only featured twice again before going on loan to Swindon. Lloyd only managed four goals in 32 League appearances including 20 as a substitute while Leon hit three in 24 games – coming off the bench in 10 of them. Gerald Sibon wasn't the force he'd been – finding the net only six times in 25 League appearances – so we struggled to score.

After we'd lost 3-1 at home to Burnley in early October, I was given a month to turn things around and save my job. I'd already told Martin and Willie to keep their eyes peeled when we went up to the board-room after the game. If there were no women around, the board would be wanting to talk to me about the job and those two had better make themselves scarce. That was the sign to look out for. Sure enough, when we got upstairs, there were no women there so the lads left. The board said things weren't going right but they'd give me four games to sort it out. I felt that was fair enough and I'd been in football a long time to see the signs. We lost 2-1 at Ipswich, beat Bradford 2-1 at Hillsborough and then lost to Watford away and Millwall at home both by 1-0. Five minutes before the end of the Millwall game with defeat staring us in the face, I felt a tap on my shoulder. I turned round to find this woman looking at me.

'Yes?'

'Terry,' she said, 'You're a lovely man but please do the best thing for Sheffield Wednesday and resign.'

Her words haunted me through the night and I decided that she was right. I was quite happy to let someone else have a go in the hope that they could do better. So on 31st October 2002 I resigned. The chairman, Geoff Hulley, was very good about it and he said my contract would be paid up which it was. I found out later that they'd been sounding out other people in the game to replace me but I was happy with the way I was treated. It was significant in that it was the first time I'd ever resigned because I felt I couldn't do any more. I respected the club so much that I had to do what was right – even thought it meant I was out of a job. My decision also made it a bit easier for the board. Most of the directors were nice people especially Geoff.

I must admit I was relieved to be out of it because the pressure of managing a club like Sheffield Wednesday nearly did me in. I felt totally responsible for everything – I was picking the team, sorting out the tactics and the coaching and when the team lost, it was down me as the manager. By the end of the week, my back was as hard as a board. The pressure would start as soon as training finished on a Friday. I had to do a weekly press conference and then there was the game the next day – sometimes it was a relief to play away from home. I'd never experienced this sort of pressure before. I seriously questioned whether I was cut out for the job and I now think it will be my last shot at being a manager.

I was replaced by the former Hartlepool manager and Wednesday keeper, Chris Turner. I didn't envy him at all. The club were £23 million in debt and just one place off the bottom of the table. He had to wait eight games for his first victory and despite winning four of the last six League matches, Chris couldn't keep Wednesday up. They finished 22nd – four points adrift of safety – and would be playing in the third tier of English football for the first time in 20 years. Sure, I felt partly responsible for their going down but not half as much as the board should have. The spectacular decline of Sheffield Wednesday as they've slipped from the Premiership to what is now League One in just three seasons is down to the club's directors. Just 10 years ago, the Owls finished seventh in the Premiership and runners-up in both the FA Cup and League Cup in the same season. The directors have been living in never-never land for far too long and mismanagement from the top level right the way down lies behind the sorry state of affairs at Hillsborough. The directors allowed managers to buy players who weren't up to it, handed them fantastic wages and Sheffield Wednesday are now paying the price. I must admit I wasn't surprised when Chris Turner was sacked in September 2004 after a 1-0 home defeat by Bournemouth left the team 14th in the table. Incredibly, his replacement, Paul Sturrock, is Wednesday's 10th manager in nine years.

After leaving Wednesday, I decided to enjoy myself. I spent quite a bit of time in our apartment in Spain, played some golf and went to the races a lot. For the first time in my career, I didn't think about football too much or where my next job was coming from. It was good to chill out for a while after spending such a frustrating time at Sheffield Wednesday but after a very relaxing break, I was ready to return to the game. They say you should never go back – and I'd shown the wisdom of that advice by suffering bad experiences at Swansea and Bradford in the 1980s – but this time it was different. When Peter Jackson rang me to ask if we could re-create the successful management team that had kept Huddersfield up in 1999, I couldn't resist. Mind you, until we actually began work at the McAlpine Stadium in June 2003, I had no idea what I was letting myself in for second time around.

The Terriers Bite Back

The only way was up. I suppose that's the best way to describe the situation when Peter and I returned to the McAlpine Stadium in June 2003 – four years after taking Huddersfield to 10th in the First Division, now the Championship. An awful lot had happened since the board had broken Jacko's heart by sacking him and their callous decision had backfired pretty spectacularly. The Terriers were down on their uppers and in danger of losing their fight for survival.

Four other managers had been and gone since we left; the club had just been forced into administration and, worst of all from a footballing point of view, they'd fallen into the lowest tier of the Football League. For the second time in three seasons, they'd been relegated and they were now staring into a pretty deep black hole – both on and off the pitch.

When Steve Bruce replaced Peter in the summer of 1999, he'd been given a transfer budget beyond his wildest dreams by owner Barry Rubery who was desperate to bring top-flight football back to Huddersfield for the first time for 28 years. The manager spent £3 million on new players but the club finished 8th, missing out on the play-offs by a couple of points after winning only two of their last seven games. Then, after losing seven of his first 11 League games in the 2000-01 season and with Huddersfield lying second from bottom, Steve Bruce was sacked. He was replaced by the former Swindon manager, Lou Macari, who recruited my old Leeds team-mate, Joe Jordan, as his assistant but they couldn't recover from such a disastrous start and the club were relegated in May 2001. After losing to Brentford in the semi-finals of the play-offs in the next season, Lou and Joe were fired and Mick Wadsworth, the former first-team coach at Southampton, took over. He lasted only nine months before being replaced by caretaker Mel Machin, the former Manchester City manager. Having overreached themselves by spending big money to try to get into the Premiership, Huddersfield's financial chickens had come home to roost and the Terriers went into administration in March 2003 owing £20 million to creditors and £1.4 million to players in unpaid wages. Just to rub salt into the wound, they were relegated after finishing 22nd at the end of the next month.

Off the field, a knight in shining armour came galloping to the rescue in the shape of Ken Davy who, after setting up his own photographic studio in the town, began a new career as an independent financial adviser. He founded DBS Management in the 1980s and the firm floated on the stock exchange in 1997, eventually being bought by a computer software group for £75m in 2001. Ken already owned Huddersfield's rugby league team, the Giants, and without him, I'm sure the football club would have gone under. Barry Rubery had sold out to a consortium led by David Taylor, a former director, in January 2002. After Barry had nobly waived his £12.5 million debt, Ken set about negotiating a takeover. He made a key move by appointing Andrew Watson as chief executive, a post he'd previously held at Burnley. After a lot of hard work, the deal was finally agreed only 24 hours before the 2003-04 season began.

By that time, Peter and I were back in tandem at the McAlpine Stadium. During the previous four years, we'd kept in touch as he worked as a sports agent and a local media pundit and I coached at Bradford and then Sheffield Wednesday. Peter was still watching games, meeting managers and staying involved and in fact, he turned down two or three good jobs because they didn't feel right. When Ken Davy invited him to be manager, Peter had no such reservations. His wife, Alison, told him that if he didn't take the job, he'd regret it for the rest of his life and he knew she was right. Peter asked me to meet him and although I realised money would be tight, I couldn't believe what I was hearing when he told me what was on offer as a salary: £25,000 a year! You don't have to be Gordon Brown to work out there was a bit of a shortfall between that figure and the £180,000 I'd been earning at Wednesday, but because it was Peter, I said I'd take the job. It wasn't so much that I felt there was unfinished business at Huddersfield as having a great affinity for the club. It really is a wonderful place to work and importantly it's run by people who just love their jobs. They're supporters as well as employees so they want to be at every game – whether they're working or not. There's an aura and warmth about the place and it's somewhere where you want to go and work every day. I knew I'd be walking into an environment where I'd be very happy – very poor too but then you can't have everything can you!?

When we took up the reins again, Jacko and I found the club in a bit of a mess. The training ground hadn't been looked after because there'd been no money to put down new grass seed and the whole place was on its knees. Only eight players turned up for pre-season training and we didn't have a physiotherapist until Huddersfield's former goalkeeper, Lee Martin, came on board a week later. We had no sponsors and we were virtually starting from scratch. Some of the players we'd inherited weren't good enough and we knew we needed some new blood if we were to get out of the Third Division. But thanks to the money provided by Ken and his board we were able to use our contacts and, as we had done in 1997, we managed to bring in some experienced old hands, mainly defenders, to form the back-bone of the team.

Ian Hughes, a former Welsh Under-21 cap, came from Blackpool, we brought Robbie Edwards back to the McAlpine from Chesterfield and the Nigerian international, Efe Sodje, joined from Crewe. We were also lucky to sign Steve Yates from Sheffield United while Tony Carss arrived from Oldham to add a touch of class with his lovely left foot in midfield. All these players were great pros and helped the young-sters come through into the team at various stages of the season. Players like Andy Holdsworth, Anthony Lloyd, Phil Senior, David Mirfin, Jonathan Stead, John McAliskey, Nathan Clarke and Jon Worthington were nearly all under 20 and had graduated from the Huddersfield academy and we also signed Lee Fowler, a 20-year-old Cardiff lad, from Coventry. At the start of the season, the senior players made up the team with Martin Booty, now our coach, at right-back, Robbie Edwards at left-back and Yatsey and Hughesy as central defenders. The youngsters weren't getting a game then, but we started putting them in and they kept surprising us with their temperament by being able to cope with first-team football.

From the opening game when he scored twice in a 2-2 draw with Cambridge at the McAlpine, it was obvious Jonathan Stead was going to be an important player. His nine goals in 15 League games helped us gradually to move up the table and a 2-1 win over Carlisle in late October took us to seventh. Jon was very keen – an absolute dream to work with. Every day after training, he'd ask me if he could stay on and do some more. Everything was about shooting with him – he just loved scoring goals and he would practice for hours trying to improve himself.

But a 6-2 drubbing at Scunthorpe at the beginning of November was the start of a worrying run of six League matches that included only one win – 3-1 at home to Hull. The turning point of our whole season was another away thrashing – 4-0 at Macclesfield in the middle of December. It made us realise that the team weren't as good as we thought. Efe Sodje had a terrible game and we had to start pointing fingers at him as well as one or two other people. Some serious questions were asked of the players because their performance that day lacked pride. Luckily for us, they reacted well and turned it round straightaway. We drew 1-1 at home against Oxford in our next match and then won six on the bounce.

The day after the Oxford game, my personal life changed dramatically. Christine and I separated. It was four days before Christmas. I decided to move into a flat I'd recently bought about three miles away from the family home. We had talked about me going so it didn't just come out of the blue but I don't know why I chose that particular day. I just felt it was the right time for me to leave. What with the girls leaving home, me coaching abroad and Christine becoming more successful in her various activities, we had been moving in different directions for quite a while. I'd felt better about myself since returning from Lebanon and the six years back in English football had done a lot to repair my self-esteem and restore my reputation. But gradually over the years, things had been changing in our marriage. When you're the main breadwinner in a family, you're quite powerful and decisive but it's difficult when the boot's on the other foot. I'd gone from earning a pretty good living as a player and a manager to picking up quite a bit less as a coach – apart from hitting the jackpot during the crazy days at Sheffield Wednesday! All the while, Christine has been making a lot of money by having a few fingers in quite a few pies. As well as being good at interior design, she's become a successful property developer, turning a former city council building in the middle of Leeds into 17 luxury apartments. They're fantastic – one of them sold for a million pounds – and she still runs her original skin care products firm. She employs six full-time staff to help her manage her companies. So the balance of power – in the sense that I've been displaced as the major breadwinner – had shifted immensely.

I could sense and see the way the relationship was changing. What had always seemed important to me began to appear not so important to Christine. Over the last five years, she's only been to one game I've been involved in whereas she would come to every one when I was a player. Things like that don't particularly hurt you at the time but they make you think you're perhaps not very significant anymore. The amount of alcohol I was drinking to dull my feelings about Daniel's death didn't help our relationship either but I wouldn't say I only took refuge in drink after he died. I'd always drunk in the house – normally scotch whiskey with lemonade, never lager but sometimes a bottle of wine too with a meal. Gradually, I developed a serious taste for whiskey and lemonade. I sometimes drank to relieve the pain caused by Daniel's death, to hide my grief and sometimes to blank out parts of my personal life. To everyone else, it may have looked like I was getting on with my job and behaving pretty normally, but privately I was very unhappy. I was drinking more and more to try to cope with my inner demons. I'm not a person who wakes up in the morning and craves a drink or indulges in the afternoon, but I do need a drink to get to sleep.

I honestly think it goes back to my early days as a player with Leeds. When I broke into the first team, we took sleeping tablets the night before a game. We were given something called Mandrax. It was lethal stuff – it's banned now – and it sent me to sleep within 15 minutes. I didn't need it at first but the big stars were using it so I thought I would too. Drink has replaced Mandrax and as the years have gone by, I've drunk more than has been good for me. The split with Christine was in part down to drink but we also had a problem with the way we were living our lives. Other people may want you to live your life like they live theirs but I can't do that. I have to live my own life my own way. To be honest, Christine was doing the same as me – working very hard and spending less and less time at home. Although we would occasionally go out for a meal, we spent very little quality time together. The one thing we had in common was Jordan and while I didn't want to do anything to disrupt his A-level studies, the split between his parents had been coming for a while. After looking at various apartments, I'd bought one off the Harrogate Road in Moor Allerton with a view to moving when I felt ready. I admit the timing wasn't great and Christine didn't want me to go at that particular time but I'm an Aries and once I decide on something, I do it. I thought four days before Christmas or four days after would make little difference. Whatever the timing, it was always going to be hurtful to both of us but I thought it would be for the best. I spent Christmas Eve in my new flat and then called in at Shadwell to give Christine and Jordan their presents the next morning. Louise and Gabby were spending Christmas away and it was obviously a pretty tearful return to the family home. I then drove to Colin Farrer's house on the other side of Leeds to spend Christmas Day with his family. Colin was best man at our wedding and has been an invaluable friend to me.

I had a strange Christmas – the first one without the family for more than 30 years – but the team really enjoyed the festive season. We were back on track after the blip at Macclesfield and three straight wins over Christmas and the New Year took us up to seventh in the table. Peter and I felt that we'd coped with the mini-crisis pretty well mainly because we realised that you have to handle different people in different ways. I suppose you could say that we're 'Mr Nasty' and 'Mr Nice'. Peter bollocks the players and they come to me for a bit of tender, loving care! His way of dealing with Efe Sodje is to give him a bollocking. As soon as that happens, Efe treats me like a sort of father figure, I put my arm around his shoulder and reassure him that we need him as a leader. If I tell Efe something, he knows it's right and he never disputes anything with me.

My relationship with Peter couldn't be better. He handles all the contracts and transfers while I do about 90 per cent of the coaching. We'll discuss beforehand what we're going to do on the training ground and he comes out with me every day. Peter watches what's going on but never too quietly! Never a day goes by without his enthusiasm for the game bubbling to the surface. Sometimes I see the players looking at him as if he's barmy and I admit he's a bit of a one-off. Paul Jewell had that same level of enthusiasm when he was manager at Bradford although he didn't come out with such outrageous remarks. Peter's always telling the players that he's the best-looking manager in English football and although they might disagree, they haven't the courage to tell him. Peter promotes himself very well – to the media and to the players – he's very loud and very much his own man. He's a snappy dresser – he always wears a suit on match days – and the lads think he spends the money from all the fines he imposes on them in training on his hair! If a player does something wrong, Peter says he'll let them off – as long as they bring him in 200 Benson and Hedges cigarettes the next day – and they do!

As a manager, Peter is far stronger now than he was first time around. Then he depended on me a lot more. He keeps making some decisions that I disagree with – and I tell him so – but he's paid to make them. After seeing Jon Worthington play in the reserves, I didn't fancy him but Peter decided to put him in the first team and he did really well. Jon ended up making nearly 40 appearances in the season so I held my hands up to that one – I was wrong. I make various suggestions and most of the time Peter goes along with them. He normally bows to my experience but if he doesn't agree with something, he'll just say no and that will be the end of it.

Our 2-0 win over Boston in the middle of January turned out to be Jon Stead's last game for us. Blackburn had been tracking him for a while and decided to make their move. When their forwards' coach, Dean Saunders, first rang up to ask about Jon, I told him that he'd never work with a better lad. I gave Jon a glowing reference and luckily for me it came off. He easily made the step up to the Premiership by scoring six goals in 13 games to help keep Blackburn up and win himself a place in the England Under-21 team. It wasn't a difficult decision to sell Jon. We thought the £1.2 million deal – involving £800,000 up front and the rest depending on appearances for Blackburn and possibly England – was good business – especially for a club with our financial problems. We had to consider if we would ever be offered that sort of money again because players can break down or they can dry up after a goalscoring spree.

When Jon left, after scoring 18 times in just 31 League and cup appearances, we had to dig deep and look for goals from other areas. We brought in Pawel Abbott, a Polish Under-21 striker from Preston who scored three in his first three games but then hit a barren patch. Danny Schofield, who'd been with us for six years, came through towards the end of the season scoring twice against both Yeovil and Swansea while Andy Booth, 'Mr Huddersfield Town', chipped in with four goals in his last 10 matches. Huddersfield born and bred, 'Boothy' began his career with us before going to Sheffield Wednesday and returning to the McAlpine in the 2000-01 season after a brief loan spell with Spurs. Efe Sodje scored three of his four goals in the last quarter of the season while John McAliskey came good at just the right time. He scored our last goal as a substitute in a 4-0 revenge win over Macclesfield that took us into the third automatic promotion place behind Doncaster and Hull in the middle of March. With Boothy suspended, we gave 'Macca' his first start against Scunthorpe a month later. It was one of the most exciting finishes to a game I've ever been involved in. David Mirfin gave us a fifth-minute lead but almost immediately Efe headed an own goal and then was sent off after conceding a penalty just before half-time. The referee, Lee Probert, decided that he'd fouled their centre-forward, Steve Torpey, but the same thing had happened at the other end of the pitch five minutes earlier and nothing had been given to us so at half-time I asked the referee to explain this inconsistency.

'Go away,' he said rather arrogantly.

'Why should I go away?' I asked. I didn't swear or raise my voice. I was just asking him politely. When I came out for the second half, the fourth official told me I'd been banned from the dugout and would have to go and sit in the stand.

'You're joking aren't you?' I said.

'No, Terry. Lee doesn't want you on the touchline.'

At the McAlpine Stadium, there are about eight places behind the dugout for staff to sit so I took one of them. It was business as usual because I was able to speak to Peter any time I wanted to. With three minutes left, our 10 men were still 2-1 down when 'Macca' popped up to score the equaliser and then incredibly the winner when he knocked in Danny Schofield's cross just before the final whistle. Macca is one of our most exciting prospects. He's just turned 20, he's 6ft 5in and still growing and he has feet that a lot of players would die for. During the season, I keep a diary that I write up after every match. I don't include much – just a couple of sentences about each player. After three games during the 2003-04 season, I wrote that we'd be lucky to keep Jon Stead and if Macca carries on making such quick progress, then I can see the same thing happening to him. We won't be able to hang on to him and, having snapped up Jon Stead, Blackburn have already taken a look at Macca.

That 3-2 win at Scunthorpe kept us third, we then won 1-0 at Northampton before picking up a very good point at Hull. We blew a chance to clinch automatic promotion by losing 3-1 at home to Mansfield but then had another opportunity at Cheltenham the following Saturday. If we won, we knew we'd pip Torquay to third place. We made a good start when Boothy put us ahead in the 16th minute and we dominated the first half. After the break, they had a man sent off and, as often happens, the team with 10 men lifted themselves. All of a sudden, we had a fight on our hands. Cheltenham had a few chances to score but didn't take them and then, with about 15 minutes left, Pawel Abbott had a ball rolled to him on the half-way line. Instead of taking it forward, his first touch took him backwards to give his marker, Shane Duff, the chance to close him down so 'Pav' ended up 10 yards outside our area out wide. Their striker, Kayode Odejayi, had moved across to cut off the back pass to our keeper, Paul Rachubka, but Pav handed the ball to him on a plate. He laid it off to Duff who curled it past 'Rabs' for the equaliser. We couldn't score the winner and although the Huddersfield supporters went wild near the end because they thought Torquay hadn't won, they had in fact beaten Southend 2-1 and they went up instead of us on goal difference.

So our campaign had ended in huge disappointment and anti-climax after we'd worked so hard all season. We felt we deserved to go up automatically and the players were devastated. A couple of the older lads, Andy Booth and Steve Yates, were crying because they thought it was the last chance they were going to get – especially Yatesy who was coming, if not to the end of his career, then very close to it.

We had to make sure the players went over to our fans and applauded them for their support at Whaddon Road. Back in the dressing room, I could tell Peter had been crying. He was really upset and obviously Pav was hoping the ground would swallow him up. The rest of the players were stunned into silence. Nobody could speak. But it wasn't a cup final we'd lost – we were still alive because we were into the play-offs.

'Listen lads,' I said. 'We're not getting relegated, we've not had a bad season and we've been given a second chance so let's take it.'

There wasn't the best atmosphere on the coach going back from Cheltenham to Huddersfield. Whatever the result, I always like to wait for about 15 minutes on the journey home before going to mix with the players. I did it as a manager and I do it as an assistant. You just can't sit and brood about something that's gone and I think the lads are pleased when you go and talk to them and don't just sit and stare at them. It seemed to work after the Cheltenham draw because when we got back to work on the Monday morning, it was if the result hadn't happened. There was the usual banter in training and we just got straight into it. The lads were brilliant – apart from Pav.

We could understand that he was upset – his mistake had cost us automatic promotion – but we didn't like the way he sulked all week as we prepared for the first leg of our play-off semi-final against Lincoln. He also had a little go at certain people in training. I suggested to Peter that he should pull Pav to one side and tell him what was what so Peter did just that in front of the players. He told Pav he should stop brooding and walking around with his head down. As the game at Sincil Bank drew nearer, we had to sit down and pick the side. We decided to take a risk by dropping Pav and bringing in Iffy Onuora who had started his career with Huddersfield. After scoring goals at the rate of one in every four games at a host of clubs including Gillingham (twice), Swindon and Grimsby, Iffy was a bustling centre-forward who was big friends with Peter and had rejoined us from Tranmere on transfer deadline day. Although he hadn't scored in three appearances as a substitute, we had a hunch he might unsettle Lincoln. Iffy was almost 37 and he wasn't match-fit but the gamble paid off because he scored in the fifth minute by heading in a Rob Edwards corner from the right. After Gary Fletcher had equalised for

Lincoln just after half-time, David Mirfin snatched a rather lucky winner for us in the 72nd minute. Boothy's firm header from Danny Schofield's right-wing corner was brilliantly saved by Alan Marriott and as the loose ball dropped to the ground, 'Big Mirf' went for it with Lincoln's wing-back, Mark Bailey. The ball ended up in the back of their net but David didn't know he'd scored! When he stood up after the tackle, he had no idea where the ball was. When he found out, he couldn't believe it!

Fletcher's goal was about the only time he'd escaped from Andy Holdsworth all afternoon. We realised that Fletcher – now Taylor-Fletcher after his marriage – posed a threat with his two very good feet. Lincoln played three up front and we couldn't allow him to drop a little deeper into midfield to pick up the ball. So we asked Andy to man-mark him and he did a great job. Andy had been one of the eight who'd turned up for pre-season training in July 2003. He signed for the club when he was 13 and seven years down the line, I'm convinced he has the ability to become a top-class player because he can slot in wherever you want him to – apart from striker that is.

We knew that it was only half-time in the two-legged tie and that Lincoln would come at us with all guns blazing at the McAlpine four days later. They'd reached the play-off final the previous season and under their manager, Keith Alexander, had become very difficult to beat. Although Pav Abbott had reacted brilliantly to being on the bench at Sincil Bank and had replaced Iffy with about a quarter of an hour left, we started having problems with him again during the build-up to the second leg. I wouldn't call him a typical Fancy Dan but his attitude wasn't right. Some players think coming to a Third Division club is going to be a doddle – they're bigger than the club if you like – and they've quickly got to be put in their place. We decided to leave Pav out of the home leg completely to teach him a lesson. Although born in York, he'd come to us from Poland via Bury and Preston and it was a case of getting him to come around to our way of doing things. Pav wasn't very happy about not even making the bench and stormed out of the McAlpine dressing room once the team was announced. I think he realised he wasn't in the squad because his attitude wasn't right – he was still sulking.

I always felt our 2-1 win at Lincoln would be enough to get us to the Millennium Stadium. With nearly 20,000 supporters packed into the McAlpine, we went out to win the second leg and after a pretty scrappy opening 20 minutes, chances started to fall to both sides. Seven minutes before half time though, Lincoln took the lead when their talented midfielder, Richard Butcher, scored with a lovely lob from the edge of the box and then Bailey ran through to fire home from just inside the area a minute later. Down near the dugout, we were shell-shocked. We were losing 2-0 on the night, the aggregate score was now 3-2 to Lincoln and we were in real danger of blowing it. For the first time since the defeat at Macclesfield, the players were told a few home truths in the dressing room at half-time. Peter started and I contributed. Fingers were pointed at certain players because too many of them weren't performing. I think it must go down as one of our best half-time team talks ever. We asked the players a simple question: having worked so hard all season, did they really want it to end this way? We told them that if they lost, nobody would ever remember the fantastic season they'd had. After getting themselves into this mess, they knew they had to deliver and they did. Just over two weeks earlier in that 1-0 home defeat by Mansfield, the young lads had frozen. We'd kept reminding them that they couldn't let it happen again but it had happened in the first half against Lincoln. We were really on the edge – one more goal and we would have been gone. Some of the younger players hadn't been into such unknown territory before but this time they held their nerve brilliantly.

We didn't change it tactically – apart from pushing Andy Holdsworth further forward as a right-back – and the turning point was the penalty we were given on the hour. Jon Worthington crossed from the right and as the ball headed for the far post, Andy Booth stumbled under Jamie McCombe's challenge. The referee consulted his linesman and despite Lincoln's understandable howls of protest, then pointed to the spot. I think McCombe was unfortunate when he challenged Boothy but it was a half-hearted challenge. I think he was drawn into a situation where he couldn't pull out of it. If the penalty had been given against us, I would have been very annoyed. I was pretty confident Danny Schofield would score. He's got great bottle, he's prepared to stand up and be counted and he did so again that night by slotting home the penalty. We were all square again. It was really fitting that the crucial goal should be scored by Robbie Edwards, our club captain, especially with his right foot – he normally uses that just for standing on! The chance came from a mistake by John McAliskey after a mazy run across the box from the right by Jon Worthington. Macca couldn't control the ball and when it fell to Robbie on the edge of the area, he lashed it home with just seven minutes to go. There was no coming back from that for Lincoln, although they nearly pinched another goal at the death. The relief at the final whistle was amazing and I was pleased to see Pav back in the dressing room for the post-match celebrations. Peter decided not to take any action against him for storming off in a huff before the kick-off. It was now a case of congratulating the players but then reminding them that the job was only half done. We still had one more game to go and the next day we watched Mansfield beat Northampton on penalties to reach the play-off final at the Millennium Stadium on May Day Bank Holiday Monday.

We now had 12 days to prepare for the climax of what had been an incredible season. It was business as usual during the week or so before travelling down to Cardiff three days before the final. The players had one day of hard work and then one day off and we spent a lot of time working on possession. They were fit enough – we just had to top it up and keep them on the boil.

Our main problem was finding somewhere to stay in Cardiff. We'd actually been booked into the Vale of Glamorgan Hotel on the outskirts of the city where the Welsh rugby and football teams base themselves before games. But when they rang in midweek to tell us they'd double-booked our rooms, we found ourselves going into our biggest game of the season with nowhere to stay! Because of my local connections, I gave the club a list of all the hotels I knew in the Cardiff area and Jury's, right in the middle of the city not far from the Millennium Stadium, was last on the list. Ideally, we didn't want to stay there but beggars can't be choosers and that's where we ended up. In hindsight, it turned out well because being based right in the middle of Cardiff meant the players were kept busy – they had things to do like talk to fans. Instead of staying somewhere very quiet where they could have got bored, there was always something going on in a bustling hotel in the heart of the city.

It was nice to be back in Cardiff and after arriving on the Friday before our game on the Monday, I spent a bit of time visiting family. I'd been bragging about the Millennium Stadium to the lads – what's Wembley compared with this?! – and they loved it when we got there for the First Division play-off final between West Ham and Crystal Palace on the Saturday. Because it was only a quarter of a mile from the hotel, we decided to walk to the ground. As the boys were wearing their club tracksuits, it was clear where they were from and as we walked through the hordes of West Ham fans, they started throwing abuse and fag ends at us. We just made sure we stayed together and got through to the stadium in Westgate Street. Once inside, the lads really soaked up the atmosphere and they loved the two pre-match entertainers who were juggling the ball in the penalty areas at either end of the stadium. They particularly liked the Asian guy who you see on TV lying on his back in a park keeping the ball up in the phone ads. They were up out of their seats clapping him at the end of his party pieces!

The West Ham-Crystal Palace game turned out to be a shocker but we learned from it – as well as the Second Division play-off final between Bristol City and Brighton the next day which we watched on TV in our hotel. All four teams were determined not to lose and their negative approach killed both matches as spectacles. The two more attacking sides, West Ham and Bristol City, ended up losing because they hadn't had the bottle to go for it. Before our training session on the Sunday, we talked to the players about being more positive when we faced Mansfield. We told them we wanted them to follow the SAS motto – 'he who dares wins.' If they played crap and lost then we would be disappointed but if they had a go and got beaten, then that would fine. At least they could look back and say that they'd played at the Millennium Stadium and done their best. We didn't want them to go out thinking that they mustn't lose. For the first time in my career, I found myself saying that winning wasn't everything. I admit it went against the basic philosophy on such big occasions, that having worked so hard, you mustn't lose at all costs. I believe if you think you're good enough to win a game, then you should go out and win it. OK, I accept that for West Ham and Crystal Palace, there was far more money involved than for the lower division teams. Millions of pounds and a place in the Premiership rested on that game and there was a huge responsibility on the managers of those two clubs. But I still say that if West Ham had gone out to win it, then they probably would have done. Another dreadful final between Bristol and Brighton reinforced our message and I'm pleased that Mansfield adopted the same positive approach to us. Both of us dared to win. The game was a cracker and somehow it ended up going to penalties but for all the right reasons.

It was fantastic for me to be involved with a team at the Millennium Stadium for the first time in my career. It's an absolutely beautiful ground, the set-up is fabulous and we had a fascinating drive to the stadium from our hotel. We had to co-ordinate our arrival with Mansfield – all the teams who play there have to follow this procedure – so we went on a sort of guided tour around the docks in Cardiff Bay. We actually passed the site of the Cambridge pub in Tyndall Street where I'd lived with my parents 40 years earlier! It was a nice trip down memory lane for me and the other member of our party from Cardiff, Lee Fowler, and it was very nostalgic to pass places where I'd played as a kid.

Once again, we had a couple of difficult decisions to make in terms of team selection. Despite scoring the winner in the semi-final, Robbie Edwards was replaced in midfield by Tony Carss, who'd recovered from a thigh strain and we recalled Pawel Abbott in place of Iffy Onuora up front. In fact, Iffy didn't even win a place on the bench. It was a straight choice between him and Lee Fowler and I made my pitch for Lee to Peter.

'We've got him on a three-year contract, the game's being played in his home city and if we don't make him substitute, we might lose him mentally.'

It was a really difficult call for Peter and he went away to think about. As the day of the final drew nearer, I asked him what he'd decided. He said he'd spoken to his wife, Alison, who'd told him Iffy would be devastated not to make the bench.

'Peter,' I said. 'You're the manager, you make the decision and sometimes you have to be brave.'

In the end, he left out his friend and picked Lee Fowler. It must have been very hard for Peter. Not only was Iffy a good mate, he'd scored our crucial first goal at Lincoln but in the end, it all worked out well – especially for Lee and me. I had a good feeling about our chances of winning as we watched the game unfold from the touch-line. It was amazing that in such an open and exciting game there were no goals – although just near the end of normal time, my heart sank when Colin Larkin looked to have scored for Mansfield. Luckily for us, the linesman ruled that the ball had gone out of play before he put it in the net. I've watched it on the video since and it was definitely the right decision. I'd immediately turned to look at Peter and his head had dropped about six inches! There would have been no comeback for us from there. We thought we'd won it in extra-time when Anthony Lloyd's shot looked to be heading towards the top right-hand corner but their captain and keeper, Kevin Pilkington, made a brilliant save.

As the clock ticked on, I was happy about the prospect of the game going to penalties. We'd practised them quite a few times during the week and we'd told the players to tell us if they didn't want to take one. It wasn't a case of seeing them as cowards – we just wanted to know who was up for it and who wasn't. A couple of them turned down the chance and that was fair enough. Mansfield had scored five of the best taken penalties I'd ever seen against Northampton and they must have fancied their chances as the shoot-out began. Club captain Robbie Edwards, having come on for Lloydy, led by example and scored our first before Rabs saved Wayne Corden's kick. Danny Schofield then put us in the driving seat with his penalty and then Liam Lawrence, Mansfield's most exciting player who's now with Sunderland, incredibly missed by chipping over via the bar. Tony Carss made it 3-0, Neil MacKenzie gave Mansfield hope by slotting home his penalty and then it was all down to Lee Fowler. If he scored with our fourth kick, we'd be up. The pressure was really on Lee. His parents run a pub on the coast at Barry not far from Cardiff and he knew lots of family and friends were watching him but he wasn't fazed by the occasion. He coolly put the ball along the deck to Pilkington's right as the keeper headed in the opposite direction and that was it! We'd made it and Lee's selection as a substitute had been fully vindicated. What a fairy-tale ending for him to score the winning goal in his home city!

I think I was almost as chuffed as Lee. To come to Cardiff and win promotion at the Millennium Stadium in front of my family meant an awful lot to me. I felt pure elation when Lee's penalty hit the net but as I've grown older, I've started to think about other people a bit more so I went straight over to the Mansfield manager, Keith Curle, and told him that despite losing he'd had a great season. Understandably, he didn't have much to say other than thanking me and I then joined in the celebrations with our lads. I turned down Peter's invitation to stand with them all on the winners' podium because it was their day – they'd worked hard for it so I wanted them to enjoy it. That's what they'd been flogging their guts out for when I put them through pre-season training in the summer of 2003. Peter likes everybody to join in and when we saved the club from relegation in 1997, I reluctantly went round on a lap of honour with him but this time I declined. Once the players had picked up the trophy, I was happy to join in and went down to the corner of the ground where our wonderful supporters were – all 23,000 of them out of a crowd of 37,000. During his post-match interviews, I was particularly pleased to hear Lee thanking Peter and myself for helping to get his career back on track after he'd lost his way at Coventry. We'd taken a bit of a punt on him but he'd come through with flying colours. That made it all the more worthwhile.

As the celebrations continued in the Millennium Stadium, my thoughts turned to our chairman, Ken Davy, who was up in the main stand with the Huddersfield party. Quite simply, without him, we wouldn't have been so successful and who knows if there would actually have been a football club if he hadn't stepped in? Later, I heard that Ken had been crying his eyes out at the final whistle and I could understand why. Over the last 10 months, he and his board had done a fantastic job in rescuing the club and then supporting what Peter and I were trying to do. Things were changing from day to day but Ken pushed the financial boat out to make sure we could bring in the players we felt we needed and we repaid him in the end as the club won promotion back to Division Two, now League One, at the first attempt. In fact, he gave us more money than was in the original plan and I felt that Ken, chief executive Andrew Watson and the rest of the board deserved a huge pat on the back for everything they'd done for the club. From administration to promotion in a little over a year must go down as one of the most remarkable achievements in the history of the club.

The people of Huddersfield showed their appreciation by turning out in their thousands during an open-top bus ride around the town three days later. By then I'd gone off on holiday but from what I've heard, it was another moment to savour and everybody enjoyed all the publicity generated by our success. It worked wonders for Lee Fowler because when he saw the pictures of himself running away to celebrate after his penalty, he realised how fat he looked! He sat down with his mum, Alison, and girlfriend Lucy and decided he had to get his body in shape for the new season. While he'd been out injured, Lee had put on a lot of weight by drinking too much and eating junk food so out went beer, chocolate and crisps and he came back in much better condition for pre-season training in July 2004.

As for me, I had mixed feelings as I looked forward to a three-week holiday in Spain and a three-year contract with Huddersfield that was said to be in the pipeline. I was obviously delighted that our season had ended on such a high note but it had been a difficult year for me personally. Christine and I had gone our separate ways and my mother, Mary, had died at the age of 87 after suffering a stroke in April 2004. If one of us needed something, Christine and I were still talking on the phone and I obviously wanted to keep in contact with Jordan. After 33 years of marriage, we were living apart and I must admit I found it lonely being by myself. But as I flew off to the Spanish sun at the beginning of June 2004, I had no idea that when I returned, my life would never be the same again.

The Bottom of the Glass

I don't know why I said it. It was probably the drink talking. 'This is the worst thing that's ever happened to me.'

What I meant to say when I was interviewed by the police straight after knocking down Raziya Aslam about half a mile from my new home in late June 2004 was 'this is the worst thing I've ever done in my life.'

I certainly should have said that – for two reasons. The worst thing that's ever happened to me was Daniel dying but the drink-driving incident is without doubt the worst thing that I have ever done. I still can't believe I was so stupid as to put my life and, more importantly, other people's lives at risk by driving when I was more than three times over the limit. I still shudder when I think about what could have happened to Raziya. She fractured her pelvis as a result of my moment of madness but it could have been so much worse. I couldn't have lived with myself if I'd killed her. I can't begin to express how sorry and ashamed I am about what happened that night and I only hope that one day Raziya will be able to find it within herself to forgive me.

I had just returned from a very relaxing holiday at our apartment in Estepona between Marbella and Gibraltar in southern Spain where I'd spent three very quiet weeks winding down after an exhilarating but exhausting season. I walked along the beach for a couple of hours at a stretch, sunbathed and went out for meals in the evening. There were a lot of Brits over there who knew that Huddersfield had won promotion and they were delighted for me. The holiday was just what the doctor ordered and I came back refreshed on Wednesday 23rd June – all fired up to begin pre-season training in a couple of weeks' time. The next day, I played a round of golf at my local club – about 10 minutes in the car from the flat – and had a few drinks, mainly lagers, in the bar afterwards. I had intended to go home to watch England take on Portugal in the quarter-finals of Euro 2004 but when some friends suggested we go for a meal, I agreed. Four of us then went to The Flying Pizza, an Italian restaurant in Leeds, where I had some wine and a couple of whiskies with the meal.

When we'd finished, I looked at my watch and realised that I could still catch the second half of the football match on the box. But instead of taking a taxi home, I foolishly decided to drive the three miles to my flat in the northern part of Leeds. I climbed into my Jaguar X-type car and headed north, passing the family home on the ring road in Shadwell and heading towards the Moor Allerton district of Leeds. As I approached the roundabout at the junction of the ring road and the A61 Harrogate Road, my car mounted the central reservation and hit Raziya who was crossing the road. She was on her way home from a karate class with her younger sister, Shazana. I'd tried to swerve to avoid her but the left-hand side of the car clipped her hip and the right-hand side hit a speed warning sign. I immediately stopped and got out to see how Raziya was. She was lying unconscious on the pavement. I couldn't believe what I'd done and my only concern was her condition. I stayed with her until the police and ambulance arrived on the scene. She was rushed to hospital and I was taken to Chapeltown police station, about five minutes away by car, where I was breathalysed. It came as no surprise that I badly failed the test. There were 120 micrograms of alcohol in 100 millilitres of my breath. The legal limit is 35 micrograms.

I spent an absolutely terrible night in a police cell. As they do with everyone, the police took everything off me – including my belt and my money. Not surprisingly after what I'd done, I couldn't sleep at all. I just lay there on a two-inch-thick rubber mat on the bunk bed thinking about what an idiot I'd been. I could have killed an innocent woman who was now lying seriously injured in hospital. On top of that, I realised what I was about to put my family through and I felt so ashamed of myself. The police asked if I wanted to ring anybody but I declined their offer. At that stage, I didn't think my solicitor could have done anything for me. I knew I was guilty – as I told the two policemen who interviewed me. I was completely honest with them because there was nothing else I could be. I was three times over the limit and I'd knocked down a young woman. Full stop.

When the sun came up on the Friday morning, my first thought was how I was going to get out of the station. I knew the police would only let me go when they'd finished with me. As soon as the questions began again, I asked about Raziya. They said they thought she was OK after spending the night in hospital. When I was allowed to leave the police station, I took a taxi home and immediately made arrangements to see my solicitor, Richard Manning, who's also a judge. All over the weekend, I kept ringing the hospital but they wouldn't tell me anything about Raziya's condition because I wasn't a relative. I felt dreadful. Having lost Daniel, I knew what is was like to have a child snatched away and I realised that because of my stupidity, somebody could have lost their daughter.

When I met Richard at his office on the Monday, he was very up front with me. He laid everything very firmly on the line. He showed me a guidelines book used by magistrates in which, when dealing with breathalyser offences like mine, they're asked to consider custodial sentences. Richard said I could be looking at spending at least a month in jail. It frightened the hell out of me.

At the beginning of July, I returned to the McAlpine for pre-season training. After the last couple of weeks, it was a welcome diversion to get back into the routine of coaching the lads. There was a fantastic atmosphere around the club after we'd won promotion, but I couldn't stop thinking about the incident. I kept going over and over what had happened and I would find myself waking up in the morning and immediately thinking of Raziya. Sometimes, I just buried my head in my hands in despair. I was very relieved when I heard that she'd been allowed home from hospital and I received some more good news when the police told me I was going to be charged with drink-driving and driving without due care and attention rather than the more serious offence of dangerous driving.

My first appearance at Leeds magistrates' court took place on Tuesday 3rd August. I couldn't sleep at all the night before but I must have eventually dropped off before waking up at about seven o'clock. A taxi took me to Richard's office not far from the court building. We arrived there by a quarter to ten and as we expected, the press and media were waiting. Once inside the courtroom, I sat and listened to two other cases – one man had been charged with growing cannabis in his garage and the other with stealing and crashing a car and driving it without insurance. When my case was called, I pleaded guilty to both charges and more details of the incident were revealed to the court. They heard that Raziya had been 'crossing the road quite properly' when I hit her. She had broken her pelvis and suffered bad headaches ever since and had been granted six to eight weeks sick leave by the call centre she worked for. The prosecution read out the statement I'd made to the police on the night – 'it's the worst thing that's ever happened to me. I hate it. I just feel sorry for the girl' – and then Richard got to his feet to explain the background to the incident.

'He lives his life in the public eye and his life has been beset by tragedy,' he said before explaining Daniel's death and the fund-raising work I'd done for the Cardiomyopathy Association.

'The circumstances simply are that in addition to that tragedy he has recently split from his wife. He had intended going home after a round of golf on the day in question but his friends, seeing he was low, asked him out for a meal and some drinks. He had no idea what he had had to drink, but it didn't seem to him or his friends to affect him.'

When Richard had finished, the district judge, David Kitson, called for a probation report to be written on me. He said he would adjourn sentence for three weeks but he was keeping all options open. I felt a little better leaving the court than when I'd arrived there. At least I was walking away from the building and not on my way down to a cell. I realised that a lot of people in Leeds would now know for the first time that Christine and I had split up. I imagined the news would shock a few of them but I felt relieved it was out. Richard had told me he expected the judge to ask for a probation report. Before we left the building, I had a preliminary chat with a probation officer who remarked on how much remorse I'd shown. Once outside, the reporters wanted me to comment but I couldn't because the case was only half way through. I was relieved the day was over but I knew the next three weeks were going to be very, very difficult. I would have to go through it all again. I was determined to face up to whatever the court decided – jail, a lengthy driving ban, community service and a hefty fine or a combination of all four. I was just glad that Raziya was on the mend.

Three days later, I met my probation officer. It was a very emotional meeting as I discussed my private life and my lifestyle with a complete stranger. We went through everything – from my playing career to Daniel's death, my time in Lebanon, my drinking and obviously the breakdown of my marriage. It was gruelling but quite therapeutic – I suppose you could call it a sort of belated counselling session. I felt pretty drained by the end and I now knew there was nothing else I could do but wait until my next court appearance in a little under three weeks time. The probation report would be written and it would then be up to the judge to decide my fate. For the moment, I had to concentrate on my job because the next day saw the start of the new football season. On the Monday after the drink-driving incident, the club's board had met to discuss my situation. Peter Jackson rang me later to explain they were obviously concerned but I had their full backing – for which I was very grateful.

Over the summer, we'd brought in a couple of new players – striker Junior Mendes from Mansfield and Chesterfield midfielder Chris Brandon. A couple had left including our goalkeeper, Paul Rachubka, who'd joined Northampton. But although the squad was basically the same, our ground would now be known as the Galpharm rather than the McAlpine Stadium. The club had put the naming rights out to tender and a local pharmacy firm owned by Graham Leslie had come out on top. It was obviously a good deal for the club but it was sad to see the original name of the stadium disappear as we celebrated the 10th anniversary of it being built. Although the Galpharm Stadium doesn't quite trip off the tongue as easily as the McAlpine did, I suppose we'll soon get used to it – as we have done with Coca Cola taking over the sponsorship of the Nationwide League. Plans to build a bigger shop, new ticket office and new reception area at the ground by May 2005 have also been announced. The £500,000 scheme will also provide 5,000 square feet of first-floor office space to let to businesses so these are exciting times for Huddersfield Town. The dark days of administration are firmly in the past.

The Football League fixtures computer had decided we would travel to Stockport County for our first game in the newly named

League One and we made an amazing start to the season by winning 3-2. A late double substitution and a change of formation had done the trick as Pawel Abbott scored an injury-time winner after coming off the bench. Moments like that make you feel good as you stand on the touchline trying to change the course of a game. It was the ideal way to kick off the season. We drew 0-0 at home against Chesterfield in our next game and then lost 2-0 to Hartlepool – again at the Galpharm – so we had the set – a win, a draw and a defeat.

The morning after the Hartlepool match, I got up and made myself a cup of tea before going to pick up my mail. As I returned from the hall to the lounge, I started to flick through the post and noticed an official-looking envelope with a Leeds postmark on it. It seemed as if the probation report had arrived. The key to my whole future was contained in this document. So much depended on its contents. Although I dreaded what was inside, I was desperate to know. I sat down on the sofa, opened the envelope, took a deep breath and started to read. Two paragraphs in the report shook me to the bone:

> 'Mr Yorath's current frame of mind leaves me with great concerns about his potential for suicide especially if he receives a custodial sentence. The isolation and loneliness which currently exists would be exacerbated in custody and I fear for Mr Yorath's ability to deal with such a sentence. Mr Yorath's acute feelings of having brought shame on his family could also affect his ability to cope.'

A little further on, the writer of the report repeated his assessment before introducing the possibility of Huddersfield sacking me:

> 'The impact of a custodial sentence on Mr Yorath could be the loss of his life. As I have stated earlier, I am concerned about his ability to cope with such a disposal. A less serious but nonetheless further potential consequence would be the loss of his job as the Deputy Manager of Huddersfield Town.'

I couldn't quite believe what I'd just read so I went back and read it again. It was weird and a real shock to actually see those comments in black and white from somebody in the probation service who didn't really know me. He had come in cold to my case and had given his professional opinion after meeting me just once. It shocked me to think that somebody would consider me to be in that frame of mind. In my view, I hadn't been suicidal but I had been stressed out and depressed about everything – especially since my first court appearance as I waited to be sentenced. It had been a lousy time but I had never felt like ending my life. I hadn't come near that position at all.

In the week before my sentencing, I made a less than pleasurable return to Sheffield Wednesday – because we lost 1-0 – and spent the next few days preparing myself mentally for my court appearance. On the morning itself, I woke up about five o'clock and took a taxi down to my solicitor's office in the centre of Leeds. Richard and I discussed the probation report and despite its observations about possible suicide, he again laid out a few things for me – including the very strong possibility that I could be sent to jail. But Richard did say that Judge David Kitson was fair. We then walked the short distance to the magistrates' court to find, as expected, all the press waiting for me. They were really in my face, perhaps hoping I would show some kind of emotion. I felt awful and walked straight through the pack of journalists, cameramen and photographers into the building without speaking. Luckily, when the court began sitting at 10 o'clock, mine was the first case to be heard. As soon as I arrived in the dock, I just wanted to get to the verdict as soon as possible but I knew the judge had to consider the new evidence. A copy of the probation report had been given to him, the prosecution and the defence but it wasn't read out in open court. Everything depended on his reaction to it. In mitigation, Richard told the court that my life had been beset with 'difficulty and trauma' and referred to Daniel's death, the Bradford fire and my split from Christine. He said I had earned a reputation as a 'hard man' during my playing career and added that 'sometimes it is difficult for a man in that situation to recognise he needs help.' Richard told the court that, contrary to newspaper reports, I had tried to contact Raziya at least 10 times when she was in hospital.

When the judge said he was 'just able' to avoid sentencing me to a spell in jail because of my personal circumstances, the relief was almost overwhelming. I kept staring straight ahead as he addressed me personally:

'You have had to cope with tragedy in your life but your behaviour on this occasion, which is recognised in this report, could also have inflicted tragedy and heartbreak on another family, namely that of your young victim. The combination of these offences aggravated each other and I am quite satisfied that the custodial threshold has been crossed.'

At that point, I must admit my knees gave way a little. Had I heard the judge properly? Hadn't he just said that I wouldn't be going down?

'However,' continued Judge Kitson, 'I am required to carry out a balancing act and consider personal mitigation – the fact you stopped immediately after the accident, gave assistance to the young girl, co-operated with police and pleaded guilty at the first opportunity.'

I breathed another sigh of relief and kept looking straight ahead. Judge Kitson said he thought I was truly remorseful and he accepted that I had played an active role in a number of charities. He then gave me a 12-month community rehabilitation order, to include 60 hours of community service, a £500 fine and a 30-month driving ban. I was also ordered to pay £40 costs.

Obviously, I was a very relieved man when I stepped down from the dock. I'd been preparing for the worst but I'd been spared jail. I knew I had been very fortunate. I shook Richard by the hand and as we left the court building a little later, the media scrum inevitably materialised. I ignored the cameras and questions and kept walking with Richard a short distance away from me until we reached his office. Although the judge mentioned Daniel's death, my marriage problems and my charity work, I think what saved me from prison was the probation report. I don't think anything else would have done. I have to say that I don't think I would have committed suicide if I'd been sent to jail but obviously I would have found prison very difficult, on top of everything else that had happened to me. A little like the writing of this book, the probation officer was going through my life with me – especially the last 12 years. We were discussing the way my life has been disrupted and he had to make a professional judgment about the mental state I was in at that particular time.

Although I have lived my life in the public eye, I'm quite a private person and I was surprised that Richard felt he had to use a lot of personal details as a means of keeping me out of jail. But how he did it was up to him. The result was the one I was looking for. I know some people think I should have gone to prison because I was more than three times over the limit and I knocked down an innocent woman. I've had about a dozen letters saying as much and another dozen from well-wishers – complete strangers who have taken the time to sit down and write to me. The nasty ones I've read and taken on the chin – and taken in what they've said. They're perfectly entitled to have a dig at me and the court. One person wrote that I'd only got away with not going to prison because I'd been a famous footballer, a name. But some people I spoke to thought it could have worked the other way – that precisely because I'm quite well known, I could have been made an example of by being sent to jail. Do I feel guilty about not going to jail? Well...it's not up to me to make that judgment. The only thing I feel guilty about is the incident and my part in it because I was drinking on that night and I could have killed Raziya.

Serving the community service part of my sentence has been a very humbling experience. As part of my rehabilitation order, I have to attend a farm on the outskirts of Leeds every Wednesday. For a minimum of five hours a week, my job is to help disabled people to ride horses. I also muck out the stables, sort out the saddles and lead the animals around the yard. It really is sad to see how badly disabled the people who come to the farm are. Some are blind and they can't speak and I find it amazing how they manage to stay on the horses. I was surprised I wasn't given football coaching as part of my community service but I think that would have been seen as me doing something enjoyable so it wouldn't have been a punishment. I suppose I ought to be grateful I wasn't given painting and decorating or gardening. I hate them all and it's good to be out in the fresh air – even with all the horse dung around. I'm doing something useful.

My drinking was one of the risk problems mentioned in the probation report. I'm doing two courses – one for two and a half hours every week for convicted drink-drivers and the other an ongoing rehabilitation course with my own personal probation officer which began at the end of September 2004. It's aimed at helping me to cut down on my drinking, I've been given a lot of literature and the importance of quantities has been explained to me. I didn't realise that a drink you might pour yourself at home is completely different to one you might get in a bar in terms of measures and units. When I was given a jug of tea with a glass and asked to pour a measure, I poured three or four times the amount of drink I'd be served in a pub. The idea is for me to become more aware of how much I'm actually drinking. I have to keep a diary as part of the course. I know I have a problem but I'm not going to Alcoholics Anonymous at the moment. I think I drink too much at home in the evening but I honestly don't know if I'm an alcoholic. I'll have a meal and maybe a bottle of wine and a glass of scotch whiskey. Sometimes I won't get home from watching a game until half past midnight so I'll have a drink to make myself go to sleep. I can't seem to drop off without a couple of scotches. An alcoholic to me is somebody who wakes up in the morning and craves a drink – or who drinks in the afternoon. I drink at the golf club and at night but if my probation officer comes to the eventual conclusion that I do need some extra help then I will go and get it.

I'm using taxis and trains to get around – plus lifts from friends every now and then. It's obviously more inconvenient and expensive but it's a small price to pay for my freedom. I was encouraged by Judge Kitson's comments that if I successfully complete the drink-impaired drivers' course, then I can re-apply for my licence in 18 months. I've also been heartened by and am very grateful for the support I've received from Huddersfield Town and especially Peter Jackson. He's been marvellous about it, a real rock all the way through – as has everyone at the club. I think it was quite reasonable for them to have held fire on offering me a new three-year contract. They had to wait to see if I was going to jail before they took it any further. Had I been jailed, I couldn't have done my job so what would have been the point in offering me a contract? I was particularly touched by the statement the board issued after I was sentenced:

'Terry is a big part of Huddersfield Town Football Club and he will continue to be so in his role as assistant manager to Peter Jackson.'

That simple statement of support meant a lot. People like the chairman, Ken Davy, chief executive Andrew Watson and secretary Ann Hough have been there for me when I needed them and I'm determined not to let them down. One of the directors, Martin Byrne, who recently left the board, had been unfortunate enough to lend me the car I was driving on the night of the incident so I'm particularly grateful to him for his support.

There's been a mixed reaction to my sentence at football grounds since I appeared in court in late August. On the same day, we travelled up the road to Leeds for a Coca Cola Cup game which we lost 1-0 in front of a crowd of more than 30,000. At one stage of the evening, up went the cry from the terraces 'Taxi for Yorath!' but the supporters at Doncaster almost a week later when we lost 2-1 were a lot more abusive. The things they were saying were so near the knuckle that I couldn't repeat them. I expected some stick but I was more than a little upset when grown men started shouting such abusive comments. I wasn't at all surprised by Raziya's reaction to my behaviour. I completely understood why, after my first court appearance, she said I should be jailed. She'd suffered the shock of being knocked down and spent a few days in hospital but I hope in time she will be able to forgive me.

I deeply regret the shame I have brought on my family especially my daughter, Gabby, who's in the public eye through her work as an ITV sports presenter. She used to come to watch me play with Christine when she was a kid and like her sister, Louise, she was pretty good at gymnastics. She finished 11th at the 1990 Commonwealth Games in Auckland and also competed in the British Championships. Gabby has always been very intelligent and hard-working. While reading law at Durham University, she was involved with the student radio station and magazine and after graduating, she worked for a series of local radio stations, including Metro in Newcastle, before being offered a job on Sky Sports in 1996. She then moved to ITV two years later and I'm so proud of everything she's achieved in her career. Everyone I speak to is full of praise for her. She's married to Kenny Logan, the Scottish rugby player, so spends quite a bit of her time commuting between London and Glasgow.

I haven't had any problems with coping with the fact that my daughter is the most well-known member of the Yorath family. The first time I realised my fame as a footballer was fading was when we were having a meal in a restaurant in Leeds. A young girl was heading towards our table armed with a piece of paper and a pen and as she walked towards us, I put my hand out to take them from her and she just carried on past me and asked Gabby to sign her autograph! I knew the writing was on the wall then but the family banter is all good humoured. It causes a laugh down at my local golf club too and at the various grounds that I go to with Huddersfield. I find that although children don't recognise me any more, their parents still do.

'Ask Terry for his autograph,' they say to their kids. 'You know who this is don't you?'

'No.'

'This is Gabby's dad!'

'Off the telly?'

'Yes!'

'Oh...'

And then as the kids just look blankly at me signing my autograph, I'm trying to recall the days when I used to be known as a footballer rather than as a very proud father!

It's obviously been a difficult time for the three children as their parents have split up but they realise that people do have their differences. Luckily they're of an age where they can understand what's going on and they're all just getting on with their lives. Louise's modelling career in America is going very well and Jordan got an A, two Bs and a C in his A-levels. He's now working for Christine's property company during his gap year before going to university. He can see there's quite a few bob to be made in property and he's talking about taking a course in estate management in Newcastle. Jordan has his own social life with his girlfriend and he plays in goal for Halifax Town's youth team. He wants to be a footballer but I've never pushed him and I'd never want to – even though he thinks I should take him round to various clubs. If he's good enough then somebody will sign him. I secretly wish someone would give him a chance.

It's almost a year since Christine and I separated. I don't know if the marriage is over but I can't see either of us saying to each other that we've perhaps made a mistake so I suppose the next step is a divorce. I'm obviously very saddened by the break-up. Christine has been a tremendous support throughout my career and a fantastic mother – especially considering how much time I spent away from home when the kids were growing up. I now only see her when I've got something to collect from the house. She's become a successful businesswoman who's got her life in order. I'm trying to do the same with mine.

I know the next couple of years are going to be difficult but I'm going to get on with it. Writing this book has been a huge help as I've been able to look back at my life – at the good times and the bad. I sometimes feel that perhaps I've said too much in these pages but I'm determined to be honest. I feel I've been very fortunate to have had the life I've had – even though I've had more than my fair share of set-backs. In the past, I seemed to be able to cope quite well and I got on with my job in football. I hope that continues. I think anybody in the game has to take the pressure off themselves somehow because they're in the public eye all the time. My problem is that I choose to have a drink and sometimes I drink too much. My life continues to be dom-inated by football and I'm pleased to say that my problem hasn't stopped me from doing my job at Huddersfield. I've never been late for work and I'm proud of my professionalism. I want to stay in the game for a long time and I'm very happy with the way things are going with the team. I'm slightly disappointed because, during my career, I don't think I've coached at the level I should have. True, I've won pro-motion with Bradford, Swansea and Huddersfield, I've coached in the Premiership with Bradford and I've managed Wales and Lebanon. People might look at that record and say I'd done enough but I would still like to help take Huddersfield into the Championship and maybe even the Premiership. If I could do that, then I'd think I'd been suc-cessful.

I'll always have a soft spot for my old club, Leeds, and it's sad to see how they've fallen on hard times. Their decline has been pretty spectacular – starting with that FA Cup defeat by my home-town team, Cardiff, in January 2002 – but if they can steady the ship and stay in the Championship for a couple of years, then there's hope for them and they could get back into the top division.

Over the last two months, my life has become more structured. There's the community service every Wednesday, the rehabilitation courses and as much golf as I can manage in between times! When I come home to the flat from work, I fix myself something to eat, watch a bit of television, go to bed and then travel to Huddersfield by taxi and train the next day. Although I'm obviously less mobile, I'm hoping to see more of Jordan. I'd like us to play more golf together but it's hard getting hold of him as he's either working for his mother or seeing his girlfriend – it doesn't leave much time for his old man! I love all my family dearly but I've decided to dedicate this book to Jordan. I want to try to make up for the way I've unintentionally neglected him since Daniel died.

The thorny subject of counselling is definitely on my mind. I've told stories in this book that I've never told before; I told the probation officer things that I probably wouldn't have admitted before so perhaps it's all part of the process. At first, I thought I could control my own grief. I didn't want to share it with anybody. I wouldn't even communicate with anyone at home – even though Christine tried to get through to me to support me – and I'm afraid the mediums I visited weren't much help. I'm a stubborn person, perhaps too stubborn. Maybe I'm not brave enough to go to counselling in case it hurts me more. Deep down, I suspect I don't really want to leave my grief behind, even though it doesn't do me any good. The picture I have in my mind of Daniel falling to the ground on the day he died still torments me. We were sharing the joy of the game we both loved and that awful moment is my recurring nightmare. Even after all this time, the tears start again.

The drink-driving conviction has been a turning point in my life. Despite everything that's happened, I'm confident about the future. I think I've bottomed out with the accident. I couldn't go any lower and it's time to move on. I can't keep sitting around crying. I know I have to look forward not back. The judge has given me a second chance and I must take it.

Acknowledgements

I would like to thank the following people who have kindly helped me to produce this book: Bjorn Andersson, Mel Booth, Peter Bibby, Ryan Giggs, John Giles, John Helm, Simon Hicks, Jane Hiles, Julian Hughes, Peter Jackson, Des Kelly, Emily Lewis, Robert Mager, Richard Manning, Matthew Phillips, Jack Rollin, Phil Shaw, Ceri Stennett, my sister Pauline Stephens, Harry Swales, Alan Sykes, Lynda Thwaites, Peter Walker and Tony Woolway. Special thanks must go to Grahame Lloyd, whose persistence has paid off because, after years of us talking about writing my life story, we've finally got round to doing it.

I'm very grateful to the following individuals and organisations for allowing me to reproduce their photographs: BBC Wales, Empics, the Huw Evans Agency, the *Huddersfield Daily Examiner*, Chris Laws, Simon Morley, Popperfoto, the *South Wales Echo*, Dave Spurdens, the Andrew Varley Picture Agency and the *Western Mail*.

Extracts from John Helm's commentary on the Bradford fire were kindly supplied by Yorkshire Television.

Bibliography

Clough, Brian (with John Sadler), *Cloughie: Walking on Water: My Life* (Headline, 2002)

Corrigan, Peter, *100 Years of Welsh Soccer* (Welsh Brewers, 1976)

Davies, Gareth and Garland, Ian, *Who's Who of Welsh International Soccer Players* (Bridge Books, 1991)

Lloyd, Grahame, *One Cap Wonders: The Ultimate Claim to Football Fame* (Robson, 2001)

Mourant, Andrew, *The Essential History of Leeds United* (Headline, 2000)

Rollin, Jack, *Rothmans/Sky Sports Football Yearbooks* (Queen Anne Press, Headline – various editions)

Rollin, Jack, *The Rothmans Book of Football Records* (Headline, 1998)

Writer and Publisher

G rahame Lloyd has been a freelance broadcaster and journalist for more than 20 years. As well as commentating and reporting on football for independent radio and television, he covers the game in Wales for the *Sky Sports Football Yearbook* and writes for *The Guardian* and *The Independent*.

He is the author of *Daffodil Days: Glamorgan's Glorious Summer* (Gomer), the official celebration of the county's 1997 championship win, *Jan the Man: From Anfield to Vetch Field* (Orion), the life story of Jan Molby, the former Liverpool midfielder and current Kidderminster manager, *C'mon City! A Hundred Years of the Bluebirds* (Seren), Cardiff City's official centenary book, *One Cap Wonders* (Robson), a celebration of British and Irish footballers who have played just once for their country and *One Hell of a Season: Imps, Pilgrims and Tales of the Unexpected,* a book covering Lincoln City and Boston United during the historic 2002-03 football season. His company, Celluloid, publishes books and makes television and radio documentaries.

Index

Index

Index

Index

Index

Index

Withe, Chris 132

Withe, Peter 132

Woolley, David 139

Worthington, Frank 27

Worthington, Jon 223, 227, 232, 233

Wragg, Dick 134

Wright, Rick 187, 188

Wurtz, Robert 123

Wylie, Ron 83

Yates, Steve 223, 229

Yorath, Ben 14

Yorath, Christine 9, 10, 11-12, 23, 78,
81, 85-6, 88, 89, 96, 100, 126, 129,
130, 135, 136, 142, 147, 149, 150,
151, 169, 170, 171, 172, 173, 175,
187, 190, 191, 192, 193, 202, 224-
5, 238, 242, 245, 250, 252

Yorath, Daniel 9-12, 78, 81, 121, 129,
169-76, 178, 188, 189 -90, 201,
225, 239, 241, 242, 243, 245, 246,
252

Yorath, David (brother) 13-14, 18,
21-2, 79, 121, 134

Yorath, David (father) 13-14, 17, 18,
21, 134, 135, 136, 137,

Yorath, Gabby 9, 11, 51, 78, 100, 123,
124, 129, 135, 136, 140, 169, 171,
172, 174, 190, 226, 249-50

Yorath, Jordan 9-10, 11, 130, 169,
188, 190, 191, 226, 238, 250, 251-2

Yorath, Louise 9, 11, 78, 100, 129,
135, 169, 171, 172, 173, 190, 226,
249, 250

Yorath, Mary 14-15, 18-19, 21, 135,
136, 137, 238

Yorath, Pauline 14

Yorath, Terry:
Birthplace 14
Education 13-22

Nicknames 25
Playing career:
League debut 30
Leeds United 23-81
Coventry City 81-97
Spurs 88-97
Vancouver Whitecaps 97-103
Wales 103-128
Management career:
Bradford City 130-141, 149-151,
208-213
Swansea City 141-9, 151-4
Wales 147-149, 155-186
Cardiff City 187-88
Lebanon 189-201
Huddersfield Town 202-8, 228-252
Sheffield Wednesday 213-9
Young, Eric 7, 157-8, 161, 164, 1668,
177